C000241767

LEEDS

THE STORY OF A CITY

DAVID THORNTON M.Phil., Ph.D.

FORT PUBLISHING LTD.

First published in 2002 by Fort Publishing Ltd, Old Belmont House,
12 Robsland Avenue, Ayr, KA7 2RW.

Illustrations courtesy of Leeds City Local and Family History Library, with
the exception of Quarry Hill Flats courtesy of Aero Films.

Front cover: 'Boar Lane Leeds by Lamplight 1881' (oil on canvas) by
John Atkinson Grimshaw – courtesy of Leeds Museums and Galleries
(City Art Gallery)/Bridgeman Art Library, London W2 4PH.

Back cover illustrations of Kirkstall Abbey (top) and Leeds Town Hall (bottom)
by D. Shaw.

Graphics by Paul McLaughlin.

Printed by Bell & Bain, Glasgow.

Typeset in 10.5pt Garamond by Senga Fairgrieve, 0131 658 1763

ISBN 0-9536576-6-3

A catalogue record for this book is available from the British Library.

to June

CONTENTS

Prehistoric Leeds ✦ Stone Age to Bronze Age ✦ Brigantes ✦ Roman Adel and Leeds ✦ The Kingdom of Elmet ✦ The Venerable Bede and Loidis ✦ The Anglian Cross ✦ Viking Leeds ✦ The Shire Oak ✦ William I and the Harrying of the North ✦ Domesday Book ✦ Everyday Life in Norman Leeds ✦ The Parish of Leeds ✦ Norman Law and Order ✦ Ralph Paynel

Evidence about Kirkstall Abbey ✦ Monastic England ✦ Dispute at St Mary's Abbey ✦ The Establishment of Fountains Abbey ✦ Henry de Lacy ✦ Barnoldswick ✦ Kirkstall and its Hermits ✦ Cistercians arrive at Kirkstall ✦ Lay Brothers ✦ Choir Monks ✦ Architectural Layout ✦ Abbots of Kirkstall ✦ Obedientiaries ✦ Daily Life ✦ Offenders ✦ Corrodies ✦ Financial Difficulties ✦ Sheep Farming ✦ Granges and Properties ✦ Disputes and Political Events ✦ Bubonic Plague ✦ Changes to Cistercian Life ✦ Dissolution

Villeins and Freemen ✦ Countryside and Field System ✦ The Lord of the Manor's Demesne ✦ Assarting ✦ Decline of the Manor's Value ✦ Paynel's Charter ✦ Maurice Paynel ✦ Leeds, Lancaster and Edward II ✦ Bubonic Plague ✦ Commutation of Service ✦ Economic Recovery ✦ Maintaining the Manor ✦ Mills ✦ Occupations ✦ Coal ✦ Woollen Trade ✦ Religious Ownership in Leeds ✦ The Knights Templar ✦ St Peter's Church and the Chantries ✦ Reformation and the Pilgrimage of Grace ✦ Leeds Grammar School ✦ Crime in Leeds

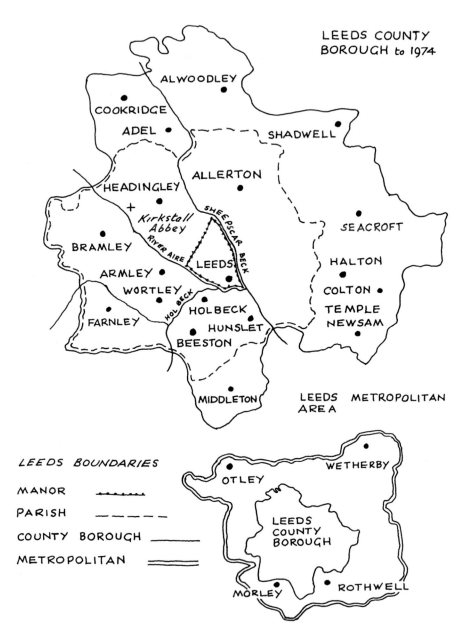

1. Map showing Leeds up to 1974 and the Metropolitan Borough to 2001
The old parish of Leeds incorporated both the manor and the out townships. By 1974 the population of the county borough had reached half a million and by the end of the twentieth century that number had swelled in the metropolitan area to over 700,000.

ACKNOWLEDGEMENTS

I was born in Leeds, educated there and spent my working life teaching in the city. For thirty years I have lectured on, and for ten years taught, local history to adult students. One of their oft-repeated comments was that they felt a book was needed which told the history of Leeds as a story. I hope this book will answer that need.

As a boy I remember Leeds as a place of grimy buildings and clanging tramcars. Nothing important, to my young mind, had ever happened there or ever would happen there. History was made in other places. I still remember the delight in reading in an old geography book that Leeds was famous for its rhubarb industry. I knew that was true because three streets away from our school great fields of rhubarb – 'tusky' as we called it – stretched down to Farnley Beck. I must confess I only half believed my grandad's tale that the Town Hall was really white. When they had finished the building, he said, two workers sat on the top, opened a bottle of beer and spilt it. Thus was the building turned black. And I only half believed him about the lions in front of it who, he said, jumped off their pedestals when the clock struck midnight and began to run around. It was my father who pointed me in the right direction, showing me where the local windmill used to be and the site of the old slaughterhouse. It was he who enthused over names such as Pipe and Nook Lane and who talked of the people who walked the streets of Leeds and told me the stories of their lives. And I still recall the hushed tones my mother always used when referring in reverential awe to that dreadful evening of New Year's Day 1891 when eleven children were burned to death in the Sunday school at nearby Wortley Church.

Through the years, I found Leeds had its place in history. It gave us the clinical thermometer, Portland Cement and 'the oldest railway in the world'. I realised that the story of Leeds was a microcosm of the history of Britain and a story told not simply in the hundreds of books which have been produced over the years but in the buildings around us and the places we walk. In writing this book it became all too obvious that I would need to rely on the help and advice of numerous people. I list them here in alphabetical order. Some have aided me much, others a little, but all have contributed something in the course of its writing: Dr Arnold Aspinall, Gary Atack, Ann Blackburn, Jim Brindle, Jack Carter, Ann Clark, Don Cole, Margaret Elphick, Elsie Firth, Geoffrey Forster, Sheila Gaunt, Brenda Gill, Revd Nicholas Horton, Alan Humphreys, Ivy Lawson, Brigid Murphy, Michele Lefevre, Mick Rainford, Alan Scott, Patricia Scott, David Sheard, Maurice Shore, Pat Shore, Jack Thornton,

John Tilbury, Frank Watkinson and to Fort Publishing, in particular my editor, Susan Milligan and my publisher, James McCarroll.

The following institutions have also been most helpful: Armley Mills Industrial Museum, Department of Archaeological Science Bradford University, House of Commons Information Office, The Leeds Library, Leeds City Libraries, Leeds City Local and Family History Library, The Second World War Experience Centre, Thackray Medical Museum, Temple Newsam House, The Thoresby Society, The Women's Library and the University of Leeds.

In particular I would like to thank Brian Chippendale, Ellen Fahey, Lorna Walker, my wife, June and our family, all of whom have given me every encouragement and wholeheartedly helped me in any way they could. I would point out, however, that any mistakes in this book are mine or my computer's – it does have a mind of its own!

David Thornton
Leeds 2002

LIST OF ILLUSTRATIONS

INTRODUCTION

In 1795, a Dr John Aiken visited Leeds. Apart from being a medical man, Aiken was also a scholar who was researching a book to be called, *A Description of the Country from Thirty to Forty Miles Around Manchester*. After his visit to the West Riding town he wrote: 'The parish of Leeds is situated on the River Aire, which runs nearly through the middle of it. . . . It is divided into ten townships, exclusive of the township of Leeds. . . . Leeds has a general infirmary . . . an excellent workhouse, alms-houses, charity schools and other institutions belonging to a great town.'

The story of Leeds and its out townships – Allerton, Armley, Beeston, Bramley, Farnley, Gipton, Headingley, Holbeck, Hunslet and Wortley – is inextricably linked. Although these townships were manors in their own right they were all part of the rambling parish of Leeds. Just as their story is closely linked to that of Leeds, so the story of Leeds must be seen against the backdrop of English history.

When Roman legions marched across the country the invaders established themselves in this area at Adel, where they built a fort and a *vicus*, or civilian settlement, of some importance. When the great age of monasticism swept across western Europe, the Cistercians built an abbey at Kirkstall, which today is one of the finest monastic ruins to be found anywhere. When the nation was torn apart by civil war and Parliament and king fought to determine where ultimate power resided in the country, Briggate echoed with the sound of musket fire as Parliamentarian and Royalist forces clashed to gain control of the town. When the 1812 Luddite outrages erupted across the North there were violent disturbances in Briggate, Hunslet and Holbeck. With the outbreak of the First World War, a recruiting tram clanged its way around the city. The young men of Leeds came forward to volunteer and, tragically, 9,640 of them never returned home. When the waves of Luftwaffe bombers droned over Britain dropping tons of high explosives, Leeds did not escape. Though suffering far less than Coventry, Liverpool and London, nevertheless, seventy-seven Leeds people were killed, 197 buildings were destroyed and some 7,623 damaged in raids on the town.

But there were also bizarre events in the history of Leeds that were unique to the town. One was the famous Dripping Riot of 1865 that broke out when a cook was sentenced to a month in Armley Jail for stealing some dripping from her employer's kitchen. Even more bizarre was the macabre money making event that occurred in 1809. Surgeon

William Hey dissected the body of the executed murderer Mary Bateman in public, charged an entrance fee and raised £80 14s. 0d. for Leeds General Infirmary!

The story of Leeds encapsulates the story of Britain. But it is not just a story of great national events. It is a story of burgeoning industries: wool textiles, the ready-made clothing industry, linen manufacture, mining, pottery, brick making, printing, engineering and many more. Indeed by 1890, in the leather trade alone, Leeds was producing some 100,000 pairs of boots a week. By the year 2001, the city had become Britain's e-commerce capital handling thirty-five per cent of the country's e-mail traffic. It was that vast diversity in Leeds's industries, and its willingness to keep abreast of a changing world, which proved to be two of the town's greatest assets and provided the basis for its ultimate prosperity.

But any history is inevitably a history of people and the history of Leeds is no exception. Some became famous on the national stage, like Richard Oastler, who campaigned vigorously to improve the appalling conditions that existed in Britain's nineteenth-century factories. More locally recognised was John Harrison. He generously gave St John's Church in Briggate to the people of the town and, along with others, helped to secure for Leeds its charter of 1626.

Some individuals were unwitting participants in history, like poor thirteen years-old John Brice. His claim to fame was that he had the unfortunate distinction of being one of the first people in the world to be killed by a railway steam engine. It happened in 1813 on the Middleton Railway. Other individuals are no more than shadows in the history of Leeds and their personal dramas and tragedies remain untold. A good example is Maria Fisher, a gypsy woman, who in 1845 resided in Paley's Galleries at the top of Marsh Lane. With her husband and eight half-starved children, she lived in a two-room house. They occupied one room that had no furniture, with only straw to sleep on. Their horse was kept in the other room. Without food for her family, she waited for three hours at the Parish Office begging for help but was finally turned away empty handed. Her story would have been long forgotten had not the case been brought to the attention of the local magistrates, assistance finally offered and the story made the columns of the Leeds press.

Where, though, is the story of Leeds told? Eyewitness accounts of Leeds through the ages have been recorded by many visitors to the town. Celia Fiennes, riding around England on horseback, arrived here in 1698. She found it had: 'good houses all built of stone, some have good gardens and steps to their houses . . . this is esteemed the wealthiest town of its bigness in the country'.

In about 1720 Daniel Defoe also arrived. He, too, left a vivid description of the place, in particular of its famous cloth market, 'a prodigy of its kind and not to be equalled in the world'. He noted that between £10,000 and £20,000 worth of business was completed there in just over an hour.

Sarah Siddons, the great actress was far less complimentary. When she appeared at the Leeds Theatre on Hunslet Lane in 1807, she stayed at the Star and Garter inn at Kirkstall. She did so, she said, because there she found 'pure air and perfect quiet' rather than in Leeds, 'the most disagreeable town in His Majesty's dominions'. She had reason to find it disagreeable. On one occasion, so the story goes, whilst playing Lady Macbeth in Leeds, she paused dramatically before a hushed audience. Slowly she raised a glass to her lips, but the illusion was shattered. A wag in the 'gods' shouted out, 'Sup it up, lass!'

Her view of the town was echoed by George Bernard Shaw. Cynical, as ever, he felt that to improve the city: 'It would be necessary to get rid of the people of Leeds and replace them with a rather different sort of people.'

Official reports, private manuscripts, and records all add to the knowledge that can be pieced together to build up a picture of Leeds as it used to be. Was there ever a more graphic official report anywhere than that by Robert Baker, the town's surgeon, written in 1842?

> In one *cul-de-sac*, in the town of Leeds, there are thirty-four houses, and in ordinary times, there dwell in these houses 340 persons . . . during the periods of hay-time and harvest . . . at least twice that number are then congregated . . . the name of this place is the Boot and Shoe-yard, in Kirkgate . . . where now exists a surface of human excrement, of very considerable extent.

Records also enable research students to determine the pattern of voting in Leeds's early elections. The Leeds Poll Books from 1832, when Leeds gained its first two Members of Parliament, to the introduction of the secret ballot in 1872, are still available to examine. These list every individual who voted and how they cast their two votes. Of course, such information was open to abuse. Disappointed at the Tory success in the Leeds election of July 1841, Samuel Smiles, the editor of the *Leeds Times*, published the names of the 'Tory Shopocracy of Briggate', to show 'how many men in one street have not come to their senses'.

The local historian in Leeds is fortunate that the town, at various times, has been served by a wide range of newspapers. The *Leeds Mercury*, and the *Leeds Intelligencer*, which became the *Yorkshire Post*, were both founded in the eighteenth century. Later the *Leeds Patriot*, the *Leeds Independent*, the *Leeds Times*, the *Daily News*, the *Yorkshire Evening News*, the *Yorkshire Evening Post*, the *Leeds Weekly Citizen* and the *Leeds Other Paper* were all launched at different times. And though only the *Yorkshire Post*, the *Yorkshire Evening Post* and the free sheet *Leeds Weekly News* now remain, each has left behind, in differing degrees, a legacy of fascinating detail of the events that occurred in the town. The trial run of Matthew Murray's famous steam engine crossing Hunslet Moor in 1812, the violence of the general election of 1832 when the celebrated so-called Battle of the Standard was fought out on the streets of Leeds between Whig and Tory supporters, the great celebrations carried out by the Sunday evening crowd that massed in Briggate at the end of the Boer War, the election of Leeds's first woman MP, Alice Bacon, in the Labour landslide of 1945, are all graphically chronicled in the columns of the Leeds press. And most of these newspapers are still available on microfilm in Leeds Reference Library for the local historian to consult.

One, however, is not. The *Leeds Wednesday Journal* was founded in January 1841. It was published on a Wednesday because the other Leeds papers appeared on a Saturday. That meant many people would read them on a Sunday which 'is not a day for political discussion or the amusement of light reading,' or so it claimed. It survived only a matter of weeks!

The ordinary people of the town, too, have added their observations and concerns about Leeds, and many of those concerns have a remarkably modern ring about them. In January 1810, a correspondent calling himself 'Aquarius' expressed the view that carrying water in lead pipes was 'disadvantageous very serious'. 'Septimus' in a letter to the *Leeds Times* in 1845 also expressed concern about pollution. He wrote 'the dark and murky cloud . . . has I fear choked the lungs of Leeds people. . . . Let the atmosphere be cleared.'

Most letter writers to newspapers during the nineteenth century were men. But, on 20 March 1841, the *Leeds Times* featured a letter from 'Laone' and the paper felt it necessary to emphasise it had been written 'by a woman'. Her comments, once again, could well have been written 160 years later and they demonstrate that even in provincial, Victorian Leeds there were women prepared to express radical views: 'Laws have been passed most injurious to the interests of women, both as females and as citizens. . . . It cannot be asserted that women are indifferent to political existence . . . there are many women in England who think.'

In 1715 Ralph Thoresby produced the first history of Leeds, his famous *Ducatus Leodiensis*. Since then numerous books on the town's history have appeared. The Thoresby Society, founded in 1889, is dedicated to furthering the study of the history of the town and Leeds is the proud possessor of a Local and Family History Library whose resources can match any local history library in the land. Numerous local history societies have also mushroomed over the latter years of the twentieth century, many producing valuable information about their own locality.

But history is not always recorded in books. Anyone walking around with their eyes open can see it written in the bricks and mortar of the buildings of the city. What can the stones of those buildings reveal? They typify the age in which they were built. Adel's Norman church, the fifteenth-century Stank Hall Barn at Beeston, the magnificent Jacobean Temple Newsam House, Barran's Moorish style factory in Park Square, Gott's great mill at Armley, now the home of the Industrial Museum, and Cuthbert Brodrick's two masterpieces, the Corn Exchange and his classic Town Hall, each reflect their period. In 1858, the people of Leeds were euphoric when Queen Victoria came to open that new Town Hall. One local chemist, Mr Trant, went to the extreme length of perfuming the very air outside his Park Lane shop as the queen was scheduled to pass by! However, in evaluating evidence the local historian must be wary. Many a stranger, looking westwards to Armley Jail, has remarked that they never knew Leeds had such a magnificent medieval castle. The jail was opened in 1847!

The very street names, too, give an indication as to what was there in the past. Lady Lane is a reminder of the site of the chantry chapel built to Our Lady in the Middle Ages, Butts Court stands near the old archery butts that were on Butts Lane, now known as Basinghall Street. Park Row also has a medieval ring about it, because from here the great manorial park stretched westwards. Mill Hill led directly to the great corn mill by the river, whilst Mabgate could well indicate it was the ancient red light district of the area. A 'mab' was a woman of loose character.

To different people the history of Leeds offers different objectives. Academics have examined its political infighting, the diversity of its religious sects, the structure of its social classes, or pursued specific topics like the development of health, housing and education in the city. They would, for example, analyse the Leeds Public Library Committee report of 1870-2 which showed that 1,215 professional and middle-class people borrowed books compared, in the same period, to 4,434 working-class borrowers and try to explain why such a discrepancy occurred.

Some people simply want bald facts. They relish knowing, for example, that one of the earliest moving pictures filmed anywhere was made at Leeds Bridge in October 1888 by Louis le Prince, a French photographer based in the town; or that, in 1867, Dr Clifford Allbutt of Leeds General Infirmary invented the clinical thermometer as we now know it.

Some want to pore over pure statistics and are absorbed in facts such as those which show that in 1801 the population of the town coupled with its out townships numbered 53,276, whereas a hundred years later the number had soared to 428,968; that the Leeds Co-operative Society of 1896, with over 33,000 members, was the largest in the world or that in 1926 there were 107 people employed in the town making umbrellas, gloves and corsets.

History is about change and the lack of change. Those seeking to find comparisons between the Leeds of the past and the Leeds of the present will not be disappointed. In the columns of the *Leeds Mercury* alone readers can find numerous examples. In December 1801 a letter appeared deploring the fact that modern Christmases are not what they used to be. In August 1811 vandals were criticised for smashing street lamps; in November 1814 'indecorous behaviour' in the streets on a Sunday was bitterly condemned; and in September 1827 another letter claimed that surgeons at Leeds General Infirmary were devoting too much time to private practice.

Some things did alter, of course, and sometimes people were reluctant to accept those changes. D. H. Atkinson writing in 1868 was one such person: 'Once it was my delight to walk through the fields from the foot of Merry Boys' Hill (Headrow) to Woodhouse Moor, but changes on that side put a stop long since to my walks westward. Soon I fear we shall have nothing but street all the way to Kirkstall Abbey.'

Other people simply want to know why such is such. Why, for example, is St James's Hospital called St James's? The answer is not for any religious association with the saints, James the Great or James the Just. It was to honour two men who had served the hospital through the years; Dr James Allen and Mr (later Sir) James Ford.

Or perhaps people simply enjoy the trivia of Leeds history: like tales of the Prince of Wales's incognito visits to the City Varieties to see his favourite, Lily Langtry; the fact that when the Hull to Leeds Railway line was extended from Marsh Lane into Leeds in 1865, it had to be laid on India Rubber sleepers as it passed the Parish Church; or that the Australians played cricket at Headingley before the Yorkshire County team ever did!

But where did the name 'Leeds' originate? And why did Leeds grow into the place it has become? Why did not Adel or Beeston, Headingley or Seacroft develop into a major European city? Why was it that they eventually were absorbed into Leeds and not Leeds into them?

The first question has no definite answer. Over the years, Leeds has been known as Leedes, Ledes, Ledis and, originally, Loidis. It should be remembered, though, that when the Venerable Bede made that first ever mention of the place, he was referring to the area around Leeds, as well as Leeds itself. It is possible that Loidis meant 'the people living by the Aire' and that the Angles who lived there pronounced the British name of the river 'Loid'. But no one can be sure.

The reasons why Leeds grew where and how it did are more certain. First, it is fortunate that it nestles in the valley of the River Aire. Crucially, it stands at a point where the water can be crossed. It appears from archaeological evidence found in 1819 that here, in all probability, a Roman ford had been established. Local tradition also claims that a ferry operated near the bottom of Briggate. By the late fourteenth century a bridge had been erected but it is possible one existed much earlier than that. In effect, Leeds was the place people would make for if they wished to cross the River Aire and inevitably it became a convenient meeting place.

It was also ideally sited for early travellers crossing the country from coast to coast. To the west lay the Aire Gap, the easiest crossing point of the Pennines anywhere between Derbyshire and Scotland. For those travelling north to south, Leeds was also a convenient point to aim for as it lay between the low-lying wet lands that were to the east and the steep-sided valleys of the Pennine foothills to the west.

The water supply to the town was another key factor in its growth. The flowing waters of the river brought with it power. It worked the fulling mills so vital in the finishing process of making cloth in the Middle Ages and later it helped to power the great mills of the woollen industry in the late eighteenth and early nineteenth centuries. But it was not simply the waters of the Aire itself that were important. The becks flowing from the north of the town coursed their way over areas of millstone grit resulting in soft, pure water, ideal for washing, scouring and dyeing cloth. To the south lie layers of sandstone and shale, water bearing rocks that would provide invaluable supplies when the river waters became polluted as the effects of the Industrial Revolution so mutilated the environment.

In earlier times the river was also a waterway if, on occasion, open to the vagaries of varying levels. In November 1700 when the Aire and Calder Navigation was opened, it became a dependable link to the North Sea and beyond. Then in 1816, with the opening of the Leeds and Liverpool Canal, the manufacturing towns of the hinterland of the West Riding could transport their goods through Leeds to both coasts and thus on to the valuable markets of Europe and the Americas. By the 1820s regular services also sailed between Leeds and London.

These waterways helped to make Leeds a focal point. It developed into an important transport centre for, apart from its valuable river and canal, a series of roads radiating from the town was constructed over the latter part of the eighteenth, and early part of the nineteenth, centuries. These enabled goods and raw materials to be brought into Leeds and finished products transported to various parts of the country. In 1781 twenty-five carrier firms were operating in Leeds. Similarly, a thriving coaching industry developed. By the 1830s over a dozen coaching inns around Briggate were dealing with up to 130 arrivals and departures daily. And even at the dawn of the twenty-first century, Leeds still is one of the hubs of the nation's motorway system.

There were other natural assets that also benefited the town. Coal was a vital one. Thoresby had noted in 1714 that there were 'pits without number' around Leeds. But what he could never have envisaged was how those coal deposits of Leeds would influence the growth of the town. With transport costs minimal, cheap fuel was readily available and on hand for any entrepreneur willing to become part of the great Industrial Revolution that so changed the face of Britain and the way of life of its people. That coal would fuel the factories and mills and heat the homes of the burgeoning workforce as the population soared and the industries of Leeds multiplied.

No single history book could ever hope to tell the whole story of Leeds. This book is no different. It should be read like the guidebook of a journey that points out certain places to visit, certain sights to see. Readers can then in their own time choose which topic or period has a particular interest for them, and pursue it at their leisure. It is a journey that begins thousands of years ago, long before people foraged their way along the banks of the River Aire, and long before 'Septimus's' 'dark and murky cloud' spoilt the landscape.

CHAPTER ONE

THE DAWNING

Without the River Aire there would have been no Leeds. The Aire springs in full flow from under the towering limestone cliff of Malham Cove, high in the rugged Pennine mountains. From there it meanders south-eastwards where it flows into the Humber and thence to the sea. But what was the Aire valley like before human beings arrived there? Like the rest of Britain in the great Ice Ages, it would have found itself blanketed under huge sheets of ice and shrouded in bitter snowy wastes.

About 124,000 years ago the third Ice Age receded. The climate became sub-tropical and hyenas, lions, elephants and rhinoceroses roamed across the Yorkshire landscape. By the banks of the River Aire hippopotamuses wallowed and straight-tusked elephants rambled over the surrounding hills. The coming of the last Ice Age saw these sub-tropical animals disappear, no longer able to survive the severe Arctic conditions. Now mammoths, woolly rhinoceroses, and aurochs or wild oxen inhabited that bleak landscape and crossed and re-crossed the hillsides of the Aire valley where Leeds sprawls today.

Historians, or rather palaeontologists, are able to claim that these animals hunted and roved across the Yorkshire countryside by examining the evidence that has come to light over the years. The remains of such beasts have been found across Yorkshire from Settle in the Pennines to Sewerby on the east coast. In Victoria Cave at Settle the remains of hippopotamuses, elephants and rhinoceroses have been unearthed. Their carcasses had been dragged there by scavenging hyenas whose bones were also found scattered among those of their victims. From Sewerby have come the bones of mammoths, giant deer and slender-nosed rhinoceroses. Leeds is no exception. In 1852 the bones of the famous 'Armley Hippo' were discovered in a clay pit. But they turned out to be the remains of not one but three hippopotamuses, two adults and a young, and they were found not in Armley but in Wortley. Again in West Leeds, the bones of an auroch and a mammoth have been found, whilst at Thwaite Mills the huge tusk of another mammoth has also been unearthed.

Between 10,000 and 11,000 years ago the ice began to melt. Hunters of the Old Stone Age or Palaeolithic Age, pursuing herds of reindeer, woolly rhinoceros and mammoth moved from Europe to

1

Britain, crossing the land mass that later became the southern half of the North Sea. They settled in a tundra-like landscape of scattered pine and birch trees. But a sudden dramatic change in climate between 10,900 years and 10,300 years ago saw the land become much warmer. More luscious vegetation reappeared and the Aire valley became heavily forested with oak, birch, hazel, alder and pine. Large tracts of the land were boggy. The word 'carr' means 'wet boggy ground' and perhaps the names Sheepscar, Hunslet Carr and Carr Crofts at Armley each reflect those marshy tracts that may well have existed in prehistoric times.

But the old cliché about being 'shrouded in the mists of time' has a definite application when related to the early history of Leeds. It was not until 1086, when William I's commissioners arrived in the town to record their findings for the Domesday Book, that the first detailed account of the place was written. It is true that the Venerable Bede made the first mention of it in AD 731. He did it twice, in fact, in his *History of the English Church and People* but the scholarly monk gives us little detailed information. What information we can glean about the years before 1086 has to come from archaeological evidence. It comes from artefacts such as tools, weapons and pottery or the remains of ancient earthworks and the scattered bones of animals.

It was such a discovery, between 1963 and 1966, of some stone tools at Thorpe Stapleton a few miles to the east of Leeds, which showed that human beings of the Mesolithic or Middle Stone Age had settled in the area. These people were hunters and gatherers, foraging for nuts, berries and roots and tracking the auroch, elk, wild pig and red deer that ranged across the land.

About 6000 BC copper and gold were being used in Asia and by 3000 BC smiths discovered that by adding one part tin to nine parts copper, bronze could be produced. It was a vastly superior metal and migrating tribes moved westward taking the new technology with them. Between 2000 BC and 1800 BC some of them entered Britain, probably by the Humber estuary and settled across what is now Yorkshire. But the coming of the Bronze Age, like the coming of the Industrial Revolution, did not occur overnight and many of the old techniques continued to be used along with the new. A flint scraper, for example, found at Ireland Wood in 1968, was not made in the Stone Age but during the Bronze Age.

These Bronze Age people were known as the Beaker People from their practice of burying a finely made drinking vessel or beaker with their dead. Such a beaker was found at Tinshill in 1960. They grew wheat and barley, domesticated cattle, sheep, goats and pigs and bred bees, not so much for their honey, but for the wax needed for casting bronze. They lived in thatched stone huts but the extensive development of Leeds over the centuries has obliterated any remains of their settlements there.

Artefacts, however, have been discovered which prove that these people were present in the Aire valley and its surrounds. At Roundhay four palstaves or bronze chisels were found and at Hunslet a socketed bronze axe. In the past, reports have claimed that at Thwaite Gate a bronze spearhead had been found, at Chapel Allerton a bronze dagger, and in Briggate, in 1745, an urn containing burnt bones. But, like the two Bronze Age burial mounds, or barrows, that are said to have been on Woodhouse Moor, they have now disappeared. However, the strange 'cup and ring' markings, carved at that time on a stone in Gab Wood above Horsforth, still remain.

The Beaker People were of an industrious nature and, as the Bronze Age was a fairly peaceful period, trade developed. The Aire valley became a major trade route where amber from the Baltic and jet from the Whitby area were ferried westwards. Flat bronze axes and gold were transported east from Ireland.

Further invasions of Britain occurred from the continent. These Celtic peoples brought with them another great technological advance – the use of iron. About 650 BC iron working arrived in Britain and the period known as the Iron Age began but, like the Bronze Age, it developed over a long span of time.

The Celts were a tribal people and among their tribes were the Iceni of Norfolk, made famous by Queen Boudicca's revolt against the Romans, and the Parisi of East Yorkshire. But without doubt one of the most powerful tribes in Britain was the Brigantes, a federation of tribes whose kingdom virtually covered the entire north of England, taking in the area where Leeds now lies. Aldborough was their capital but most of these people did not live in the nine Brigantian towns. They lived on scattered farms eking a living out of the land, and faced a colder and wetter climate than we do today. Like the Bronze Age farmers before them, they cleared the woodland to grow wheat, barley, oats, rye and flax. They reared cattle, sheep, goats and pigs, and traded in horses.

Their farmsteads consisted of circular stone huts about eight metres in diameter, with thatched roofs and rectangular walled enclosures for their animals. Remains of such circular hut settlements have been found near Cookridge Hospital and off Iveson Rise. They ground their corn into flour by hand using beehive querns. The bases of four of these querns and a quern top were discovered in the area in 1908 and some russet-coloured earthenware pottery was also recovered in 1923. At Ledston near Leeds, where another Iron Age settlement was found, pits used for storing grain have been excavated.

The Brigantes were a highly organised and artistic people but periods of inter-tribal warfare often broke out. Thus they built themselves defensive enclosures where, when danger threatened, they could take their families and herd their livestock. Such defence works were constructed at Gipton, Temple Newsam, Chapel Allerton and probably on Woodhouse Moor. But whereas the remains of the first three are still visible the latter site has long since disappeared. Rampart Road which runs across the Moor may well indicate that long-lost fort.

However, whatever defences the British tribes had devised they were unable to withstand the onslaught of the Roman armies. In AD 43, Emperor Claudius launched his successful invasion of Britain. As the Roman conquest spread north, Cartimandua, the Brigantian queen, managed to maintain her tribe's independence by allying it with Rome. In so doing, she eventually split both her tribe and her marriage. Many of the Brigantes, including her husband Venutius, opposed her treaty with the invaders. The final straw came when she handed over the British resistance leader, Caractacus, to the Romans. Now in open revolt, Venutius gathered his forces together at Stanwick, but in AD 74 Petillius Cerialis and his IX Legion heavily defeated him. The authority of Rome was stamped on the area.

Four years later Agricola became governor of Britain. He realised that to maintain Roman authority meant acknowledging the threat the Brigantes still posed. To enable him quickly to subdue any further outbreaks of resistance, he embarked upon building a series of roads across the country. One of these roads ran through Burgodunum, the present day Adel, linking York (Eboracum), Tadcaster (Calcaria), Ilkley (Olicana) and Ribchester (Bremetennacum).

Opinions are divided over the site at Adel. Unquestionably, Roman objects such as roof tiles, brooches, coins and pottery have been found there. Excavations have gone on intermittently from the 1930s to the present and the extent of the discoveries at Adel indicate that Burgodunum was a substantial Roman settlement and a site of some considerable importance.

The dispute centres on whether a Roman fort existed there. Earlier writers from Ralph Thoresby onwards believe that one had been built. More recent historians have disputed this and argue that as no Roman evidence has been found in the area of the supposed military site, such a claim cannot be made. However, during the 1990s, a geophysical survey by the Department of Archaeological Science at Bradford University unearthed evidence that verifies the theory that a fort had been built at Adel, but it was located some distance from the site that Thoresby had examined.

Its layout was that of a traditional Roman fort, shaped rather like a playing card with gates on four sides and at Adel surrounded by a single defensive ditch. It stood directly on the Ilkley to Tadcaster road and was roughly equidistant from the Roman forts at Ilkley and Newton Kyme near Tadcaster. The civilian settlement or *vicus*, which was itself a major site, stood to the west of the fort. If the position of Adel is considered geographically, it is clear that Burgodunum would have been ideally placed strategically as a military base to oversee the Brigantes of the Wharfe and Aire valleys.

As far as Leeds itself is concerned, no direct evidence of Roman buildings has been found but numerous finds of Roman objects indicate a strong Roman presence. Coins have been recovered in Wade Lane, Burmantofts and Headingley. Pottery was found near the Headrow. At Chapel Allerton both a Roman altar and a burial have been discovered and a further burial has also been located in Hunslet. But the most intriguing issue is whether the Romans built a fort in Leeds. Once again all archaeological evidence has long since disappeared but it is thought that one possibly stood at Quarry Hill, near the site of the present day West Yorkshire Playhouse.

Historians have long known that Cambodunum, a Roman fort, existed on the York to Manchester (Mancunium) road some twenty Roman miles from Tadcaster. Its site, however, has always been uncertain. It is now thought that there is a strong possibility that its actual location was Leeds. It has been contended that the York to Manchester road crossed the Aire at the ford discovered in 1819 south of Leeds Bridge and then ran up a line to the east of Briggate. It is easy to see how the Quarry Hill site would have been strategically ideal, in order to control the only river crossing for miles around. And the very name of Cambodunum indicates that Leeds was the site, for it meant 'fort by the river bend'.

For almost four hundred years the Roman occupation continued. And though there were, occasionally, local uprisings like the one that destroyed Ilkley in AD 115, most of the time people had to get on living their lives as craftsmen, traders and farmers. Large farms were known as villas and east of Leeds, at Dalton Parlours near Wetherby one was built about AD 200. The area it covered had previously been one of the largest Iron Age sites in the north of England. The villa was an extensive building with living quarters that had mosaic floors, a bath-house and a typical Roman hypocaust, or underfloor central heating system.

By now Britain was a Christian country, but in the fourth century pagan Anglo-Saxon invaders began terrorising the Yorkshire coast. In AD 367 they destroyed Malton. Other pagan tribes in central Europe challenged the authority of Rome and in AD 410 the Eternal City was sacked. Emperor Honorius declared that Britain must look to defend itself from then on and the last Roman troops departed these shores. It was the beginning of the so-called Dark Ages. But it is from this period that we begin to see Leeds slowly emerging as a place of some consequence in the region. It was a position from which it has never faltered.

When the Romans withdrew, the small kingdom of Elmet was established, stretching from the marshy land at the head of the River Humber to the foothills of the Pennines. Loidis or Leeds and the area around it, was probably a subdivision of that kingdom. The pagan invaders swept across the south and east of Britain: the Saxons principally occupying Essex, Wessex and Sussex; the Jutes Kent, the Isle of Wight and Hampshire; and the Angles the Midlands and the North. Here however, they were confronted with Elmet, a British buffer state curbing the heathen's expansion and one of the last outposts of Christianity in an increasingly hostile country. In all probability, Grim's Ditch, a defensive earthwork about three miles east of Leeds, may well have been constructed to help deter these invading hordes, as were Becca Banks and Woodhouse Moor Rein near Aberford. It is now thought, too, that the mounds at Adel, once considered to be the remains of Thoresby's Roman fort, were in all probability erected as defences at this time.

Eventually in AD 617, Edwin, King of Northumbria overcame the resistance of Elmet. Nennius, the eighth-century Welsh historian, records in his *Historia Britonum* how Edwin conquered the small kingdom and expelled Certic, its king. The invasion could well have been an act of revenge. Hereric, a relative of Edwin had been driven into exile by Ethelfrith, the King of Bernicia, a kingdom which stretched north of the River Tees. He sought sanctuary with a certain British king, known as Cerdic. Hereric was poisoned and if the Certic of Elmet is the same as the Cerdic in the story, it may well have been that the murder was one of the reasons which precipitated Edwin's invasion. Whatever the causes for the Northumbrian expansion, the small kingdom was absorbed and Leeds became part of Northumbria. Edwin eventually converted to the Christian faith and possibly set up his capital in Leeds.

The evidence for this is substantiated by the Venerable Bede if the town truly was the site of the Roman Cambodunum. Writing in his *A History of the English Church and People,* he makes only a minor change of spelling when he makes the first-ever mention of Leeds, or Loidis as he calls both the town and the area round it.

> A basilica was built at the royal residence of Campodunum; but this, together with all the buildings of the royal residence, was burned by the pagans who killed King Edwin, and later kings replaced this seat by another in the vicinity of Loidis. The stone altar of this church survived the fire, and is preserved in the monastery in Elmet Wood.

Edwin was killed in battle at Hatfield Chase near Doncaster but his conqueror, Penda, the pagan King of Mercia, was himself later killed in the vicinity of Leeds. The Battle of Winwaed was fought in AD 655 and Bede again recounted the event: 'This battle was won by King Oswy in the region of Loidis on the 15th of November'. The exact location of the battlefield is unknown, but the course of the Cock Beck in the Stanks and Seacroft area is a favoured site. Certainly, Penda's name is perpetuated in the area in the streets named Penda's Way, and Penda's Walk.

Little archaeological evidence from this period has been found in Leeds but Christianity must have been re-established there by this time. In 1809, when work was being carried out on the old Parish Church, the head of an Anglian wheel-cross was discovered. Then, in 1838, work began on the complete rebuilding of Leeds Parish Church and this in turn produced a major discovery from the Christian Anglian period. As the old tower built in Edward III's reign was being pulled down, workmen found some stones with strange interlaced runic-like characters engraved on them. Robert Chantrell, the architect, offered rewards for any similar stones that turned up.

He was perfectly within his rights, as the terms of his contract enabled him to claim any 'old material' found on the site. Eventually a large collection of fragments of at least five stone crosses was recovered and Chantrell had the finds taken to his home in Little London where he meticulously catalogued them. The result was that he was able to fit together one almost complete Anglian, or as many people refer to it, Saxon, cross.

When he retired to Rottingdean near Brighton, he had the cross re-erected in a rockery in the middle of the lawn of his home, Ivy Cottage. Chantrell died and when news of his widow's death reached Leeds, steps were taken to recover the ancient object. Dr Gott, the Vicar of Leeds, entered into negotiations to buy it back.

A Court of Chancery placed a value of £3 on it but the new owner, a grocer, flatly refused to sell, threatening to break it up into rubble.

Gott then privately visited his shop and offered £25. The grocer demanded £100. But Gott persisted, eventually buying the cross for the price he offered and that very night removed it. Thus the Anglian Cross was returned to Leeds and was re-erected on the altar flat of the Parish Church in 1880.

But most important, its presence on the site indicates that a church of some importance stood there in ninth-century Anglian Britain. It is difficult to see so magnificent an object, along with several other crosses, belonging to a church of little consequence and if Leeds possessed a church of considerable significance, it follows that the town itself must have reached a position of importance. It was certainly important enough to be considered as a place suitable for the safe handing over of a person of some note as the eleventh-century *Life of Saint Cadroë* indicates.

The invasion of Britain by the Vikings saw Northumbria thrust into a state of turmoil. The invading Norsemen set up their capital at York and from the north-west the British Kingdom of Strathclyde expanded southwards through Westmorland and Cumbria. It is even claimed that Leeds was on the boundary of the two kingdoms.

About AD 842, St Cadroë visited the King of Strathclyde and then set off for Winchester. King Domnall, his relative, accompanied him as far as : '. . . the city of Loidis, which is the boundary of the Northmen and the Cumbrians; and there he was taken up by a certain nobleman, Gunderic, by whom he was led to King Eric in the city of York.'

Whatever its importance, the people of Leeds would have been faced with the arrival of the Vikings and the establishment of the Danelaw, the huge kingdom that covered the Midlands, East Anglia and Yorkshire. Here Danish legal customs operated. The image of marauding Norsemen in horned helmets wreaking havoc and devastation wherever they went is far from the whole truth. Certainly, the *Anglo-Saxon Chronicle* graphically describes atrocities carried out by the invaders, but these people were also skilled craftsmen, farmers and traders. Many eventually embraced Christianity. They introduced a sophisticated system of government dividing the county into ridings or thirdings and subdivided these into wapentakes. The one thing they did not do was wear horned helmets!

The people of Leeds were part of the Danelaw. Unfortunately, little hard evidence from that period has been found around the town. Thoresby tells us that a 'Danish fortification' was built at Giant's Hill, Armley, overlooking the River Aire. Later suggestions have been made that it may well have been a motte and bailey or ring-work and bailey castle. However, whatever earthwork was present there has long since been eradicated. But the *Coucher Book* of Kirkstall Abbey for 1300 refers to 'Castel Armelay' and the district is still called Castleton. Both facts indicate some fortification probably existed in Armley but whether the site was Viking or relates to a later period is impossible to say.

What has been left behind is the language of those Norse settlers. Scholars have examined the place names of Yorkshire during the eleventh century and have been able to draw a picture of how that settlement probably took place. The Vikings set up their kingdom at York but it appears that the newcomers preferred the Vale of York and East Riding Wolds areas to settle in. The West Riding, including Leeds, was part of that Viking kingdom. However, the lack of many Norse place names in the riding suggests that although some of the invaders would have settled there, the majority of people living in west Yorkshire were the indigenous Anglo-Saxons.

These different peoples would have worked together and intermarried and much of the invaders' language was absorbed. Today such Viking words as *beck* for a stream are used and, in the name of the Leeds street Kirkgate, are found two Viking words: *kirk* meaning *church* and *gate* or *gata* which meant *road*. But if words can indicate where people settled, they can also give an impression of what the area around Leeds and its surrounding villages was like. Beyond the manor of Leeds it appears to have been, on the whole, a heavily wooded landscape with clearings known as assarts where the small settlements were established. Alwoodley, for example, meant Athelwold's forest-glade or clearing; Headingley, the forest clearing of Headda; Seacroft, an enclosure near a pool; Shadwell, a spring in a shady place; Armley, Earms(a)'s woodland glade or clearing; Bramley and Farnley, a woodland glade or clearing overgrown with broom and fern respectively.

Leeds and its surrounding villages fell into two wapentakes. Wapentakes were the Scandinavian equivalent of the Saxon Hundred. Here all freemen gathered each month to solve local disputes, oversee the peace and punish crime. To signify agreement the members of the assembly took their weapons and flourished them, hence the word *wapentake*.

Those villages south of the River Aire such as Armley, Beeston, Farnley and Bramley attended the Morley wapentake which stretched from Hunslet in the east to Todmorden in the west, and probably met at Tingley. North of the river lay the Skyrack wapentake reaching as far north as Arthington and Pool, as far west as Bingley and as far east as Aberford. It gathered at a suitable focal point in Headingley, a massive oak tree known as the Shire Oak. The name may have originally meant 'bright oak' or *siaraches* and *Skyrack* may have been a variation on this word. Today both Shire Oak Road and the Skyrack Inn perpetuate the name. For over a thousand years that oak tree stood at Headingley but, on 26 May 1941, it finally collapsed. It was to this Skyrack wapentake that the men from the manor of Leeds came.

No specific records relating to Leeds at this time exist but there is no reason to suppose its inhabitants escaped the plagues that regularly ravaged the country such as those in AD 987, 1001 and 1046, or the famines that occurred just as regularly, such as the one that lasted from 1041 until 1066.

That year, 1066, was to herald a significant change in English history when Duke William of Normandy launched his invasion of England. Riding roughshod over the indigenous population, he effected the most sweeping and brutal transformation of English society ever perpetrated either before or since. Every man, woman and child was affected to some degree but for the inhabitants of Yorkshire it resulted in the most calamitous event that the people of the county have ever experienced. Mysteriously, for the people of Leeds it appears to have had just the opposite effect.

On the death of Edward the Confessor in 1066, Harold Godwinson was chosen as successor to the throne of England, but, at the Battle of Hastings, Duke William of Normandy, by skilful generalship and some luck, defeated the new English king. Within two years of assuming the throne, William had to face three revolts in the North. The final out-break, which started in Durham, soon spread to Yorkshire and the Norman garrison in York was besieged. In the latter part of 1069, William resolved to put down the uprising with a ferocity which would ensure that never again would his rule be challenged. The Harrying of the North began.

After an initial setback when the swollen River Aire held up his punitive force for three weeks, William finally crossed at Ferrybridge, and designated Ilbert de Lacy, one of his Norman barons, to quell the uprising in the west of the county. William himself attended to the rest and ensured that the land from the Humber to the Tees was turned into a virtual wilderness. As the writer of the *Anglo-Saxon Chronicle* says, 'King William marched into that shire and completely devastated it.' With their crops destroyed, their cattle slaughtered and their homes demolished, the bulk of the population became either wandering refugees or simply starved to death as famine swept the land. Of 1,900 settlements listed in the Domesday Book in Yorkshire, 850 were totally destroyed and a further 300 partially so.

William then set about resolutely imposing his authority across the country. He distributed estates to his followers on condition they gave him undivided loyalty. One vast tract of land was granted to Ilbert de Lacy, a baron from an estate a few miles east of Rouen in Normandy. De Lacy's new estate ranged from Pontefract, where Ilbert built his castle, to Blackburn in Lancashire and was known as the Honour of Pontefract. Leeds and its surrounding villages were part of it. But much of Ilbert's newly acquired land had been turned into little more than a wasteland. The exception was Leeds itself, for the town appears to have been spared the brutal subjugation meted out by the Norman force to the surrounding villages.

A few days after Christmas 1085, William determined to know exactly what his new kingdom contained in order that the correct amount of taxes due could be assessed. He directed commissioners to cross the country and compile a record of the places they visited. That record would explain, among other things, who owned it when Edward the Confessor was king, and who now owned it; how much woodland and pasture there was and how many people lived there; what was its value when Edward was reigning and what now. It was the most comprehensive survey of England carried out until the nineteenth century. It listed 45,000 holdings and 14,000 places. It is claimed it was so authoritative that people likened it to the Last Judgement, hence its name Domesday Book, and certainly by the 1170s it was known as such.

For some reason it missed out both London and Winchester but, fortunately, it included Leeds and thus gives the first detailed account of the town as it was in 1086 when the commissioners arrived. In so doing it also graphically identified the devastation Ilbert had brought to this locality during the Harrying of the North.

Headingley had been worth 40 shillings and was now worth just 4. Newsam, later Temple Newsam, dropped from a value of 60 shillings to 6. Armley and Reestones, which later became Wortley, originally valued at 20 shillings was now worth 10. Gipton and Colton, though boasting a church, had plummeted from 40 shillings to 2 and carried the gloomy observation that it was 'waste'. The value of Seacroft's woodland and pasture had dropped from £4 to 20d. but the commissioners considered that too was 'waste'. It was not alone. Coldcotes, Manston, Bramley, Beeston, Halton and Allerton, later Chapel Allerton, all carry the same grim description whilst Hunslet was given no value at all.

Leeds was a different story. The vill or township actually increased in value from £6 to £7. Even at £6 it was valued far more highly than any of the surrounding settlements. Before the Conquest, the manor of

Leeds had been divided between seven thanes, men who held a position between that of freeman and hereditary nobleman. In 1086, there were twenty-seven villeins, sometimes described as villagers, living there. Though not slaves, they were not freemen and were obliged to provide a variety of services to the lord of the manor in exchange for their cottages and land. There were four bordars who, though working sometimes for wages and performing menial tasks for the lord of the manor, cultivated some land for themselves. There were also four freemen or sokemen, farmers who rented their land from the lord at a fixed rent. Those thirty-five men, together with their families, meant Leeds would probably have had a population in the region of about two hundred in 1086.

The town itself stretched eastwards down Kirkgate as far as the church. To the west near the river lay the corn mill and a further small group of buildings. Farther north were two more small hamlets at Buslingthorpe and Great Woodhouse, which stood on the sides of a ridge north-west of Leeds. To the east lay the tiny settlements of Hillhouse, now Richmond Hill, and Knostrop which flanked the Aire. There was also a small pocket of land that belonged to the manor in the out-township of Holbeck known as Cat-Beeston.

Much of the woodland in the manor itself had been utilised over the centuries and the only valuable sources of timber left were found in what became the manorial park to the west of the town and to the north on Woodhouse Ridge.

The buildings would probably have been a collection of wooden structures with smaller outbuildings. Agriculture was the principal occupation as it was throughout all of England and, from ancient man-uscripts of the period, we can see how the people of this time farmed. Grass was scythed for haymaking in July. The corn harvest was reaped in August and threshed in September. Sowing was carried out in October, and those beasts not retained for breeding slaughtered in November. And so it would have been for the inhabitants of Leeds.

Their diet consisted of fish, eaten particularly on a Friday, a Christian tradition borrowed from the Roman followers of the goddess Venus. Cattle, hens, geese and pigs were reared for food. They bred sheep principally for wool and milk. Only the older animals were slaughtered for mutton. The pig was the poor man's animal and left to wander the moor at Woodhouse under the watchful eye of the local swineherd. Wheat and rye produced bread, and butter and cheese were eaten with it. Their drinks were ale, beer made without hops, and mead, fermented honey and water, though this was mainly the drink of the aristocracy.

The manor boasted a mill and ten acres of meadow. The mill, powered by a series of goits or watercourses from the Aire, was built about where the old Swinegate tram depot and later Queen's Hall stood. This, again, indicates the growing wealth of Leeds. Only one third of the manors listed in the Domesday Book possessed a mill. There were also fourteen plough teams, each team being made up of eight oxen.

Many churches were in existence at the time of the *Domesday Book* survey but were not included in the record. Perhaps it is an indication of its importance that Leeds Parish Church is recorded. The commissioners noted that there was a church with an attendant parish priest. His responsibility, however, lay not only for Leeds itself. The parish took in Allerton, Armley, Beeston, Bramley, Farnley, Gipton, Headingley, Holbeck, Hunslet, Osmondthorpe and Wortley.

Inevitably, one crucial question is asked: why was there such a mystifying increase in the value of Leeds, when the surrounding villages had suffered such devastation and been reduced to such little worth? The historian can do no more than hypothesise and recognise that, in the end, no satisfactory explanation will ever be forthcoming.

It may be that Leeds did suffer devastation during the Harrying of the North but that the lord of the manor, appreciating its potential value, decided to send more plough teams into the place and stimulate its growth. In so doing he would strengthen its economic base and thus increase the overall value. It may be that the Normans realised its strategic value at a river crossing and so deliberately left it untouched. Thus, it would have been in a position to expand economically unhindered while the ruined villages of the surrounding area were left to languish well behind it. Is it possible that, as Leeds was clearly far wealthier than the surrounding settlements, it could afford to buy off its would-be destroyers? It would not be the first time in history that bribery had averted catastrophe. Or is it feasible that the punitive expeditionary force inadvertently overlooked Leeds? It was, after all, nestled in a valley, surrounded by marshy ground, woodland and inhospitable countryside that lay beyond its outskirts. There were no maps at the time and the roads running from village to village were no more than rough tracks.

The student is even bound to wonder whether the Domesday commissioners themselves almost missed the town. The entries for the places listed in the Domesday Book are arranged in two neat columns, yet the Leeds entry appears scribbled across the bottom of a page almost as if it were an afterthought.

But all this is conjecture. The answer will never be known and once again the historian is reminded that the study of history so often ends with questions remaining unanswered. What is certain is that Norman Leeds had reached a vastly superior economic position to any of the villages around. It was a position from which it would dominate the area for the next millennium.

William knew that he must be ever vigilant if he wished to maintain the subjugation of the defeated Anglo-Saxons. Across his kingdom he established a series of castles and fortified manor houses as a constant reminder of his all-embracing power. His Norman barons ensured that his will was exercised in their fiefdoms and, in the Leeds area, that government rested in the hands of Ilbert de Lacy. De Lacy, who was directly answerable to the king, governed from the massive castle he had built at Pontefract. Some time between 1086 and 1100 he sub-let the manor of Leeds, and that of Headingley, to Ralph Paynel.

Paynel, who had loyally supported the Conqueror, was rewarded with estates in various parts of the country. In Yorkshire he was granted Drax, Armine, Camblesforth, Barlow and several estates in and around York. Adel, Arthington, Burdonhead and Eccup devolved to him by marriage. But his main Yorkshire lands lay between the Ouse and the Aire.

Paynel built his castle at Drax. But it was also felt necessary to have a strong Norman presence in the manor of Leeds, and thus Paynel built, not a castle, but a fortified manor house there. It was built in the area bordered by Boar Lane, Bishopgate Street and Mill Hill at the edge of the wooded manorial park. The remains of its moat were found when workmen uncovered it in 1836 whilst working by the Scarborough Hotel. This, then, was the centre of government of the manor of Leeds.

Ralph Paynel was a devout Christian and like many of his generation believed in practical expressions of gratitude to the Church with the hope of gaining suitable rewards in the afterlife. In 1089, he founded the Priory of the Holy Trinity on Micklegate in York. The opening words of Ralph's charter establishing the foundation give an illuminating insight into the medieval mind and why Ralph had acted as he did:

> I, Ralph, surnamed Paynel, inflamed by the fire of divine love, desiring to treasure up in heaven what I can after this life receive a hundredfold . . . (have) a certain church constructed in the Honour of the Holy Trinity . . . I have delivered it to the blessed Martin Mourtier, and to his monks, to be in their possession for ever.

It was to be a cell of the wealthy Benedictine Abbey of Marmoutier near Tours, and Paynel's charter granted to the monks of his new foundation the advowson, or right to appoint a priest, to the churches at Leeds and Adel. He also granted them the tithes from the churches. A parish priest was entitled to claim one tenth of the produce from both land and

2. Adel Church
The church of St John in the Baptist at Adel, built in the mid-twelfth century, is an excellent
example of Norman architecture. Ralph Paynel's charter of 1089 granted the monks of Holy
Trinity, York the advowson, or right, to appoint the priests to the churches at Leeds and Adel
and to receive the tithes from both churches.

beasts from his parishioners. From Leeds the priory took two-thirds of
the tithe and altarage, the fees paid for marriages and burials. The priest
in Leeds retained the other third. Paynel's gift also included the buildings close to the church and a parcel of land in Holbeck where the
monks established a monastic cell. From then on, it became an enclave
within the manor of Leeds known as the rectory manor of Leeds
Kirkgate-cum-Holbeck.

The Roman Catholic religion played a central role in the everyday
life of all the men, women and children of Norman England. Noble and
peasant, craftsman and knight were deeply dedicated to the Christian
faith. That religious compulsion had already spawned a whole way of
life before the Normans had arrived. Monasteries had long been established in the country and as Bede shows one already existed in the Leeds
area in Elmet Wood during King Edwin's reign.

But in the centuries that followed the coming of the Normans, a dramatic increase in new foundations came about. In Yorkshire alone, from 1069 when Selby Abbey's Benedictine monastery was founded, to 1398 when the Carthusians founded Mount Grace, 100 monasteries were established in the county. One of these was at Kirkstall.

CHAPTER TWO

THE MONKS OF KIRKSTALL

Only three miles from Leeds city centre stands Kirkstall Abbey, a dignified and solemn monastic ruin, gazing down on the busy A65 Leeds to
Skipton road. It reminds the passer-by of another age, another culture
and the romantically inclined pause to wonder what tales those stones
could tell if only they could speak.

Yet from June 1950, when Dr David Owen, the Director of Leeds
City Museum, organised the first archaeological dig on the site, those
stones and the artefacts discovered at the abbey over the years have
yielded up some of their secrets and been used to piece together a fascinating picture of the life that went on behind those walls for four centuries. However, some questions remain unanswered. Why for instance,
in an order so devoted to simplicity of style and austerity of living, is a
most beautiful carving of interlaced stone ribbonwork to be found in
the nave at the base of one of the columns and next to it the beginning
of similar carving that was never completed?

Fortunately, there is a considerable body of written evidence available
to help piece together the daily doings and concerns that occupied the
monks of Kirkstall. Several original documents, mainly legal charters,
have survived as have copies of other records. The thirteenth-century
manuscript telling of the foundation of Fountains Abbey, the fourteenth-
century *Kirkstall Chronicles*, the fifteenth-century document on the
founding of Kirkstall, and the *Coucher Book* of Kirkstall which contains
115 leaves of parchment, all help in building up the story.

No famous man ever lived within its precincts; no great event ever
took place within its walls, yet Kirkstall, as an ancient building, has a
genuine claim to fame. It is one of the most extensive monastic ruins to
be found in Britain, it is possibly the country's finest early monastic ruin
and, according to the historian Chris Given-Wilson, 'it is probably easier
here than at any other ruined monastery to visualise what the abbey
must have looked like when it was completed and in use.' Professor
John le Patourel went even further and claimed it was 'more valuable
archaeologically than Rievaulx or Fountains'.

Its picturesque, ivy-clad walls, the idyllic rural landscape in which it
stood and the meandering river that flowed by its buildings, stirred the

imagination of British artists and poets of the eighteenth and nineteenth centuries. Here, the followers of the Romantic Movement found inspiration from its crumbling stones. Samuel Buck, the eighteenth-century engraver who specialised in works of picturesque ruins, Thomas Girtin, the great watercolourist and his friend and rival, Joseph Mallord William Turner, all painted Kirkstall in its ruined glory. Horace Walpole, wit, author and son of the Prime Minister, visited the site to record that the abbey stood 'in a most picturesque situation, on the banks of a river that falls in a cascade among rich meadows'. Even Sarah Siddons, though she considered it 'too sombre for a person of my age' had to admit, 'It is, however, extremely beautiful.'

But to see Kirkstall as they saw it in all its romantic splendour, or to see it today with its well manicured lawns, its spring blossom trees in bloom, or a carpet of white snow lying evenly over the ground, contrasting dramatically with the dark stones of the building is to see Kirkstall very differently from the way it looked in its heyday. For four centuries the abbey at Kirkstall was a place of work, prayer and dedication. Men came here to devote themselves to the glory of God through a life committed to obedience, chastity and poverty.

Kirkstall was but one small piece of the vast mosaic that made up monastic England. For centuries hundreds of men and women had committed themselves to following the Rule of St Benedict, engaging in a communal life of harmony and pursuing a love of humanity that was born of the spirit of Christ. With the coming of the Normans those numbers increased dramatically.

William the Conqueror, a pious and austere individual, believed devoutly in close ties between Church and State. Not surprisingly, the year after his victory at Hastings he established the Benedictine monastery of Battle Abbey on the site of his triumph. Two years later he founded a Benedictine abbey at Selby. It was an effort to revive the fortunes of the Church in the wasteland that the north had become.

The Benedictines believed in a well-regulated life of prayer and manual labour, dedicated to contemplation, scholarship and missionary work. Their monasteries became the great centres for learning and literature and these grew in both size and wealth. In Yorkshire several Benedictine houses were founded including, in 1088, St Mary's at York. It was here in this Benedictine monastery that Kirkstall's story really began.

By the end of the eleventh century there were those who felt that a certain laxity had eroded the strict discipline to which the Benedictines were dedicated. In order to get back to a more austere, secluded and simple way of life a group of French monks attempted to introduce reforms. Eventually they broke away from the Benedictines altogether, formed a new order and established themselves in the middle of a swampy forest at Cîteaux in Burgundy. They took their name from the Latin for Cîteaux, *Cistercium* and so the new order became known as the Cistercians.

The first chapters of Kirkstall's story followed a similar theme. The monks at the Benedictine abbey of St Mary's in York, like their counterparts in Cîteaux, had also become a divided community. The rules of St Benedict were regularly being ignored. The vow of silence was broken day and night and idle gossiping had become the norm. The strict dietary regulations had given way to the excessive over-eating of 'exquisite delicacies' and 'flavoured sauces'. Hugh of Kirkstall, writing in 1207, gave the graphic details. 'The full and over-gorged belly [has] hardly a scrap of room left in it,' he wrote and went on to remark on the 'splendid variety of drinks' taken and the 'elaborate delicacy of raiment' worn.

For six of the monks at St Mary's it was contrary to everything they held dear. They raised their concerns about the loss of the strict and simple way of life in which they so believed with their prior, Richard. In him they found an ally and he, in turn, pointed out their worries to the abbot, Geoffrey of York. He, however, was not sympathetic. An old man and set in his ways, Geoffrey rejected Richard's objections and bitterly resented the idea that a small rump of radicals should try to hold the rest of the community to ransom.

The dispute dragged on through the summer. By autumn the dissidents had risen to thirteen and included several senior members of the monastery. Richard now played his trump card and, ignoring his abbot, directly approached Thurstan, the Archbishop of York, who, as it happened, was a personal friend. Geoffrey, too, was not idle. He invited representatives of various Benedictine and Cluniac monasteries to come and support him. When Thurstan arrived he was confronted in the cloisters. Fighting broke out, and the archbishop was forced to herd the thirteen protesting monks into the church and blockade the door.

He then escorted them to his palace and in December took them to celebrate Christmas at Ripon. On 27 December 1132, he guided them to the desolate valley of the River Skell. Here he encouraged them to set up their new home and to elect Richard as their abbot. Serlo, thirty years-old, joined the order six years later and described the location as 'a place remote from all the world, uninhabited, set with thorns . . . fit more, it seemed, for the dens of wild beasts than for the uses of mankind'. Numerous springs flowed down the rocky hillsides and as the Latin for springs is *fontis*, the site became known as Fountains.

They sheltered first under an elm tree and then built a simple hovel with a turf roof. Thurstan supplied them with bread and the nearby river provided their drink. They sought adoption by the Cistercians who had already set up a monastery at nearby Rievaulx. They were taken in as a daughter house of Clairvaux in Burgundy, and St Bernard, the abbot there, despatched Geoffrey d'Ainai to Fountains to teach the English monks the ways of the Cistercians. But life was difficult in those early years and things reached such a pitch that at times they were driven to making gruel from the leaves of the elm tree. In 1135 the situation was so critical that Abbot Richard asked permission for the monks to leave England and relocate to France. Had they done so there would ultimately have been no abbey at Kirkstall.

As it happened the move never materialised. Hugh, a dean of York, upon reaching retirement decided to join the beleaguered community. He brought with him his considerable wealth and his library. Two more York canons followed him and Fountains' future was finally guaranteed.

Now they could concentrate on the life dedicated to poverty, chastity and obedience they so desired. So austere was that life that paintings were forbidden for it was felt that they detracted from worship; manuscripts had to be written in but one colour and even the belfries of their churches should not be 'of immoderate height which are unbecoming the simplicity of the Order'. They wore no cloaks, fur-lined boots, shirts or drawers. They rejected warm bedding and even combs. Their churches had no stained-glass windows and their altars were clear of richly decorated vessels and finely embroidered cloths. No stone statues were to be found in their churches, no saints' relics were to be seen. No special services for saints' days were performed. Every Cistercian abbey was dedicated simply to St Mary the Virgin.

They were also expected to set up daughter houses. Thus the monks of Fountains founded Newminster in Northumberland in 1138 and by 1151 they had established eight new monasteries. One of these, the monastery that eventually became Kirkstall, was founded in 1147. Years later, its story was graphically told to Hugh of Kirkstall by Serlo, an ageing monk who as a young man had witnessed the events he described.

Henry de Lacy, the Earl of Lincoln and grandson of Ilbert de Lacy, fell seriously ill. He believed he had somehow offended God and vowed to atone for his sins by building a Cistercian abbey in honour of 'the glorious Virgin and Mother of God, Mary'. When he recovered, he approached the Abbot of Fountains, Henry Murdac, with the offer of founding a new monastery. Murdac welcomed the suggestion.

Henry offered a site at Barnoldswick on the bleak and windswept Pennine hillside. What he did not say was that he rented the land from Hugh Bidgood, the Earl of Norfolk, one of King Stephen's chief officers; nor did he mention that he had defaulted in paying that rent for some years. On 19 May 1147, Alexander, the prior of Fountains, twelve monks and ten lay brethren made their way to their new home. Alexander was elected abbot and initially erected several small simple buildings. Mount St Mary was begun.

The local inhabitants, however, objected as the monks began to dominate the area and when they saw their parish church pulled down by the over-enthusiastic Cistercians they took the matter to the Archbishop of York. Their objections eventually reached Rome but the Pope ruled in favour of the new monastery.

But Alexander had more to contend with than truculent locals. For almost a year rain swept the Pennines destroying their crops. Worst of all, civil war ravaged the land as Stephen of Blois and his cousin Matilda vied with each other for the throne of England. Villages were destroyed, crops left unattended and famine stalked the land. The people were brutally terrorised and their possessions plundered. It was a time when men said 'Christ and his saints slept.' The monks at Barnoldswick fared no better. Their cattle were driven off, their goods stolen. Poverty, and lack of food and clothing forced Alexander to consider changing their site.

One day Alexander, on abbey business, passed through a shaded and woody valley with a pleasant river flowing through it. Here he found a group of hermits, men dressed in religious garb. Their leader was a man called Seleth. He explained that he originated from the south but a vision of the Virgin Mary had instructed him to go to Yorkshire and find a place called Kirkstall in Airedale.* Guided by a cowherd to the spot, he settled there living off roots and herbs and the generosity of local people. Others gradually joined him.

Alexander saw the potential of the site. Though it was something of a wilderness, wood, stone and water were on hand. He persuaded the hermits to see the sense in the Cistercians developing it and approached de Lacy at Pontefract Castle. The lord of the manor gave the idea his blessing but although the land was part of his vast estate, it had been sublet to William of Poitou. William raised no objection to the monks occupying the site. The Cistercians from Barnoldswick had finally found

---

* If Seleth's story is correct and the first syllable of 'Kirkstall' refers to a 'kirk' or 'church', it implies that a church must have existed in the area before either the hermits or the monks arrived there. Edward Parsons, the Leeds historian, rejects this, arguing the 'name was unknown until after the foundation of the Abbey'.

their new home. Here they would remain for the next four hundred years but Alexander, perhaps in deference to the hermits who had settled there previously, opted for a new name for the abbey of Mount St Mary, calling it Kirkstall.

The land south of the river was tenanted by William de Reinvill. He agreed to the Cistercians occupying the valley floor as far as the hill that led to the village of Bramley. To the west lay the vast tract of Hawksworth wood. A mile and half to the east and north lay the small hamlets of East and West Headingley. Southeast, a similar distance away was the small settlement of Burley and three miles farther on lay the growing town of Leeds.

On 19 May 1152,* some of the monks and lay brothers left Barnoldswick and made their way to their new home at Kirkstall. It would have taken some time for all the monks to transfer and even when the community had finally moved, a few lay brothers remained on the old site to convert it into a sheep farm or grange.

At Kirkstall they cleared the ground, felled the trees, removed the scrub, and turned what the monks described as 'the niggard soil' into rich arable farmland. Simple temporary wooden huts were constructed to accommodate them but work soon commenced on their great basilica or church, with Henry de Lacy even laying the foundation stone. Throughout, Henry proved a generous patron. He was eager to support them whenever he could, providing them with food and money, and paying for some of the buildings. Nor should William of Poitou be forgotten for though the documents say little of his contribution, the Cistercians used his coat-of-arms as that of the abbey.

Millstone grit, known as Bramley Fall, was brought from the quarries at Bramley and with remarkable speed the buildings rose. The bulk of the monastery was built in its first thirty years.

Whereas the Benedictines built their abbeys near and in populated areas and could use local labour for menial tasks, the Cistercians lived well away from other people. So it was that they created their own work-force, known as lay brothers or *conversi* who originally outnumbered the choir monks. The lay brothers were the basis on which the Cistercians built their highly successful commercial business. However, lay brothers were monks, not servants, and often came from good families. They entered the order as novices and eventually became brothers. They took the same vows as the choir monks and observed the same rules of silence

---

* The date of the founding of the new abbey has been disputed by a few historians but most accept this as the probable one.

and abstinence. Their clothes differed from the choir monks in that they wore brown tunics along with a hood covering the shoulders and breast, a cloak, stockings and boots and their heads were not tonsured. Expressly forbidden to learn to read or write, they were taught a few prayers and psalms by heart. Their role was to work on the buildings, grow crops and tend the abbey's flocks and herds. Some of them were based in the sheep granges. Those who were not on the farms attended Kirkstall's evening service of compline. They worshipped daily but not as regularly as the choir monks and their services were held in a separate part of the church, just as they dined and slept in separate quarters. As one Cistercian monk in the twelfth century remarked to a Cluniac monk, they had 'two monasteries under one roof, one for lay brothers and another for clerics'. Lay brothers held their chapter or meeting with the abbot only on Sundays and certain feast-days.

The choir monks spent their days in prayer and worship and, unlike the Benedictines, initially avoided intellectual pursuits to any degree. However, in about 1280, Rewley Abbey was founded at Oxford as a centre for Cistercian studies. In 1433 the General Chapter at Cîteaux acknowledged that Willelmus Gason, a Kirkstall monk, had worked so well at Oxford and brought such credit to his house that he should remain at the university to study for his doctorate in theology. What manual labour the choir monks did is not clear but they probably grew vegetables and herbs, took care of the orchard, tended the poultry and worked in the dairy.

They wore a cowl, stockings and shoes and when these were replaced the old ones were given to the poor. They were also issued with a girdle, knife, needle and handkerchief. Should anyone have to make a journey from Kirkstall they were given better quality clothing and drawers to wear. However, they rejected the black habit worn by the Benedictines and favoured instead a white habit of undyed wool as more in keeping with their austere views. Over this they wore a black scapular, a piece of cloth which hung down the front and back and was joined at the shoulders. It represented the yoke of Christ mentioned in St Matthew. Another symbolic rite they employed was that of tonsure. This was the shaving of the top of the head. The fringe of hair that was left symbolised the crown of thorns. It was carried out when a man was initiated into becoming a cleric. The heads of the monks were then shaved every three weeks to retain it.

Kirkstall was laid out to the same architectural design as every Cistercian monastery. The cloister was the heart of the monastery. On its northern side lay the magnificent church. This was divided up into a

3. Kirkstall Abbey as it was in c. 1230.
A model of Kirkstall Abbey as it probably appeared in the early thirteenth-century. Note the low belfry tower. The Cistercian Order insisted that belfries should not be 'of immoderate height which are unbecoming the simplicity of the Order'.

number of areas. At the west end was the place where the lay brothers would worship. Then came a bay containing two chapels and beyond that the retro-choir, the place set aside for the old or sick monks. A stone screen or pulpitum divided these bays from the rest of the church. Behind the screen was the area known as the choir, where the choir monks worshipped and then came the high altar in the presbytery at the very east end of the building.

Immediately outside the church was the cloister and sharing the church's south wall was the cloister walk known as the scriptorium. Here the choir monks sat at wooden desks known as carrels and copied out manuscripts. On the eastern cloister were the library, the chapter house and the parlour, the place the monks had to go if they wished to speak to each other. Above the whole of the eastern walkway was the choir monks' dormitory and at the rear of it the monks' privies.

The south walk had the warming room, the only place the monks could warm themselves in winter and above it the muniment room where all of the abbey's documents were stored. The laver, a long washing trough was placed in the south walk so that monks could wash before going into the refectory for meals; the kitchen was next to that. Later, a passage was constructed which led from the cloisters to the infirmary where old monks and the sick were catered for. A small prison was constructed here and nearby was the abbot's lodging. A separate abbot's lodging was also built to cater for the visiting abbot from Fountains.

Whereas each Benedictine abbey was autonomous, the Cistercians organised themselves into an extended family. Each new monastery they established was visited annually by the abbot of the abbey which founded it, hence the Abbot of Fountains would visit Kirkstall each year. Kirkstall, however, never founded a daughter house.

Each year a General Chapter was also held at Cîteaux which every Cistercian abbot was obliged to attend. For the Abbot of Kirkstall it meant a four-to-five week journey, a round trip of over 1,000 miles travelling across rough country on unmade roads and often through areas infested with bands of outlaws.

Originally, at the western end of Kirkstall's cloister, a huge wall separated the lay brothers' quarters from those of the choir monks. Above the western buildings was the lay brothers' dormitory and beneath it their refectory and a large room used for cellarage.

Most of the church and buildings around the cloister were built between 1152 and 1182. Some changes occurred over the centuries. Originally, stone pantiles covered the roof and the east end had three arched windows with a circular one above them, but in the fifteenth century the present great east window was fitted. Between 1509 and 1528, William Marshall, the abbot, raised the belfry, lowered the roof and added corner turrets. The original pantiles were replaced with lead.

The intriguing thing about the early buildings at Kirkstall is that they clearly show two styles of architecture. Whereas the windows and doorways have the typical round-headed shape of the Norman style, the arches of the piers in the nave are pointed, hinting at the Gothic style that was only just beginning to be used. It may be that these new ideas had been brought over from France, for certainly the twin entrance to the chapter house at Kirkstall is typical of that found in some monasteries in Normandy. A typical example can still be seen there at the Benedictine abbey of Hambye.

The monastery's precincts covered about forty acres of ground. This area was surrounded by a wall which stretched from what is now Morris Lane to the river. The outer gatehouse was on Morris Lane. Once through that the visitor would see that the site was divided into two courts. To the north-west lay the outer court where stables, workshops, a smithy and farm buildings would be found. In the northern part of the court a pond had most likely been created to supply the water for the abbey and power for the small corn mill that stood near the present day entrance to the car park.

Opposite the mill was the inner gatehouse, the present Abbey House Museum. This led into the inner court where the great church towered above the other buildings. To the west of the court stood the guest house. Here distinguished visitors, nobles with their families and retainers and wealthy merchants would find hospitality. The guest house had all the amenities of a self-contained small manor house. There was a main hall where a fire burned in the middle of the room. At the north end a two-storey private chamber provided some privacy for the more important guests. At the south lay the kitchen, scullery and bakehouse. A short distance away were its stables and smithy. When guests arrived at the abbey the rule of St Benedict insisted that they should be received as if Christ himself had arrived at the gate and thus whenever possible, the abbot came to greet them.

It was the abbot who was the head of the monastery. He was often elected to his position by the monks of another house of the same order. From 1147 to 1231 six of the Kirkstall abbots had previously been monks at Fountains. Over the four hundred years of Kirkstall's existence the abbots proved themselves to be capable administrators, incompetent leaders, devoted men of God and outright villains. In effect they demonstrated all the qualities, both good and bad, that can be found in any group of individuals.

Undoubtedly, the first abbot of Kirkstall, Alexander, would rank among its greatest leaders. Not only did he establish the monastery and show considerable foresight by preserving the woods nearby for future generations of monks to come, but also had the satisfaction of seeing the vast bulk of the buildings completed before he died in 1182, or as the Kirkstall histories more poetically tell us, was 'gathered to his fathers'.

His successor was Ralph Haget who had once been a soldier but was now considered to be a man of piety. Though he had inherited an establishment that was by no means wealthy, nevertheless it was one unencumbered with debts. Sadly he lacked the skills needed to develop Kirkstall. A series of internal disputes broke out in the community, crops failed and disease decimated its herds and flocks. Most serious of all, the abbey lost its greatest asset, the grange at Micklethwaite near Collingham when Henry II granted the land to Adam de Brus. Even Haget's attempt to bribe the king with a golden chalice failed and blame was laid at the abbot's feet. After nine years, in 1190, he finally moved on to become abbot of Fountains.

The next ten years came under the rule of Abbot Lambert, a monk who had first arrived at Kirkstall with Abbot Alexander. He, too, was prepared to leave matters to God's will. It was during his abbacy that violence erupted on one of the distant sheep farms at Accrington. In return for a gift of land to Robert de Lacy, Kirkstall had acquired land there. Taking possession, the monks embarked on establishing a new grange for their sheep and unceremoniously drove off the inhabitants of the area. They were not alone in behaving like this. Their brother Cistercians at Fountains, Byland, Holmcultren and Sawley abbeys all treated local inhabitants similarly, unrestrainedly driving them from the land in order to establish their granges. Treatment of locals could be severe in the extreme. Peter of Kirkstall, the granger at Barnoldswick, cut off the ear of a serving boy for stealing two loaves of bread. Equally, local inhabitants could react with similar severity. At Accrington, the infuriated dispossessed people returned, burnt the grange buildings and furniture and murdered three lay brothers, Brothers Norman, Humphrey and Robert.

Abbot Turgisius, who took up the position in the very first years of the thirteenth century, was probably the most devout of the abbots. He always wore a hair shirt, and in winter never donned the additional clothing that the other monks did. He never drank wine, was strictly vegetarian, and even refused to eat fish. When he conducted services he wept profusely. One thirteenth-century manuscript describes him as, 'never without tears, and so great was the flood of them that he seemed less to weep than to pour them down like rain'.

Helias, an abbot who originally emanated from Roche Abbey in South Yorkshire, was a very different individual. With a fine brain, a flair for administration and enormous energy, he was a pragmatic leader with a sound knowledge of the outside world. Initially Robert de Lacy, the local feudal lord, fell into such an acrimonious dispute with him that he refused to allow the abbot to be admitted to his presence. But over the years the lord mellowed and eventually supported Helias when he approached King John requesting permission to repossess Micklethwaite Grange. Their joint appeal succeeded in 1205.

Other abbots proved less than satisfactory. Gilbert Cortles was forced to resign in 1280 when he allowed the abbey to fall into serious financial difficulties. Even more damaging to the Cistercians, he led the Kirkstall monks in a rebellion against their mother abbey of Fountains. Probably the greatest abbot-villain was John de Thornberg. Along with five monks, one lay brother and four laymen he terrorised the neighbourhood and attacked Thomas Sergeant's house at Thorpe, near Knaresborough. Another attack was launched in about 1366, this time on the Vicar of Sandal and an archbishop's official. It arose over charges against a certain Margaret Baghill, 'notoriously defamed of many delinquencies' and whom the archbishop wished to investigate. The vicar's servant was killed and the vicar himself wounded. The culprits, however, were pardoned.

Kirkstall, like other abbeys, was administered by a group of officials known as obedientiaries chosen from the community. These included the prior who was the abbot's deputy. The cellarer, sometimes known as the second father of the monastery, was responsible for the properties of the abbey, visited the granges, and had charge of food, drink and transport; much of Kirkstall's prosperity depended upon him. The precentor organised the church services and cared for the monastery's books. The sacristan was responsible for security and cleanliness and the illumination of the church. The kitchener provided the meals whilst the fraterer organised the refectory or frater. The guest-master had responsibility for visitors to the abbey, and the infirmarian cared for the old and sick. The almoner gave money and food to the poor. The novice-master instructed the young novices who eventually hoped to join the order. Originally no one under sixteen could become a novice but this was beginning to change by the end of the twelfth century.

The daily life of the monk was strictly regulated. The first service, Matins, started about 2 a.m. followed by Lauds and Prime. At Kirkstall it is still possible to see the night stairs that led down into the church from the choir monks' dormitory. At about 8 a.m. Tierce was held, followed by Morning Mass. High Mass came about two hours later. Nones was held just after noon with Vespers in the early evening and then Compline, the last service of the day. Sundays were different in that they also processed around the cloister and sprinkled the various rooms with holy water.

Baths were taken three or four times a year and the community was also bled four times a year. Bleeding was felt to be a useful preventive against the plague. Each week the feet of the monks were ritually washed by those who had been appointed to cook for the week.

The kitchen at Kirkstall was placed between the lay brothers' refectory and that of the choir monks. The choir monks' first refectory at Kirkstall was found to be too small and so another was built on a north-south axis. The monks dined in silence listening to one of the order standing in a pulpit on the western wall, reading from a religious book. Their main meal consisted of a pound of coarse bread and two dishes of vegetables which were usually cabbage and beans, and they drank either common wine or weak beer. At the top table it was usually the prior who presided, for the abbot was often busy entertaining important guests.

But changes gradually came to the strict vegetarian diets employed at Kirkstall. From 1335, the Pope declared that the weak or sick should be allowed meat. Fish became accepted as part of the diet and fish ponds were constructed at Kirkstall near the River Aire for breeding stock.

Ewes' milk was used for making cheese. Eggs soft, hard, beaten up, fried, roasted, stuffed and minced were also consumed. By the fifteenth century the Pope made a further dispensation, this time allowing meat to be eaten by all the monks on Sundays, Tuesdays and Thursdays as long as it was cooked in a separate kitchen and eaten in a separate refectory.

At Kirkstall a meat kitchen, known as a misericord, was built southeast of the refectory. Instead of building a second refectory, the old refectory pulpit was removed and the room itself divided into two floors. Meat dishes were eaten on the ground floor and vegetarian meals in the upper. From the discoveries of numerous bones by archaeologists at Kirkstall, it is known that the Cistercians here began to consume beef, mutton and pork. Next to the meat kitchen a round dovecote was erected so that fresh meat could be enjoyed all year round. A malthouse was also built for brewing.

Their food supply may well have been supplemented by hares, rabbits, pheasants and partridges. Kirkstall had been granted free warren at Bramley, Breary, Cookridge, Headingley and Horsforth. This was a franchise from the Crown. It permitted the monks to hunt there for these creatures as well as for foxes and squirrels as they were considered harmful to protected animals such as deer. Inevitably, poaching occurred and in 1378 and again in 1385 Kirkstall's abbot was furious that locals had abused the abbey's rights with their illegal hunting.

Matters such as poaching or indeed any other business that affected the abbey were discussed daily in the chapter house. Every morning after Mass the choir monks gathered there. By the thirteenth century Kirkstall's chapter house was found to be too small for the community and had to be enlarged. Here they listened to one of the rules of St Benedict being read, were instructed as to their duties that day, remembered their dead colleagues and listened to letters from other monasteries being read out. Then, any monk who had a sin to confess did so. Punishments ranged from fasting on bread and water, being flogged or, for more serious crimes, imprisonment in the abbey's cell next to Kirkstall's infirmary. Extreme crimes could be punished with expulsion from the order and excommunication.

Some offenders at the abbey were thieves: Henry Howden stole a chalice and some other property before fleeing the community. He was excommunicated in 1304. Some, like Richard de Eckesley in 1362 and William de Otley in 1368, simply walked out of the abbey. The Pope, however, issued an order encouraging them to return and be reconciled with the community. Thurstan Lofthous's case was particularly interesting. In the 1480s he obviously grew dissatisfied with the Cistercians and left

Kirkstall to join the Carthusians at Mount Grace Priory. He lived there for some years but even so the abbot at Kirkstall refused to condemn him for so doing. Thurstan returned to Kirkstall but was still obviously unsettled for, in 1485, he finally returned to the Carthusians. In 1490 the Pope agreed to allow him to remain at Mount Grace.

Some monks were accused of sexual offences. At the end of the fifteenth century a document from Fountains claimed Kirkstall's monks were 'accustomed to inveigle females from the path of piety into that of profligacy'. Others were accused of sodomy. However, the charges against Thomas Kirkstall, Paulus Mason and Gabriel Lofthus made in the late 1530s were dropped as no proof was forthcoming and no further action was taken.

It was not only recalcitrant monks who caused concern to Kirkstall's abbots. Another source of considerable frustration to the monastery was that of the corrodians. These were lay people who had paid abbeys or granted them land in return for being allowed to live at the monastery in old age and enjoy a secure and comfortable standard of living. Others negotiated to receive an annuity for the rest of their life. Corrodies, then, were a form of insurance, but though a useful source of income or a convenient way for the monks to acquire land, it was a system which could easily get out of hand. Kirkstall, in 1539, was responsible for fifty-one annuities which amounted to a sixth of the monks' yearly income.

The source of greatest frustration was the royal corrodians, for the king could demand a monastery to provide for men who had retired after serving in the royal household in some minor post. Both Edward I and Edward II exploited the system shamefully. The drain on the monastery's resources by such appointments may explain why one incident at the abbey occurred in 1312. When the Knights Templar were suppressed, Kirkstall was instructed to admit one of them. Once he had confessed his sins, Roger Sheffield was taken into the abbey but he was there no time at all. Within months he had disappeared with the monks quite happy to connive at his speedy escape.

Eventually the monasteries formally protested to the king about the appointment of corrodies. The new ruler, Edward III, undertook only to ask for them 'where he ought'. It was no help to Kirkstall. He continued to appoint one or two corrodies there from time to time. This constant depletion of the abbey's resources reached such a pitch between 1352 and 1362 that Abbot Roger de Ledes pleaded with King Edward III not to burden the abbey further. He was not successful.

When financial problems beset the abbey, as they did from time to time, Kirkstall, like other monasteries, sought to reduce its overheads by using the system known as dispersion. With this system, permission had to be granted to disperse some of the monks to other wealthier monasteries and no more novices were admitted until the crisis was overcome. In 1284, Hugh de Grimstone took over as abbot at Kirkstall and found urgent action was needed to reduce the monastery's enormous debt of £5,248 15s. 7d. To ease the pressure on the abbey's strained resources he was allowed to disperse some of Kirkstall's monks elsewhere.

Three years later with debts still pressing, Abbot Hugh, accompanied by John de Birdesall, set off on the long journey to Gascony to lobby King Edward I and urge his help. Henry de Lacy, the Earl of Lincoln, presented Kirkstall's petition to the king. At first he categorically refused it on the grounds that it would set a dangerous precedent but later relented and granted the abbot an audience. The outcome was satisfactory for the abbey. The king guaranteed he would not take action against them for the rent overdue on their properties at Collingham and Bardsey and instructed the king's treasurer to ask the abbey's creditors to behave reasonably in their demands and give the monks time to pay off their debts.

Henry de Lacy personally offered to help. He promised to give Kirkstall an advance in return for some of the abbey's properties in Lancashire and Yorkshire. At the same time he also offered to buy, at a reasonable price, any moveable goods there. Abbot Hugh, wary of the Norman earl, instructed his brother monks to remove everything from the granges that could be moved except the crops! However, by 1301 his efforts had succeeded in reducing the debt to just £160 and had built up the abbey's herds of cattle to over six hundred and its flock of sheep to four thousand five hundred.

It was not the only time the abbey found itself with financial liabilities. During Ralph Haget's abbacy Kirkstall, along with eight other Cistercian houses, was in debt to Aaron the Jew of Lincoln. When he died in 1186 the nine monasteries collectively owed him some 6,400 marks (when a mark was worth thirteen shillings and four pence or two-thirds of £1).

It was inevitable that economic problems would confront the monks at Kirkstall from time to time. Like the rest of the Cistercians they were sheep farmers involved in international trading and subject to the fluctuations of fortune that occasionally confront any business. The General Chapter had encouraged sheep farming but with monasteries often in serious financial trouble there was always a temptation to indulge in the advance selling of wool. Cîteaux condemned this but nevertheless hard-pressed abbots found it sometimes the only option for survival. The abbots of Kirkstall were no different.

Demands on the monasteries were considerable at times. All wool exports were taxed. Indeed, the wool from the abbeys was so important to the Exchequer that no merchant could remove it from an abbey without a licence and a certificate. It was not for nothing that the Lord Chancellor sat on the symbolic woolsack in the House of Lords.

General Chapter realised that for some monasteries to survive, advance selling was essential and so in 1279, all trading restrictions were removed. The decision may well have been precipitated when a couple of years earlier the fatal disease known as scab struck at sheep flocks across England. Then a combination of a series of hot dry summers and the virulence of the infection saw the disease reappear with increasing devastation year after year. It decimated Kirkstall's sheep population. Production was severely reduced and in 1278 the abbey found itself in debt to the merchants of Florence. By 1284 scab had wiped out the entire abbey flock. Good management, however, turned the situation around and by 1292, Kirkstall was able to raise 160 marks as advance payment for their whole output for the next ten years. The flock continued to increase and by 1301 had reached four thousand five hundred.

The Cistercians were adept at sheep farming and unlike most monastic orders were fairly progressive in their approach. The sheep they reared were possibly the long-haired hornless variety of animal that was eventually developed into the Wensleydale breed. Kirkstall grazed them on their numerous granges across the North; for example at Bessacar there were 1,000 animals, at Seacroft 700, at Bramhope, Cookridge and Potternewton 300, and at Beeston 240. After clipping, the wool was brought by pack horse trains to the abbey.

Merchants arrived at Kirkstall from Italy, France and the Low Countries. It was more convenient for them to buy from Yorkshire's Cistercian monasteries. They could buy in bulk and complete their purchases in a matter of weeks whereas dealing with smaller producers would have taken considerably longer. When the wool merchants arrived at Kirkstall they were conducted to a special parlour which can still be seen. There they could discuss business without disturbing the silence of the rest of the abbey.

Even though Kirkstall, at times, supplemented its own supply by buying additional wool from local farmers its annual output could never compete with that of Fountains. Fountains, along with Rievaulx, were the largest wool producers in the country. Whereas Fountains produced seventy-six sacks a year, Kirkstall's total was twenty-five. It has been estimated that a sack was roughly 364 lb of wool, approximately the amount a packhorse could reasonably be expected to carry. But in quality Kirkstall's wool ranked second only to that of its mother abbey.

The supplies were exported first to York, Doncaster and Pontefract and then down river and through Hull, the North's primary wool exporting centre, to the continent. At times the abbey received a boost to its trading. Both Henry II and Richard I exempted Kirkstall from certain taxes. And in 1224 Henry III granted leave to Abbot Maurice to despatch one shipload of wool to whichever destination he chose. The harbour-bailiffs were instructed not to interfere with the vessel.

To engage in large-scale wool production meant a considerable number of sheep farms had to be established. Some of these were granted by generous benefactors of the abbey and others were rented by Kirkstall. But by 1279 Edward I had grown so concerned at the growing power of the religious houses that he introduced his Statute of Mortmain which forbade the passing of lands to religious orders. Thus it was that in 1323, when John de Calverley wished to make a grant of land to Kirkstall, an inquisition was appointed to investigate the proposal. It found that it would not be 'to the king's damage' and the abbey was able to acquire the new property the following year.

Some of Kirkstall's granges were widespread: Barnoldswick was in the Pennines, Bessacar was near Doncaster and Accrington was in Lancashire. Others, such as Morley, Pudsey, Calverley, Bardsey and Collingham, were much nearer home. Their site at Snydale near Featherstone was important. There the monks were able to work the coal mines whilst at Ardsley, between Wakefield and Leeds, they established iron-making. They worked a second ironworks at Seacroft between 1200 and 1287 and others at Weetwood and Haslwell between 1287 and c.1400. There is some dispute about when iron-working actually took place at the abbey site itself. Some authorities claim it occurred just before the Dissolution, others just afterwards.

Many places in present-day Leeds were monastic sites: Adel, Armley, Beeston, Bramley, Headingley, Horsforth, Roundhay, Allerton, Potternewton, Shadwell, and Farnley where they owned a mill. Originally, however, the monks did not hold property in Leeds itself. Indeed, Maurice Paynel's charter of 1207 expressly forbade anyone selling land to 'religion' there. It was not until 1459 that they acquired holdings at Little Woodhouse, Burmantofts and in Kirkgate and the 'Fleshambles' Briggate.

Although sheep farming was the main occupation, horses, cows, goats, pigs and deer were raised on their farms and references to plough oxen at Bramley and Roundhay show that arable farming was also undertaken. Lay brothers would work the farms but also available as labourers were those villeins who, being tied to the land, were given to the monks along with the estate. When Henry de Eland granted his land at Cliviger near Blackburn to Kirkstall, he stated clearly that his villeins were part of the gift, whilst at Horsforth records show that a William Potter was one of twenty-two villeins who were similarly part of the property that the abbey acquired. At Rawdon, John White, a ploughman, came with the grant of land there; at Potternewton it was a carpenter named Hervey. And some were actually bought. Adam, the son of Henry de Bramhope, along with his family and possessions, was acquired by the abbey from Ralph Fitz-Baldwin for just three marks of silver.

Some agreements with landowners were quite specific. One such allowed the monks to move 700 of their sheep from Roundhay Grange to Seacroft but stipulated that 400 of them had to be kept in the owner's sheepfold so that he could use their dung as fertiliser. Others were more favourable to the monks. In 1331, Adam de Hopton, for example, gave the monks a right of way to their pastures at Beeston.

The Cistercians may well have wished for a life of seclusion and contemplation away from the hurly-burly of everyday life but involvement in the wool trade made day-to-day contact with the outside world inevitable. Ownership of land on the scale they held was bound to generate disputes from time to time. Some disputes were with other religious houses such as Bolton Priory over land at Horsforth and Rawdon, and St Mary's at York over land at Adel. Some were with private individuals such as John Sampson, who had allowed his sheep to graze on abbey land at Bardsey. As a result Abbot Hugh de Grimstone confiscated his entire flock!

And try as they might to remain aloof from the various political issues of the time, they found themselves being caught up in the events of their day. In December 1192, Richard I, returning from the crusades, was captured by Leopold of Austria. To meet the exorbitant ransom demand of 150,000 marks, every man in England had to give up a fourth of his income. Church plate and chalices were taken to raise funds. Thus it was that in 1193, the whole wool crop from Kirkstall for a full year was confiscated along with the rest of the Cistercians' yearly output.

When Henry III's reign created such discord in England, Simon de Montfort led the rebels against the king. In January 1265, in the hope of establishing order, de Montfort summoned his historic Model Parliament. As well as the usual barons, bishops and abbots, he also invited four chosen knights from each shire and, for the first time, representatives from certain towns. It was said to be the forerunner of modern parliaments. Present at this historic gathering was Abbot Simon of Kirkstall. He was one of the five abbots called there.

In 1298, as part of Edward I's campaign against the Scots, the king moved his Exchequer and part of his administration to York. Eventually Edward was triumphant. Stirling Castle fell after a siege and William Wallace, the Scottish leader, became a hunted outlaw. Edward decided to return his treasury to London. Hugh de Grimstone, the abbot of Kirkstall, received royal orders to supply four horses, a cart and two men to help to transport the royal entourage.

Robert the Bruce, the new Scottish leader, continued his resistance to the English and Edward II moved his troops north to combat the threat. Kirkstall was ordered to supply the king's troops with victuals. Just over twenty years later Edward III demanded the same monastery should pay a subsidy towards the wedding expenses of his sister!

But these impositions paled into insignificance compared with the catastrophe that struck Europe in the mid-fourteenth century. Between 1347 and 1350 an estimated one-third of the population of the continent was struck down by bubonic plague. It appears to have reached England in 1348 but where the Black Death first struck in the country is not known. Some claim Bristol, some Southampton, and one fourteenth-century chronicler claims it was at Melcombe, in Dorset. What is known is that by 1349 it had reached Yorkshire. Between forty-two and forty-five per cent of the clergy died and that was a lower figure than in many other counties.

At the Cistercian Abbey of Meaux near Hull, the abbot and five monks perished in a single day. Kirkstall fared no better. Whereas it had at one time boasted some thirty-six monks and numerous lay brothers, by 1381 the records show that only seventeen choir monks and six lay brothers were now in residence.

Changes came. The rule of silence was abandoned. Lay brothers were phased out. More and more granges were leased rather than farmed by the monks themselves. Monasticism was no longer the great driving force it once had been. From 1400 only eight new establishments were founded in the whole kingdom.

Undoubtedly the wealth the monasteries enjoyed may well have bred a degree of jealousy and suspicion in society generally. Whereas the manor of Leeds in 1459 was earning between £70 and £80 – about the same as it had been making in 1288 – Kirkstall's income had risen from £207 to £354. Thus the wealth which the monasteries enjoyed, his dispute with the Pope and the opportunity to reduce the power of the

Church, induced Henry VIII to dissolve the nation's religious houses. On 22 November 1539, Henry's commissioners arrived at Kirkstall. Richard Layton and the other commissioners were conducted to the chapter house and there drew up the necessary documentation.

Everything the monastery owned, its buildings, its farms and granges, and its moveable goods all had to be handed over. In return the abbot, the sub-prior and the remaining twenty-nine monks each received pensions. Some abbots in the North had objected to the king's attacks on the Church and paid for it with their lives. William Thirsk, the abbot of Fountains along with the other Cistercian abbots of Kirkstead, Whalley and Jervaulx all perished on the scaffold. John Ripley, the abbot of Kirkstall, showed greater discretion. Although he attended a meeting at Pontefract to discuss the Pilgrimage of Grace he took no part in the uprising, accepted the inevitable, took the generous pension he was granted and, according to legend, lived out his remaining days in the inner gatehouse.

Of the other Kirkstall monks at the Dissolution it is known that some, such as Anthony Jackson, Richard Bateson, Gabriel Lofthouse and William Lupton became curates or priests in various parishes in the Yorkshire area. Richard Wodd appears to have married. Thomas Bertlett moved to live in the home of George Hall at Allerton Grange where he set up an altar in the house. He died in 1542, leaving his vestments to the chapel at Chapeltown.

As for the building, the lead was stripped from its roof and the windows removed from their settings. Locals came to regard it as a convenient quarry and removed the very stones from its walls. Some of those stones were used to build the steps that led down to the river by the side of Leeds Bridge. But fortunately for posterity the church and cloisters remained, on the whole, untouched.

For four hundred years the monks of Kirkstall had watched the unfolding pageant of British history and at times played their part in it. For the people of Leeds and the surrounding villages the abbey's disappearance would have had some effect. The poor for example would no longer be able to gather at the monastery's gate in order to beg for food and money. By the fourteenth century Kirkstall was already beginning to affect the economic development of Leeds. It disappearance would have caused a hiatus in the local economy.

But the disposal of Kirkstall's estates also had a positive effect in the area. It attracted new inhabitants to the district. Of the twenty-nine families that formed the first Leeds Corporation in 1626 no less than twenty-four were first or second generation newcomers with several of them from families who had settled on land previously owned by the abbey. These sons of yeomen farmers and small landowners came with a clear intent; to exploit their new properties, stimulate economic growth and develop Leeds into a viable and successful business centre. The first steps in that process, however, had been taken centuries before; in fact, just over fifty years after the Cistercians had first arrived at Kirkstall.

CHAPTER THREE

MEDIEVAL LEEDS

As the dawn of the thirteenth century broke, life in Leeds and its surrounding villages followed a similar pattern to that across the rest of England. The nation was a society based on agriculture, where life revolved around the seasons and would remain so for the next six centuries. Land was held from the king through the barons and nobles down to the lowliest peasant, on condition that specific service was rendered for it. Popularly known as the feudal system, its exact nature is disputed by some historians. They argue that feudalism related only to the political and military system of the time. They claim that the organisation of agricultural labour should be more properly known as manorialism. Whatever its designation it originated in Anglo-Saxon times, but it was the Norman invaders who regularised it and made it more or less uniform across the nation.

In Leeds, as elsewhere, the very base of that social pyramid was made up of the villeins. According to many historians they were simply unfree tenants with no legal rights to leave the estate. Should they wish to live outside the manor they had to find someone to stand security for them and were forced to pay an annual payment to the lord known as chevage. In 1385, Robert Foster stood security for Joan Buslingthorpe to live outside the manor of Leeds, as did Robert Totty for John Branden. Both John and Joan paid twelve pence chevage. Villeins were compelled to work so many days a year on the lord's land. They also had to ask the lord of the manor's permission for their daughters to marry whilst their sons were denied the right to join the Church.

In Leeds, for the winter sowing, they were obliged to give two days ploughing and a further two days harrowing along with three days ploughing at the Lent sowing. They had to mow the lord's meadow, lift and carry the hay, reap the lord's corn for six days in autumn, and for a further three days carry that corn. They were obliged to repair the water mill when needed and in return received rye bread and herrings for sustenance and a nominal sum of money. Even after death the feudal restraints continued. When a villein died the lord could seize his best beast as heriot, a form of medieval death duty.

But there were different grades of villein. The lowliest of these were the cottars. They were smallholders, renting a cottage and a small plot but having no land of their own to farm. They were obliged to give service to the lord of the manor and also worked for the local freemen and bondmen for a fixed rate of pay. To supplement their meagre income some took other jobs, as their names testify. In 1258 we find among the cottars of Leeds a Henry Carpenter, a Richard Taylor, a Simon Forester and a Thomas Baker. Others like William Beveridge and Robert Rande even attempted commercial enterprises and, in 1341, paid twelve pence a year respectively for the rent of a stall and shop in Leeds market.

Some historians argue that 'villein' as a term should only be applied to the wealthiest class of peasant. In Leeds they were known as bondmen. Manor documents for Leeds, dated 1341, identify some of these men: Robert Knostrop, Adam Birks, Richard Palfreyman, Richard Hunslet and Jordan Moode. They held approximately forty acres each, though as the population expanded this was reduced to twenty. Not only the cottars combined farming with other occupations. Among thirteenth-century Leeds bondmen were a William Carpenter and a William Shoemaker.

Finally came the freemen. In Leeds we find listed Robert Woodhouse who paid two shillings a year rent and Thomas Bywater who paid one shilling and four pence.

The countryside in which these people lived was very different from that of today. There was no urban sprawl, no neat hedgerows creating the patchwork of fields that is now so much a part of our country landscape. There was no stark division between rural and urban life. The capital, London, was semi-rustic in character. Vast areas of the country were nothing more than uninhabited stretches of moorland and marsh, scrubland and forest. Even at the beginning of the eighteenth century about a quarter of the nation still remained a neglected wilderness.

In Leeds those large tracts of wasteland rolled eastwards and westwards from the town but they were not totally without use. There, as well as on the common land of Woodhouse Moor, the inhabitants of the township would find useful additional grazing areas for their cattle and sheep as well as being able to fatten their pigs on acorns and beech-mast in autumn.

Farming itself was carried out in two places. One area lay south east of the town and stretched as far as the river. Here lay three huge open fields tended by the inhabitants of the hamlet of Knostrop. North of the town, reaching as far as the common land of Woodhouse Moor, were probably four more large open fields cared for by the bondmen of Woodhouse.

In Leeds, as elsewhere, the open field system of farming was used. Crops were rotated with one field being left fallow each year. These huge areas of farmland were often surrounded with moveable hurdles to keep out any stray beasts. Once the corn and hay had been cut, the hurdles were thrown down and the area opened up as common pasture to ensure that the field would be regularly fertilised.

In order to achieve a fair distribution of good and bad land the fields were divided into strips known by a variety of names such as 'selions', 'loons', and 'paulls'. These strips were divided from each other by furrows. The people of Leeds held about forty selions each. The shared land was used both for growing crops and for meadow.

Wheat and rye were grown for bread. Sometimes these cereals were sown together making a crop known as maslin. This was often used for baking the bread of servants and labourers. Generally only the wealthiest people ate wheat bread. Oats were grown for making porridge, oatcakes and oatmeal pottage, a kind of thick soup or stew. Oats could also be used for making coarse bread, as was barley; and like barley, particularly in northern England, oats were sometimes used for brewing.

Peas, broad beans, lentils, onions, parsnips, carrots and lettuce were grown in the tofts, small plots of land, in Kirkgate or in the hamlets at Woodhouse and Knostrop, as they would be in the outlying townships. Cattle, sheep, goats, pigs, geese and hens were also reared. Even the poorest people usually managed a few hens. Chaucer's impoverished widow in his *Canterbury Tales*, for example, had her seven hens and a cock but dined mainly on brown bread and milk. Only very occasionally did she manage grilled bacon and an egg or two. The poor of Leeds would have fared no better.

The lord of the manor of Leeds, the freemen, cottars and bondmen had to abide by the common policy of the township, for without hedges to divide up the properties it was essential everyone co-operated in running the estate. The lord had his share of the divided land and his strips were known as the old demesne. He also had an enclosed home farm known as the new demesne. In Leeds it was made up of Hall Flatt, a field of approximately fifteen acres covering the area bounded by what is now the Headrow, Briggate, Boar Lane and City Square, and three other plots. These were known as Margaret Holmes, Gallowhill Flatt and the Holmes. This stood south of the river.

In order to reclaim additional land from the wilderness and extend their holdings, some farmers resorted to assarting. Assarting meant clearing smallholdings of woodland or waste and then growing corn or hay in the reclaimed area. In subsequent centuries, as the population of

Leeds increased and the demand for land rose, it became more and more important to reclaim the wasteland in the manor. In 1341, the Woodhouse cottar Robert Fyrkild was farming an area that had previously been wasteland as was Richard Hill. Both paid a rent of two pence. As early as in 1172 Adam, the son of Hucke, and his wife and family enclosed a piece of assarted land in the settlement of Cookridge, north of Leeds.

Sometime between 1086 and 1100, Ilbert de Lacy granted the manor of Leeds to Ralph Paynel, a wealthy Norman baron who had arrived in England with Duke William's invasion force. Paynel founded the Benedictine Holy Trinity Priory in York, giving it land in Leeds and the tithes from the parish churches of both Leeds and Adel. When Ralph died, his son William inherited the manor and, like his father, he also established a priory, this time an Augustinian one at Drax. To this priory he granted the tithes from 'all the mills in Leeds', thirty bushels of unground corn from his mill in Hunslet and land in Beeston. He very probably also made further grants of land in Leeds, this time to the religious military order of the Knights Templar. Their tenants in the town were excused the need to grind their corn at the lord's mill but had to mark their homes with the distinctive cross of the order.

The erosion of the value of the manor by these several gifts was continued when, sometime between 1166 and 1176, Alice Paynel and her second husband, Robert de Gant gave two acres of land, a building with its adjacent plot and the rights to pasture there to another religious military order, the Knights Hospitallers. Between 1175 and 1185 the estate was again reduced when the manor of Northall was created. It took its name from the hall which stood between Vicar Lane and Lady Lane north of the Parish Church, and comprised an area stretching down to Sheepscar Beck.

Avice, the daughter of Alice and Robert de Gant married Robert FitzHarding who died shortly afterwards, but not before they had produced a son, Maurice. He would play a significant part in the subsequent development of the town. By this time the manor of Leeds was held by Richard I, but sometime between 1200 and 1205, young Maurice came of age and took on his family responsibility as lord of the manor. He generally referred to himself as Maurice de Gant but he occasionally adopted his grandmother's maiden name of Paynel.

Faced with declining revenues from his estate, Maurice recognised that some drastic measures were required if the fortunes of his possession were to be reversed. His solution was to follow the pattern that had been emerging in Western Europe during the previous century.

41

Numerous lords across the continent saw the future of medieval society no longer focused solely on an agricultural economy but in stimulating trade and industry. What had been small villages were encouraged to grow into walled towns. Both Richard I and King John swelled their royal exchequers in exchange for granting charters to towns where the freemen of these boroughs could develop their manufacturing and commercial potential. Across Western Europe numerous feudal barons established new towns which increased their own revenues in the form of rents and surcharges.

In the North of England nobles had also embarked upon similar projects. Robert de Roche exported wool and imported wine through the Humber estuary whilst Eustace de Vesci, another baron, had developed the town of Alnmouth. In 1207 Maurice de Gant, styling himself Maurice Paynel, decided that he, too, would follow this trend. Like de Vesci and others he decided to establish a new borough within the old manor of Leeds.

He would grant privileges to its inhabitants making them free burgesses with a freedom which would enable them to develop whatever industries or trades they wished. But Paynel reserved for himself his traditional rights. He insisted that the new burgesses must bake their bread in the lord of the manor's oven in Kirkgate. Exceptions were made, however. The accounts for 1356–7 show that Agnes Baxter paid two shillings for a special licence to have an oven 'in her house for baking bread during the term of her life'. The lord could continue to make certain financial demands on the inhabitants. Another power he demanded was the right to appoint the reeve, whose job was to oversee the running of the new borough.

The reeve played a vital part in the economy of rural England. It was he who organised the work of the manor and the repairs needed to local amenities and it was he who was often the spokesman for the rest of the community in negotiations with the lord of the manor or his steward. In return he received a money payment and often special grazing rights. In Leeds, the reeve's duty ran from Michaelmas to Michaelmas (29 September) and his payment was fixed at three shillings and fourpence or one sixth of £1. At the end of his term of office he was expected to draw up an account of income and expenditure. Fortunately for Leeds historians four reeves' accounts have survived. They were drawn up by William Widdowson for 1356–7; Adam Gibson for 1373–4; John Newton for 1383–4; and Adam Gibbarne for 1399–1400 and give us a graphic insight into life in the borough and manor of Leeds during the fourteenth century.

It was most likely on Monday 12 November 1207 that Paynel proclaimed his charter with the opening words:

> Let all men, present and future, know that I Maurice Paynel, have given and granted, and have confirmed by this my present charter, to my burgesses and their heirs freedom and free burgage and their tofts, and with each toft half an acre to cultivate . . .

It was a charter based on the one granted to the burgesses of Pontefract by Roger de Lacy in 1194, but whereas those burgesses paid 200 marks for their charter, the people of Leeds paid nothing.

As far as the charter went it was extremely limited. It failed to give the new burgesses political rights, refused them self-government, and denied craftsmen and merchants the right to establish guilds. There was no widespread exemption from tolls and tenants were strictly forbidden to sell property either to the Church or to any monastery.

But it did establish fixed rents for the burgages or tenements. It allowed the burgesses to hold their plots of land freely and lease their property, to subdivide it or even sell it if they so desired. They could build workshops on their land and thus crafts and industries could develop. Although Paynel was in no position to grant extensive trading rights, he nevertheless guaranteed a limited exemption from tolls for any burgess carrying grain or goods by river or road. Also created was a new borough court which was more suited to industrial and commercial disputes than the old manorial one, though this still continued to exist.

Trial by duel or ordeal of water was to be continued if the accused in a case wished to clear their name or settle a dispute. In 1209 William Gammary, Lord of Middleton, and Adam de Beeston held a trial by duel in order to determine the ownership of certain land south of the River Aire. The outcome is unknown. Some people have argued that as the woods are known as Beeston Woods, Adam may well have been the victor but this is conjecture.

Paynel's new town ran at right angles to the old township in Kirkgate. It was to be a single street that ran down to the river crossing and became the Briggate of today. It is probable that a bridge may have been built over the river there shortly afterwards but there is no documentary evidence of one until the fourteenth century. Approximately thirty tofts were placed on either side of the thoroughfare which itself was wide enough to accommodate a market. The charter did not establish a market as such but certainly before 1258 one was operating in Leeds, and by 1341 it was being held on a Monday.

The long narrow tofts which ran back from the street were large enough to hold a crude cottage with, perhaps, an outbuilding or two.

Here the new tenant could grow a few vegetables and rear a goat and some hens. The narrow yards and the fine shopping arcades which today still run off Briggate are, in all probability, a twenty-first-century echo of Paynel's thirteenth-century development.

In addition to these plots the new men of the borough were granted a further half-acre toft to the north-east of the town at the borough-men's tofts now known as Burmantofts. For though many were involved in developing trade and manufacturing, and this would be their main source of income, farming was still essential to supplement their needs. The people who settled in this new development were probably invited immigrants or the sons of the bondmen who worked the manorial lands. To allow the existing bondmen who farmed the lord's demesne at Woodhouse and Knostrop to settle in the new town would have caused too great a dislocation to the manorial estate.

Paynel's brave concept was a long time in coming to fruition. The manor's main source of income came from its rents. Another source was the tolls it exacted from its weekly Monday market. Tolls also came from the fairs operating in Leeds. By 1341 two fairs were being held regularly; on 29 June, the feast of the apostles Peter and Paul, and, on 28 October, the feast of Simon and Jude. The franchise for both the common oven and the great water mill by the river, the borough's greatest asset, were equally valuable as virtually every occupant of the town was compelled to use them.

But Paynel was not to enjoy his new development for long. He had followed King John to France on the king's ill-fated expedition of 1214. Then, along with the other discontented barons, he formed part of the baronial party that took the revolutionary step of demanding a programme of reform. In June 1215 at Runneymede, John accepted the charter presented to him, and Magna Carta, so often considered the cornerstone of English liberties, became part of the bedrock of the British constitution. For John it was but a deliberate ploy to buy time. Within months civil war had broken out between the rebels and their king. Pope Innocent III excommunicated the barons and thus it is recorded on 2 January 1216, 'the good men of Leeds' were ordered to 'be obedient to Philip de Albini' whom the king had appointed to oversee the estate.

John died that same year and the rebels made one last desperate attempt to overthrow the new king, nine years-old Henry III. At the Battle of Lincoln in 1217 their forces were routed and Paynel himself was captured. As a ransom he was forced to pledge his manors of Leeds and Bingley to Ranulph de Blundeville, Earl of Chester and Lincoln. After this Maurice Paynel disappears from the history of Leeds but his legacy lived on. The town he had created down Briggate slowly coalesced with the old manorial township in Kirkgate.

In 1294, Alice, daughter of the Earl of Lincoln, married Thomas, Earl of Lancaster, the nephew of Edward I. It was a marriage which would ultimately have a significant influence on Leeds. Legend may well reflect that Lancaster led the hunt that killed the last wolf in the Leeds area in 1306, but his real impact had far greater political and economic implications for the town.

When King Edward died in 1307, the son who succeeded him, though 'fair of body and great of strength', was weak and dissolute. Edward II's policies would eventually lead to civil war and his own ultimate overthrow and murder.

The king's troubles were compounded by his difficulties with the Scots. At Bannockburn in 1314, Robert the Bruce humiliated the English force and Edward was reluctantly forced to accept Thomas Lancaster, the richest landowner in England and now lord of the manor of Leeds, as the real governing power in the realm. But the Scottish victory saw highland marauders sweeping into the North of England. In 1316 the church at Adel and the homesteads around it were pillaged.

Edward regained his power but the friction with Lancaster continued and eventually erupted into outright revolt. At Boroughbridge in 1322 the opposing forces met. Lancaster's supporters were crushed and six days later the earl was executed for treason. Sir William Beeston, a supporter of Thomas, who held land at Beeston, Churwell and Cottingley, was forced to leave his son in the king's power as a guarantee of his own future loyalty.

In the aftermath of the battle, King Edward's troops commanded by Sir Andrew Harclay, Oliver Ingham and Robert Lewer, invaded the district and Leeds suffered considerably. How destructive their presence was can be judged by the fact that Thomas Forester, Roger Sargent, Robert Brown and Jordan Whitehead felt it was impossible to continue farming. Their land had been so wasted during the military operations and rendered so uneconomic, they felt they had no other option but to return it to the king.

Similarly, William Paslew and John Godfrey, who held the franchise for the water mills, common oven and tolls to the market and fairs, felt they had no option but to give these up as their profits also had been so markedly reduced by the recent turbulent disturbances. The common oven itself was described as having 'fallen down'. Whether or not it had been destroyed in the troubles or simply fallen into a dilapidated state is not clear but certainly it had to be rebuilt. A description of the manor written in 1341 also shows that the manor house itself had fallen into disrepair and was no longer in existence. Only the moat and a few farm buildings marked the spot where it had been.

But the throes of revolution were not the greatest calamity that befell the people of medieval Leeds. In July 1348 news had reached Yorkshire that bubonic plague was sweeping across Europe, decimating populations as it moved ever westwards. Archbishop Zouche of York swiftly pointed out to his flock that it was 'caused by the sins of men'. Prayer was the answer to this calamity. The reality was that it was caused by the bites of infected fleas borne by black rats. Outbreaks usually occurred in heavily populated areas. Northerners waited anxiously as the infection spread nearer and nearer to them. They realised that their chance of survival was no more than fifty per cent.

It reached York on 21 May 1349. The worst months of the outbreak in the North of England were June, July and August. Though Archbishop Zouche sat out the summer at Ripon, many of his clergy, like Hugh of Damascus, visited the sick and consecrated the new temporary churchyards needed to accommodate the soaring numbers of dead. It was a dedication carried out at enormous personal cost as over forty per cent of the clergy in the county perished.

However, though the ridings suffered considerably, Yorkshire was not subjected to the same alarming devastation as some counties. Unquestionably the plague took its toll in Leeds. Estimates put the population of the parish at this time at around 1,000 with some 350 to 400 in the borough. Records show that in 1425 the manor had only sixty-two tenants compared with 100 in 1343. There were only eleven families in the town who had lived there before the Black Death wreaked its havoc.

The effect of the pestilence on the fortunes of Leeds was also considerable. The accounts for the manor show that income was substantially reduced. Prior to the epidemic striking the manor profits were in the region of £70 to £80. By the end of the fourteenth century they had been reduced to between £62 and £66. Contributing to this was the fact that the various reeves appointed to supervise the running of the estate found it more and more difficult to insist on villeins fulfilling their obligations. So serious was the labour problem nationally that Edward III introduced the Statute of Labourers in 1351. It was an attempt to maintain wages at pre-plague rates, refused workers the right to leave their masters and denied other landowners the right to employ them. Nevertheless, newcomers arrived in the area. At Hunslet, the poll tax return for 1379 refers to John of Garforth, William from the North, Roger of Keighley and Thomas of Manningham.

In Leeds, commutation of service by making money payments in lieu of labour had already begun by 1341. By 1399, the men of Knostrop and Woodhouse who had worked the lord's estate now did so as rent-paying tenants. Adam Gibbarne, the reeve that year, recorded that eight shillings and sixpence had been received in lieu of winter ploughing and harrowing, six shillings and fourpence halfpenny for mowing and twenty-six shillings for reaping corn. Occasionally some services were required such as repairing the mill dam and fences but these demands tended to be more and more irregular.

By this time the ownership of the manor had became royal and had passed into the hands of Henry Bolingbroke. In 1399 he deposed Richard II and assumed the crown as Henry IV. Leeds was administered by the steward of the Honour of Pontefract under the supervision of the council of the Duchy of Lancaster.

Following a substantial increase in the revenues of Leeds between 1258 and 1341 a significant slowdown in the economic expansion of the borough and manor is noticeable as a result of the damaging effects of the Black Death. But it was a relative slowdown. The town suffered far less in terms of economy than many other manors, where income plummeted disastrously. Leeds was far wealthier than Bradford, Dewsbury, Huddersfield and Halifax, though, as yet, it had not reached the economic status of Pontefract or Wakefield. Nevertheless, in the years that followed the catastrophe of the plague its growing prosperity was manifested in the building of a new court-house, the extension of the parish church and the erection of several chapels-of-ease in the surrounding out-townships.

The town's economic recovery was undoubtedly enhanced by its position at the Aire crossing but Leeds also stood on two important roads. One was the cross-country York to Chester highway, and the other route, known in 1246 as Kliderowgate, ran from Pontefract, through Rothwell, Leeds, Bradford, and Haworth to Clitheroe in Lancashire. The other obvious factor stimulating local industry was Paynel's limited but effective charter.

But the gradual economic success of the town could only be achieved by careful administration of the day-to-day running of the manor and the borough. The responsibility for running the manor and maintaining the manorial buildings lay with the annually appointed reeve. The bailiff supervised the daily administration of the borough. From the reeves' accounts the situations and crises they faced can be clearly seen.

Civic amenities like the common oven, the Hall of Pleas, the pinfold, the fulling mills and the great corn mill, all had to be maintained and the reeve was responsible for their upkeep until 1492. From then on the people who farmed or leased the oven and mills were responsible for their maintenance. The old manor house was finally rebuilt, for although the old one is reported as having disappeared by 1341, a new one is recorded by 1560. The materials to effect all these repairs were acquired locally; timber was brought from the woods at Roundhay, Seacroft and Rothwell; stone came from the quarries at Headingley Moor and Armley.

Maintenance of the great double corn mill was crucial, even if at times expensive, as it was the most profitable part of the borough. Expenditure on the mill listed in the 1399–1400 accounts amounted to £1 2s. 2d., fourteen shillings of that for two new millstones brought from Rawdon.

Floods and drought could affect the revenue considerably. One hiatus came after the particularly severe winter of 1383–4. Exceptional floods had breached High Dam, now under City Station, and swept away the river banks. The complex system of goits or water courses which channelled the water to power the great mill wheel was left high and dry. For four days forty carpenters felled trees in Rothwell Park and another twenty-three worked in Seacroft Wood cutting down timber. Then the planks were cut to the required lengths to make the beams and piles needed for the repair.

Transporting the wood to Leeds was a major logistical problem. The amount required can be judged by the fact that twenty-one journeys were needed from Rothwell and twenty-eight from Seacroft. Roger de Ledes's quarry at Town End provided stone, as did the lord of the manor's quarry at Benetbank. Once again the scale of the operation is indicated by the fact that sixty cartloads were carried from Benetbank and a further 125 cartloads from Town End.

Dozens of men were employed removing the sand, gravel and debris that blocked the water courses, filling the breach in the dam with turves, sand and faggots and finally helping the carpenters to set the timber into position. It was a mammoth task costing some £15 0s. 0 1/2d. and added to that was the replacement cost of a new wheel costing nineteen shillings and eleven pence. Set against the receipts for the year of £82 6s. 4d., the expenditure shows just what an expensive operation the restitution of the mill had turned out to be.

The mill was an essential feature of any medieval town or village. Bread was eaten by all sections of society and it was also a valuable ingredient in preparing many dishes from sausages and stuffing to providing the crumbs for covering fried fish. At the time of the Norman

Conquest Leeds was unusual in that it had its own corn mill, whereas in Yorkshire generally such mills were sparse. By the fourteenth century the Leeds mill was considerably larger than others in the area, and as the town's greatest asset earned in the region of £14 a year.

But gradually some of the surrounding villages and townships acquired their own mills. As early as 1184 Serlo is recorded as being the miller at Hunslet and Beeston. In 1425 reference is made to a windmill 'to be built' within the lordship of Hunslet but its site has never been found. There were other mills grinding corn in the area. In some cases it has been established who operated them or where they were sited. In 1459 Adam Milner was the miller at Headingley. The mill at Farnley stood near the beck dividing the township from Bramley. Local monasteries were often beneficiaries of these corn mills. At Shadwell half the mill's profits went to the monks of Fountains Abbey. The monks of Pontefract benefited from the mill sited between Swillington and Garforth, and William de Somerville granted the proceeds from the mill at Seacroft to Bolton Priory.

There were not only millers in the out-townships. The occupations in these settlements during the fourteenth and fifteenth centuries were many and varied. Elena Brighton was a brewer at Allerton and Gledhow whilst Laurence More was a merchant at Austhorpe. At Hunslet, in the poll tax return for 1379, a falconer and a fletcher are listed, both with the Christian name John.

Many, of course, worked the land. About this time, Miles Hay was a farmer in Hunslet, albeit, at times, an irresponsible one. For three years he defaulted with the rent he owed to the monks of Fountains Abbey. Finally, in desperation they excommunicated him – and then with amazing rapidity he settled the debt!

That same poll tax return indicates a population of about 300 people in the town and lists the wide range of occupations which existed in fourteenth-century Leeds. John Passelaw and Johnannes Dyconson were innkeepers, Radulfus Passelaw was a lyster or tanner, Symon Passelwoman was the boucher or butcher and wealthy enough to employ a servant called Agnes. Thomas Milsson and Wilemus Snell were the local tailors, Johannes de Newton was a merchant, Johannes Masam was the local mason and Johannes Dykman was the local souter or shoemaker.

There were also market traders, like Agnes Morley, who rented a butcher's stall in 1425. Some of the stalls were rented by local entrepreneurs such as John Passelaw, the innkeeper, who rented three stalls whilst Robert Passelaw and Johannes Tymbill had interests in more than one.

The Passelaws, along with the Newtons, Snells, Dyconsons and the blacksmiths, Rynaws and de Tymbills, were the wealthiest families in the town although the richest man by far, and paying almost twice as much poll tax as anyone else, was Roger de Ledes. The Ledes family held the manor during the fourteenth century from the Dukes of Lancaster.

There were three blacksmiths at the time in Leeds, all with the Christian name Johannes: Messrs Rynaws, Arusmith and de Tymbill. The last-named was wealthy enough to employ four servants: John, Adam, Walter and William. Smiths worked not exclusively at shoeing horses but provided a whole range of services. In 1322 and again in 1399, for example, one local smith was called in to repair the spindle-housing of the water mill along with its axles and bearings.

The fuel needed for these forges in Leeds was coal. The town was fortunate in that ample supplies of coal were forthcoming from the immediate neighbourhood. Numerous medieval bell pits have been discovered between the Calls, Kirkgate and Briggate; others have been found at the out-townships of Roundhay and Allerton and one on the waste at Whinmoor. Bell or bee-hive pits were simple holes dug down and then welled or belled out in order to acquire as much coal as was feasible before the inevitable collapse ensued. Middleton Woods still show the depressions of many of these collapsed diggings and claims have been made that the Belle Isle area in south Leeds owes its name to these workings.

But of all the industries which arose in Leeds during this time, that of the woollen industry came to dominate the neighbourhood. As early as 1201 it is known Simon, a dyer, was working in Leeds – and fined for selling adulterated wine! In 1258 a weaver, William Webster, and a dyer, John Lister, were both employed in the trade whilst in 1275 Alexander Fuller was charged with selling 'cloth not the right breadth'.

Leeds now stood in the advantageous position of being at the junction of both an established agricultural area and a developing wool textile one. It was an ideal spot as a growing commercial centre but the development of the woollen industry in Leeds was to be a slow and long-drawn-out process.

In the thirteenth century the production of woollen cloth was predominantly centred on the west of England, Bristol and East Anglia. By 1300 some production had been established in Beverley and York and then through the fourteenth century it slowly expanded across Yorkshire. In the first half of that century there had been a general decline in the trade, brought about in part by the high demand for

English wool abroad and the restrictive practices of weavers' guilds. But the mechanisation of one of the most complex production processes, fulling, and the more positive policies of Edward III helped to foster the industry at home.

By 1470 it had become concentrated in the West Riding where the strict regulatory trade guilds had no power. A further additional fillip was given to the industry when severe restrictions were placed on the export of wool. Kirkstall's monks looked for new markets and found them in the fledgling local woollen industry. A further stimulant to that industry was the sumptuary laws of the fourteenth century. These compelled persons of a particular station in society, on pain of a severe fine, to wear clothes appropriate to their place in the social order. Production of cloth in Leeds increased dramatically. At the end of the fourteenth century, fifty-four weeks' production resulted in 120 cloths being completed; in 1468–9, 177 cloths were produced in just forty-two weeks.

The industry not only spread to Leeds itself but to many of the outlying villages to the west and south. By 1598 Hunslet could boast tenter frames and dye vats, and by 1610 two fulling mills. From these outlying villages the cloth was taken into Leeds for the finishing processes of dressing, cropping, fulling and dyeing, processes impossible to complete in the cottages of the local weavers. The industry had gained such a hold in the area that by 1534 when John Leland visited Leeds, he remarked that 'The Toun stondith most by Clothing.'

In its initial stages woollen cloth production was very much a cottage-based industry and one in which every member of the family was involved. The wool was bought from local farmers by a chapman who would then sell it on to individual clothiers. This was strictly illegal. From 1326 wool should only have been bought in staple towns. The nearest staple town to Leeds was York but the journey there, or to the next nearest staple towns of Newcastle, Lincoln and Norwich, was both long and, at times, dangerous. Thus the Government turned a blind eye and the local industry slowly prospered.

First the wool was sorted: there were up to ten grades of wool in one fleece. Next came the washing or scouring. In this process loose debris such as gorse and heather, picked up by the sheep from the local hillsides, was removed and the fleece washed. Leeds and its surrounding villages were fortunate. The soft lime-free waters of the Pudsey, Farnley and Hol becks to the west and south, and the Adel and Sheepscar becks to the north, provided an ideal water supply.

The matted wool fibres were then straightened. This was often a job for the younger members of the family. Teazels were pulled across the fleece to open it up and loosen the wool. Later, wires were set into leather handles. These brushes were known as cards, hence the person using it became known as the carder, or pynner.

Next came spinning the wool fibres into a continuous thread, a job often undertaken by the unmarried women of the household, the spinsters. Originally a distaff was used. Wool was fastened to the forked end of this stick, and then with a weight attached to the end of the strand of wool, the thread was slowly drawn out by the fingers. The spinning-wheel did not make its appearance until the end of the fourteenth century. As an indication of how slow the process was, it took eight spinners to meet the requirements of just one weaver.

The weavers or websters in Leeds and the West Riding wove the cloth to a length of about four metres. John Morley and Robert Webster of Leeds had been weaving cloth for twenty-two years when they are mentioned in 1399 and though the manor records do not specifically name any other weavers, no doubt many more were very much involved in the trade.

The woven cloth had then to be fulled so that the fibres were matted together. First it was scoured again by soaking it in stale urine to remove the grease used in the weaving process. It was then soaked in troughs in a solution of fuller's earth powder. Teams of a dozen or more walked on the cloth, pounding it by trampling on it whilst it was still wet. Thus the cloth was shrunken and the fibres matted together.

This fulling process was revolutionised in the twelfth century when wooden hammers or fulling stocks driven by water power replaced the walker. The first fulling mill in England was recorded in 1185. It was on the Knights Templars' estate at Temple Newsam, about three miles east of Leeds. It was obvious that fulling was a lucrative process for every cottage weaver was dependent upon it. By 1322 the lord of the manor had realised its potential and erected a fulling mill to the east of Leeds Bridge. By 1399 William and Hugh Walker were leasing it for thirty shillings for the Easter and Michaelmas terms.

By 1356 a second fulling mill, this time on the western side of the bridge, was built. And though it had fallen into disrepair by the middle of the fifteenth century, Gilbert Leigh saw the potential to develop a new mill east of the bridge, and by 1498 Richard Bank had done the same.

The wet cloth was then stretched on tenter frames, long wooden structures between four and ten metres in length and set with rows of hooks that pulled the material tight. These frames were erected on any available open space both in Leeds and the surrounding townships and were a prominent feature of the Leeds landscape until the nineteenth century.

By 1341 Thomas Kiddal and William Addy are listed as renting tenter sites in the town. In 1373, Kiddal was negotiating to extend his tenter area. Kiddal, along with a Nigel Walker, were clothiers of some distinction in the town. Not only did they use the tenter frames but were also engaged in dyeing. The year 1356 saw Kiddal paying rent for an enlarged dye-vat and Walker for constructing a new one. As the industry slowly developed, the need for more tenters was apparent and thus from 1455 nine new tenters were established on either side of Leeds Bridge. Some of the clothiers were commercial entrepreneurs like William Nettleton. In the 1480s, he combined both cloth manufacture and trading with leasing the common oven and the corn mill.

Dyeing, like fulling, was a specialist process. Cloth was brought to central Leeds, first to be dyed, then finished. This involved raising the nap or pile by brushing it with teazels and then croppers or shearmen cut it to the correct length. Leeds cloth, known as 'northern dozens', was usually about four metres long. The cloth was then sold in Leeds Monday market, which, from 1488, was already gaining a reputation for quality cloth.

If the woollen industry came to dominate the economic life of medieval Leeds and its surrounding out-townships, the Church and other religious institutions dominated not only everyday life in general but also a considerable part of the surrounding landscape.

In the southern village of Hunslet, the monks of Fountains and Sawley abbeys held land. At Holbeck, the monks of Holy Trinity Priory established a religious cell some time during the thirteenth century. A small monastic community of Benedictines remained there probably until the late fourteenth century. Drax Priory held property at Beeston and about 1233 a small hospital is referred to in the township, probably established by one of the religious orders. By the fifteenth century Kirkstall Abbey held considerable lands in the area and the religious order of the Knights Hospitallers also held land at Adel. But the religious military order which was most dominant in the Leeds area was that of the Knights Templar.

Founded in 1119 as a military order which held strict monastic vows to serve God in Palestine, the Knights Templar became extremely wealthy landowners across Europe. In England the most extensive of the Templar properties were to be found in Yorkshire. They held numerous small parcels of land rented out to tenant farmers such as at Seacroft and Horsforth, whilst the remains of one of their properties, the medieval village of Colton, can still be seen. In Leeds itself they held property in what is now the Headrow and Vicar Lane. But their largest manors in the West Riding were at Ribston near Wetherby, Temple Hirst near Selby and at Newsam near Leeds.

Newsam had been granted to the order in about 1152 by Ralph and William Hastings and about three years later, Henry de Lacy, the great benefactor of Kirkstalll Abbey, confirmed the handing over of the estate for lands in Nottinghamshire. At Newsam the new owners built a pre-ceptory, a form of monastery headed by the preceptor. It had a chapel, dormitory, stables, barns, brewhouse, dairy and hall.

The place became known as Temple Newsam, and archaeologists have been able to piece together what some of the Templar buildings there would have looked like. The chapel appears to have been rectan-gular. The great barn was over forty-five metres long, an enormous structure for the time. Other discoveries have shown the remains of pos-sibly a dovecote or granary, and pits lined with stone have been unearthed. They were probably used for tanning. An 1185 document also records two water mills at the site, one for grinding corn, the other for fulling cloth.

Their wealth came from farming: growing crops, particularly oats, and rearing sheep. But that wealth was not for self-indulgence. Most of it went to support Templar activity in the Holy Land. Indeed the goods they had at Temple Newsam appear to have been very basic: a few pots, a gridiron, a tripod and a frying pan are listed in an inventory. Even their religious objects were inexpensive: a copper crucifix and iron candle-sticks are both mentioned.

But the days of the Templars at Temple Newsam were numbered. In 1275, they were accused of hunting on their estate when they were not only forbidden to partake in such pastimes but even to associate with anyone who went hawking. They were also accused of failing to pay fines for the villages of Halton, Colton and Osmondthorpe and of ille-gally seizing land at Mickeley.

Normally only a few knights would be at Temple Newsam at any given time as the bulk of them were serving in Palestine fulfilling their vows to protect pilgrims there. Eventually driven from the Holy Land, the Templars lost their sense of purpose but not their considerable wealth. Philip IV of France, eyeing their riches and fearful of their power, urged Pope Clement V in 1307 to dissolve the order. Reluctantly, Edward II of England followed suit. Accused of idolatory, heresy and immorality, the Templars were arrested.

Geoffrey de Arches, the last preceptor of Temple Newsam and two others were taken to York for trial. Found guilty on the flimsiest of evi-dence, the Templars were despatched to various monasteries to do penance. Richard of Sheffield was sent to Kirkstall Abbey, but the Cistercians, perhaps anxious about another mouth to feed, were happy to connive at his quick escape.

Today, the presence of the Templars in Leeds is still apparent in the names of Templar Street, Templar Lane and the Templar Inn on Vicar Lane. Templar crosses on buildings at Whitkirk are constant reminders of the men who once held sway at Newsam a thousand years ago.

Whatever political calamities befell the nation, the people of Leeds had to face their own communal crises and personal tragedies. In 1550 the 'sweating sickness', a virulent infection whose victims were 'ended or mended' in twenty-four hours, descended on the town with alarming impact. Scores in the area died, with burials at Swillington up from four to twenty-five. Similarly, in 1587, another visitation of bubonic plague saw deaths in Leeds trebled. And there were sad personal, private tragedies such as that of John Webster of Hunslet Lane who buried his wife, Alice, and his son, John, on the same fateful day in 1574.

Most took consolation from the fact that the Church was ever present to support them in their times of need – and even afterwards. In 1525, Thomas Moore's will provided money so that hymns would be sung for his departed soul in Leeds Parish Church. In April 1528, Lawrence Towneley, a gentleman of the town, made a similar provision.

Wealthy patrons often established special chantry chapels where prayers were chanted for their souls when they had died. Travellers would also use these chantries in preparation for setting off on journeys. Leeds had two such chapels dedicated to St Mary: one stood just off the north-east corner of Leeds Bridge and the other on the outskirts of the town about at the junction of the present Vicar Lane and Lady Lane. Somewhere towards the top of Kirkgate, Revd Thomas Clarell established a chantry dedicated to St Catherine and had the chancel decorated with paintings and other adornments. At the junction of the Headrow and Briggate a further chantry stood. This was Sir William Eure's chapel and was dedicated to Mary Magdalene.

Chantries were also established within the chapels built at Holbeck and Farnley, while Beeston and Chapel Allerton could also boast their own places of worship. But all these chapels were part of the great rambling parish of Leeds and came under the auspices of the Parish Church in Kirkgate, known by 1420 as St Peter's.*

A church had stood in Leeds since Anglo-Saxon times, as the entry in

---

* Adel and Whitkirk were churches in their own parishes.

the Domesday Book shows, and some time between 1090 and 1100 Ralph Paynel had granted the monks of Holy Trinity Priory at York the advowson or the right to appoint the Vicar of Leeds, and enjoy the tithes paid to the church. A tenth of the produce of every man was collected and stored in the great tithe barn that stood just west of the church.

During the mid-fourteenth century the old church was destroyed by fire and an imposing new structure replaced it using much of the old Norman building. It was cruciform in shape, with a nave, choir and transepts. Dominating it was the 96-foot-high tower that stood above the crossing. It had to cater for some 3,000 communicants, for the population of the town and out-townships was rapidly expanding. By now the old town in Kirkgate and the new town round Briggate had long since coalesced and by 1560 the urban sprawl had spread itself into Mabgate, Vicar Lane, Quarry Hill and Marsh Lane as well as along the Headrow, Boar Lane and Mill Hill.

Around 1500 fire seriously damaged the building again but by the time Leland, the historian, visited the town he was able to comment on the 'Paroche Churche reasonably well builded'. But fire was not the major crisis the parishioners of Leeds, or indeed any other church in England, faced at that time. Henry VIII's dispute with the Pope, the dissolution of the monasteries and the fear of the religious changes that were being introduced led to dissatisfaction amongst many devout Roman Catholics.

Among these was Thomas Darcy, who had become the owner of Temple Newsam and the first person to build a house on the site. Darcy was a loyal supporter of King Henry VIII and served his monarch well. He had fought the Moors in Spain, and as a reward, in 1512, Henry separated the park from the manor at Roundhay and gave it to Darcy. In the autumn of 1536 Henry again asked for Darcy's help, this time to quell the rising tide of opposition to his suppression of the monasteries. Darcy locked himself in Pontefract Castle but when the rebels arrived he not only admitted them, he joined the Pilgrimage of Grace.

This northen uprising against Henry's government was diffused by the king's vague promises and the offer of a full pardon. The 30,000 men disbanded. In June 1537, Darcy, Aske, the leader, and others were arrested for treason and executed on Tower Hill. The Temple Newsam estate passed to the Lennox family whose most famous offspring, Lord Darnley, the future husband of Mary, Queen of Scots, was born there.

The impact of Henry's religious policy had a major influence on Leeds. In 1538 he granted the advowson of St Peter's to a Thomas Culpepper. This was a matter of some concern, for the vicar's position in the community was extremely important and to have him appointed by a non-resident was totally unsatisfactory. It was a situation compounded when the advowson was sold on to other non-resident owners. As a result, in 1617, the parishioners of Leeds bought the right to appoint the vicar for themselves.

The religious passion that the Reformation unleashed was felt strongly in Leeds. In 1584, when Roman Catholic Richard Lumbye of 'Chappiltoune' died, his family were refused permission to bury him in the churchyard at St Peter's. Finally, after ten days, the authorities relented on condition that he was buried at night.

Leeds developed a strong Puritan tradition. On the death of the blind Reverend Fawcett, the first Protestant vicar of Leeds in 1590, the Beeston-born, Oxford educated academic, Robert Cooke was appointed as incumbent. He was a Puritan and his appointment began the long tradition of Puritan vicars being appointed in Leeds during the seventeenth century.

In the 1540s Henry had suppressed the chantry chapels. William Sheafield was the priest attached to the Clarell Chantry in Leeds. When it closed he drew up his will dated 6 July 1552 in which he granted the rents from nine cottages and eight acres of meadow and pasture near Sheepscar Bridge to be part of the stipend for the payment of a 'Schoolmaister at Leedes'. It was the birth of Leeds Grammar School and the establishment of a tradition which has stretched unbroken to the twenty-first century. It was very probably not the first school in Leeds. The extent or survey carried out in 1341 of the lands of the disgraced Earl of Lancaster records a 'John, master of schools' as holding land in the town. In 1528, Lawrence Towneley bequeathed twenty-one marks to keep James Towneley 'at the Schole'. It has been suggested that Sheafield's endowment may have been made to ensure the future of that institution rather than establish a new one.

Whether it was a new or an already existing establishment, the Grammar School was devoted to teaching Latin, the language of the Church, the Law and Medicine, and Greek, the language of culture. Part of Sheafield's condition was that responsibility for providing the school building lay with the townsfolk of Leeds. It seems that the school opened in the chantry chapel which stood in Vicar Lane, with the chantry that stood at the end of Leeds Bridge used as a reading school. In 1579, both chapels were purchased 'to the use of the Schools'.

The initial success of the institution rested greatly on Sheafield's choice of trustees. All were substantial men of Leeds or held property in the area. One of these, Sir John Nevile, of Liversedge Hall and the owner of lands in Hunslet, was inveigled by Christopher Danby of

Beeston into joining the abortive rising of 1569 to replace Elizabeth I with Mary, Queen of Scots. He subsequently lost his estates and fled to Flanders leaving behind his wife with 'only a white frieze gown, and ten children and neither house, meat or drink'.

Treason was but one of the crimes committed in Leeds throughout the Middle Ages. There were sordid killings, such as the infamous brawl of 1319 between members of two of the leading families in the town and which erupted one Sunday outside the Parish Church, and the murder of John Paslewe on Sheepscar Bridge in 1398 by William de Leeds and his servant John Mareschall. There were thefts recorded, such as that of Thomas Awtrey of Hunslet who stole forty shillings from Emmas de Walton in 1333 but received a royal pardon because of his good services in the war against the Scots. And there were famous legal disputes such that involving Thomas Falkingham, lord of the manor of North Hall.

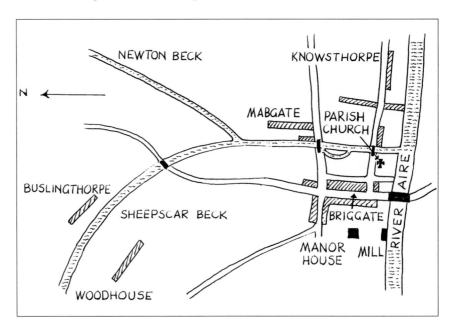

4. Tudor Leeds
The first map of Leeds was drawn up about 1560 as a result of a legal dispute. This modern reconstruction based on it shows the bridge, mill and manor house.

Around 1560, Thomas Lyndeley and his wife Elizabeth were tenants of the great corn mill in Leeds and were furious when Falkingham decided to build a mill of his own at what is now Millgarth. Falkingham claimed it was built within his own manor. For twenty years the dispute dragged on; depositions were taken and the first-ever map of Leeds was produced to clear up certain legal points, but the outcome of the judgement is unclear. It was becoming clear, however, that Leeds was growing rapidly and the ancient medieval ways of government could only restrict its further growth.

What brought matters to a head was another crime. Leeds, as Leland had said, 'stondith most by Clothing' but that very trade was in imminent danger of being destroyed. Various local clothiers had begun to produce imitation 'northern dozens', dyeing the cloth with logwood and passing it off as the real thing. It was vital for the protection of the industry and the overall economic development of the town that such practices were brought to an end. The only effective way to achieve that was to establish an agency in Leeds which was legally capable of controlling the production of local cloth and of overseeing the future expansion of the town. In effect, a charter was required that would establish a town council, do away with the restrictive practices of the Middle Ages and encourage the development of the burgeoning town of Leeds.

CHAPTER FOUR

A TOWN WITH A CHARTER

James VI of Scotland left Edinburgh in April 1603 to travel in triumph through the new kingdom he had inherited. As he made his way slowly south to take up the English throne as King James I, crowds flocked to welcome him. For James it was a relief. As he remarked, up until now he had been 'like a poor man . . . wandering in a wilderness . . . and now arrived at the land of promise'. Both he and his new subjects had good reason to see England as a 'land of promise'. English ships were now trading across the globe. Old industries were being developed; new ones such as felt making, thread making, silk weaving, and the manufacture of lace, needles and glass were being introduced. At Beeston near Leeds, the out-township became famous for the manufacture of bone lace. But all these industries paled into insignificance when compared with the growing woollen industry and here Leeds played a prominent part. In 1550, the cloth manufacturers of Leeds and Wakefield between them were making just 500 cloths a year. By 1600 their combined output was about 5,000.

The early years of the seventeenth century saw the West Riding textile boom continue as Hull revived as a port, offering greater opportunities for Yorkshire's merchants to exploit the growing lucrative markets overseas. Eventually coarse northern woollen cloths would make up ninety per cent of Hull's exports. Leeds benefited from this increased demand and was equally fortunate when four charters exempted the town's merchants from tolls at the wool markets of Ripon, Boroughbridge and throughout the estates of the Duchy of Lancaster. But it received a bitter blow in 1617. That year Wakefield was nominated as one of the twenty-three staple towns. Only at these designated towns were staplers allowed to sell wool. The Leeds cloth merchants protested that such a move would endanger their local industry. Fortunately for them, the following year, the town itself was added to the list.

James I's family inheritance brought him Temple Newsam, the birth-place of his father Lord Darnley, whilst Leeds itself remained a royal manor. James, however, quickly restored Temple Newsam to the Lennox Family who had lost it when Darnley had married Mary, Queen of Scots and Elizabeth I, in a petulant fury, condemned Lady Lennox to the Tower and seized all the family's assets. But Ludovick, Duke of

Lennox, lived an extravagant lifestyle and by 1622 he was forced to sell his house and estate to Sir Arthur Ingram for £12,000. Ingram was an astute, unscrupulous financier, secretary to the Council of the North, High Sheriff of the County and MP for York. But as far as James I and Charles I were concerned his greatest achievement, along with that of other financiers, was in being able to raise sufficient revenue to enable both kings to rule without having to resort to asking Parliament for regular grants.

At one time and another Ingram owned forty-one estates, mainly in Yorkshire. One of them was the manor of Leeds-Kirkgate-cum-Holbeck, a small estate near the parish church which had been separated from the manor of Leeds when the monks of Holy Trinity Priory acquired it at the end of the twelfth century. The manor of Leeds itself, known as Leeds Main Riding, was granted by James to his wife, Queen Anne of Denmark.* In 1612, Thomas Potts, Deputy Surveyor General, arrived in Leeds to carry out a survey of the royal estate. From this résumé the boundaries of the manor are clearly designated. Sheepscar Beck flowed by Woodhouse Carr forming the eastern limit of the estate. The boundary ran down Buslingthorpe Lane and then east of Richmond Hill as far as Pontefract Lane. The western boundary ran southwards from Pikeman Ridge, a hedge planted with trees which separated the manor from those of Headingley and Burley.** From a point where it met the River Aire at Armley the boundary followed the river to High Dam by the great mill in Leeds then down to Meadow Lane. Potts's survey also described the shops and stalls in Briggate and in the congested area around the main street could be found granaries, more shops, courtyards and gardens.

By 1628, a second survey again showed how much the town had developed over the years. Buildings now sprawled along Boar Lane and on either side of the bridge. But the growing population meant more and more dwellings and workshops were required. Behind the buildings on the main streets smaller ones were erected, forming a compact area. Many of them were 'ancient meane and lowe built; and generallie all of Tymber', despite the fact that there were numerous stone quarries about the district. Even the houses of the wealthier inhabitants, though 'large

---

* The manor of Leeds was much smaller than both the parish and the borough of Leeds. Both of these included the town of Leeds and the out-townships.

** The fact that the hedge was called Pikeman Ridge in 1612 dispels the popular belief that it derived its name from a skirmish fought in 1643 during the Civil War.

and capacious', were 'low and straightened on their backsides'. But here also were to be found orchards, gardens and the ever-present tenter grounds that were so vital to the town's premier industry. The wide main street, Briggate, where the Monday market was held, was paved with stone. It was also the site of Moot Hall.

Parish officers had responsibility for the running of the manor. One group of officers, the churchwardens, was responsible for the maintenance of the church. The parishioners appointed these wardens. The West Riding Justices of the Peace appointed the other officers. It was their responsibility to oversee poor relief, fix wages, punish miscreants, regulate the price of corn and deal with any crises that should occur.

The recurrence of bubonic plague was one such regular crisis they had to face, for the disease frequently made its appearance across the country. It affected Leeds in 1573, 1575 and 1587. York suffered over 3,000 fatalities in 1604 when the pestilence struck. To avoid infection, young Prince Charles, the future king, was diverted from there and brought to Leeds on his way to London. But Leeds itself did not escape. For the fourth time in forty years the disease struck the town. The magistrates acted swiftly. The markets were closed and substitute ones established on Hunslet Moor on Mondays and Chapeltown Moor on Fridays. It was here that the magistrates said farmers 'shall bring corn . . . to supply the town'. Only those with special 'tickets or notes' could attend the markets or continue carrying wool and cloth around the district. As a guarantee that the holder was free from infection the certificates had to be signed, 'under the hand of Robert Cooke, clerk, vicar, Edward Savile, gentleman, high constable, John Harrison, John Metcalfe, W. Lodge, or two or more of them'. Most people accepted the restrictions but one individual at least, William Lawson, refused. He was arrested, 'having carried himself in a most dissolute and contemptuous manner . . . [was] imprisoned within the prison of Leeds . . . and kept fast locked there for three days . . . [and then] upon his good carriage of time [released]'. The Justices then announced further action to be taken should it be needed. The people of Leeds were authorised 'to erect, to make and set up lodges on Woodhouse Moor, to place their visited people in'.

One of the certificate signatories was John Metcalfe. By 1615 he was appointed bailiff or principal officer, whose role was to act on behalf of the lord of the manor. About that time, together with the parish officials, he decided to replace the old magistrates' meeting place. Previously they had met in the old Hall of Common Pleas which stood above the manorial oven in Kirkgate. Not surprisingly, the justices complained at times of the heat and smoke from the bakehouse as being both 'noysom and a great hinderance'. So it was decided to erect a new building in the centre of the town's principal thoroughfare, Briggate.

But the building of Moot Hall led to a major scandal. Monies intended for the relief of the poor had been used for the project on the understanding that rents from the property would be used to alleviate poverty in the town. Apart from the courtroom, the building contained shops on the ground floor and first-floor rooms which were all available for hire, hence the hall was devised as a viable commercial venture designed to raise revenue. It was discovered, however, that for two years, Metcalfe had pocketed £5 of the £20 rent for the upper rooms of the building for himself. Compounding this crime was his abuse of the Toll Dish. This was a toll imposed on the sale of all corn in Leeds markets. It had been decreed that one-third of the revenue collected should go to the poor, one-third to repairing the roads and the final third for Metcalfe's personal use. The toll had been regularly collected but not one penny had found its way into the coffers of the poor or into maintaining the highways.

Once the facts became known there was a public outcry and King James appointed a commission to investigate. Headed by Sir John Savile and the newly appointed Vicar of Leeds, Alexander Cooke, the committee drew up its report. Metcalfe had to refund the purloined money and the commissioners insisted that in future the administration of the hall should come under the jurisdiction of a new administrative body. The Committee of Pious Uses was set up in 1620 and comprised twelve trustees and the Vicar of Leeds. Deeds and documents of the body were to be kept 'in a strong Chest in the vestry of the Parish Church'. On 5 July 1620 *The First Decree for a Committee of Pious-Uses in Leedes* identified the areas where the charitable funds had to be used: for aiding the poor, maintaining the highways and in supporting 'the free grammar school of Leeds'. In addition to this the corn toll was to be collected by a representative of the bailiff working with a representative of the new committee. But as this saga unravelled, two of those involved, Metcalfe, the bailiff, and Cooke, the vicar, clashed publicly over their differing religious views.

It was not only Cooke and Metcalfe who held different views about religion. The country as a whole was bitterly divided. Although England was now a Protestant nation, there still existed a small group of devout Roman Catholics. The Church of England itself was disunited. The High Church Party believed in all the panoply of church ritual and in episcopacy, the government of the Church by bishops. The Puritans, on the other hand, favoured simple dress, lived strictly moral lives, condemned ceremonies in worship, laid great emphasis on personal conversion, rigorously observed the Sabbath and were bitterly opposed to the appointment of bishops. Some Puritans, unable to accept the manner of worship in Anglican churches, chose to become Dissenters such as Independents and Baptists. One such group, the Pilgrim Fathers, emigrated rather than compromise their principles. But most remained as members of the Church and worked for its reform.

One such was Alexander Cooke. He was appointed Vicar of Leeds on the death of his Puritan brother Robert in 1615. The new incumbent followed in his brother's Puritanical tradition. For many Leeds people, Alexander Cooke's strict emphasis on the austere way of life his Puritan beliefs demanded was anathema. The announcement of his appointment caused uproar in the town. It was claimed that Cooke had already been replaced in one parish because of his extreme beliefs. A petition was sent to Queen Anne claiming the new vicar 'came not in by their consent', and urged her to replace him with 'some learned and godly divine'.

Cooke was in fact a 'learned divine', an accomplished academic but with a passionate, obsessive loathing of the Church of Rome. To this end he published numerous critiques attacking the Romanists. *Work for a Masse Priest, More Work for a Masse Priest, Yet More Work for a Masse Priest* and *The World Turned Topsy Turvey by the Papists* were but a few.

But Cooke remained at his post in Leeds and for many it seemed the fun had gone out of life. The Puritan way meant that the costly hangings in the Parish Church were removed, the stained glass destroyed, the multi-coloured frescoes obliterated with whitewash. Cooke railed against those who dared to work or play on a Sunday. He thundered from his pulpit at the 'irreligious atheists, whoremasters, drunkards, epicures, infidels and abbey-lubbers'. He condemned confirmation and the use of the marriage ring as superstitious practices, preached that there should be no praying on Good Friday, 'Cursed' Friday as he called it, and argued that Christmas should be in summer on the basis that shepherds did not watch flocks in winter.

To many of his parishioners he was a man of 'giddy, brainless, distempered disposition'. One local poet lamented:

> And thou my native towne, which was of old, Leede
> (When as thy bonfires burn'd, and Maypoles stood,
> And when thy wassall-cups were uncontrol'd)
> The Sommer bower of peace and neighberhood,
> Although since these went down, thou ly'st forlorn
> By factious schisms, and humors overborne.

These factious schisms led Cooke to take to walking about his parish carrying a brace of loaded pistols. Matters came to a head when John Metcalfe was accused of misappropriating the funds from Moot Hall and the corn tolls. In 1619, Cooke accused Metcalfe of being absent from church. Metcalfe argued his duties had prevented him from attending. The dispute between the two men dragged on. Metcalfe filed a suit in the Court of Star Chamber for slander and libel against Cooke, 'a perverse, factious sectary and Puritan'. It was claimed that the vicar had damned Metcalfe both from the pulpit and at prayer meetings, including reciting a poem about his adversary in which Metcalfe was accused of immorality and corruption. Compounding this, Cooke had brandished a halberd and cried out 'I wish I had . . . Metcalfe here!' He was even accused of forcing a father who was a friend of Metcalfe's to bury his own child.

In 1618 James I, wary of the Puritans' political power and their strict Sabbatarianism which forbade sport and merry-making on Sundays, yet conscious of the feelings of their opponents, published the *Book of Sports*. In it James argued that denying sport to the 'commoner and meaner sort of people' led to discontent. He listed what he considered were suitable pastimes for the Sabbath once church had been attended, among them maypole dancing, morris dancing and rush bearing. The Puritans were outraged.

That year, people in Leeds attempted to hold a rush bearing ceremony when rushes and garlands were to be carried into the Parish Church. There they were to be strewn over the floor and used to decorate the walls. Cooke was incensed as the crowd approached the building beating drums and playing pipes. The vicar and his supporters physically prevented the celebrations developing by the simple ploy of attacking the revellers. Cooke then preached hell-fire against those who indulged in the festivity, but on St Bartholomew's Day 1619, his adversary Metcalfe encouraged a further celebration to take place.

Metcalfe employed a drummer to parade round the parish for a week advertising the forthcoming ceremony and not surprisingly on the day a large crowd turned out to see what would happen when the rush bearers arrived at St Peter's. Cooke locked the church doors and once more led an assault against the revellers. One woman was seriously injured but Cooke claimed that the only person he had attacked was his own sexton and that for ringing a bell. As far as he was concerned the whole episode had been organised to annoy him. The incident then turned into farce when a man wearing a visor and ram's horns created a diversion and the crowd, many of whom had been drinking, then broke into the church. Not surprisingly, the service was ultimately abandoned!

Not all the problems of the Church in Leeds hinged on theological matters. In 1615 a bill of complaint by the town's leading citizens was made to the Court in Chancery. It pointed out that, 'the Town and parish had become very large and populous and consisted of more than 5,000 communicants and that though some of them were three to four miles distant from the church yet three to four thousand of them ordinarily resorted thither every Sabbath'.

It was obvious that overcrowding was a major problem. In previous centuries some provision had been made in the out-townships to ease the problem. A chapel of ease had existed for centuries at Bramley and was said to have been built by the monks of Kirkstall. Another had existed at Farnley since at least 1240 and in 1417 Henry V had granted Sir William Harrington the right to build another in recognition of his services at Agincourt. Beeston's chapel dated from 1597 and Headingley's from 1616. In West Leeds a grudging Ralph Hopton allowed the worshippers from the two townships of Armley and Wortley to hold services in his private chapel at Armley Hall. It was not until 1649 that the two communities finally built themselves a chapel in Armley. In these out-townships, as in Leeds itself, the tradition of Puritanism was strong.

But the man who came to the rescue of the parishioners in Leeds was accused of being both a Puritan and a High Churchman. John Harrison was one of the truly great benefactors of the town. A successful clothing merchant, he devoted time and money to alleviating the suffering of the poor and provided twenty almshouses for those in need. In 1619 he paid for the erection of a market cross in Briggate and in 1624 he provided land and paid for a new grammar school building to replace the existing medieval one. Harrison Street near the Grand Theatre commemorates the site. The overcrowding of the Parish Church led him to propose that a new church be built in Leeds at the northern extremity of the town on what is now New Briggate.

A deeply religious man, he has been accused of being a Puritan whilst others have argued that his plan to build a second Leeds church was a deliberate attempt to counterbalance the severe puritanic regime at St Peter's. The Archbishop of York had already expressed his concern about the project, fearing that it would become a rival to the nearby Parish Church. Being a Laudian or High Churchman himself, he equally feared that a Puritan incumbent might be appointed. His fears regarding the appointee were justified. Harrison chose Robert Todd as curate. Todd had been a Reader at the Parish Church and he was a Puritan. He became a major embarrassment and an appointment Harrison lived to regret.

The consecration service for St John's was arranged for 21 September 1634 and in some ways that day perfectly encapsulated the conflicting views which were vying with each other for the soul of the Anglican Church. Dr Cosins, Archbishop Neile's chaplain, conducted the morning service and his preaching reflected the beliefs of High Church Anglicanism. At the afternoon service, the congregation must have been totally perplexed. Todd launched into a tirade in defence of Puritan dogma that virtually contradicted everything Cosins had said. The Archbishop was furious and St John's first curate was suspended immediately after his first service. Only the pleading of Harrison and Sir Arthur Ingram saw him finally reinstated.

5. John Harrison
John Harrison (1579-1656) one of the great benefactors of Leeds. His gifts included St John's Church in Briggate and the new Grammar School on what is now Harrison Street. He was a leading proponent in the campaign to gain Leeds its first charter in 1626.

John Harrison's magnificent church is still one of the architectural gems of Leeds, but his greatest contribution to the long-term future of the town came in his efforts to see Leeds granted a royal charter. For Harrison, like other notable Leeds families, the Hoptons, Skeltons, Hodgsons, Cassons, Sykeses, Bensons, and Hillaries, was concerned not simply about the reprehensible behaviour of the local bailiff. A far more serious threat to the town's major industry came from unscrupulous local manufacturers producing inferior cloth and passing it off as the genuine article, generally known as 'northern dozens'. It was felt that a much closer regulation of the trade was required and the only way to achieve this effectively was to have Leeds granted a charter of incorporation.

The new king, Charles I, agreed, and on 13 July 1626 a charter was granted. The local corporation could now dictate not only the quality of the local cloth produced but also take responsibility for the development of the town. It was a charter which gave the council the right to govern not only the town but the out-townships of the parish of Leeds as well. Oddly enough it made no mention of Paynel's charter of 1207.

Although it was similar to many other charters of the period its opening is very specific to Leeds. It makes it quite clear why it was being granted before going on to lay down the administrative responsibilities of the new body:

> [D]ivers clothiers of the . . . town and parish had begun to make . . . deceptive cloths, and to dye the same with wood called logwood, to the damage and prejudice . . . of the clothiers of the town . . . [T]hey most humbly have besought us . . . to extend our royal favour and munificence to . . . create, for the . . . better rule and government and improvement of the town and parish . . . a body corporate . . . AND . . . all houses, buildings, lands, waters, watercourses, soil and ground . . . within the town and parish of Leedes . . . shall be called and known by the name of the BOROUGH OF LEEDES IN THE COUNTY OF YORK . . . and shall be at all times . . . able . . . to have, purchase, receive and possess lands, tenements . . . and also goods and chattels . . . and shall be able to . . . defend and be defended . . . before . . . judges and justices . . . [O]ne of the more honest and discreet . . . inhabitants of the borough . . . shall be named the alderman of the borough . . . [N]ine of the more honest and discreet . . . inhabitants . . . to be elected . . . and shall be called the principal burgesses . . . [T]wenty other of the more honest and discreet men . . . shall be called assistants . . . [T]he alderman and common council . . . shall be enabled to impose . . . penalties and punishments . . . [and] fines . . . [T]hey shall . . . have full power and authority yearly and every year, on the day of the feast of St Michael the Archangel . . . themselves . . . be assembled in the common hall . . . and there to continue until they . . . have nominated and elected one of the principal burgesses . . . to be alderman . . . AND if . . . one or more of the . . . nine principal burgesses . . . die, or be removed . . . it shall . . . be lawful for the . . . alderman and others of the common council . . . to elect, nominate and make one other or others of the assistants . . . into the place or places of him or those . . . [A] discreet man, and learned in the laws of England . . . shall be named, the recorder of the borough . . .

[The] alderman, recorder and the principal burgesses . . . [shall hold] the office of justice of the peace . . . AND FURTHER we will . . . grant to the . . . alderman and burgesses . . . two officers, who shall be . . . sergeants-at-mace . . . [who] shall . . . carry gilt or silver maces . . . [T]he alderman and principal burgesses . . . from year to year may elect . . . one coroner, and also one clerk of the market . . . [and] shall have within the borough . . . one prison or gaol, for the custody of . . . prisoners . . . [And] . . . shall have the inspection . . . of the assize of bread, wine, ale and of all kinds of victuals sold . . . within the borough . . . WHEREAS in the town of Leedes . . . there hath . . . been held and kept one market . . . on every monday [sic] in each week . . . the inhabitants . . . [have] found it better to be holden on a tuesday [sic] . . . [T]he borough of Leedes . . . shall . . . hold . . . one market in every week . . . forever on tuesday[sic] . . . AND FURTHER . . . the inhabitants of the borough . . . especially the workers and labourers . . . shall have . . . reasonable guilds . . . WITNESS ourself at Westminster, the thirteenth of July, in the second year of our reign.

The local knight, Sir John Savile of Howley Hall was appointed the first alderman and the new borough's coat-of-arms included in it the silver owls which formed part of Sir John's own shield. But his regular attendance at court meant that the duties of his office were more often than not carried out by John Harrison.

The charter itself was not universally popular. In the first place it failed to grant Leeds the right to have a Member of Parliament. In the second place, the council that it set up was not democratic. It was self-perpetuating. Its members were empowered to replace any vacancies by people of their choosing and ultimately the corporation became dominated by a Tory-Anglican oligarchy, to the anger of the Whigs and Dissenters in the town. Hundreds of townsfolk were furious that the new corporation had been established to satisfy the requirements of 'some of the ablest men in Leeds for their own ends' without gaining the consent of the majority of people. They made their objections but to no avail. The charter stood. Nor did the establishment of the trade guilds meet with approval. Many clothiers resented the fines and other penalties that could be imposed on them for failing to meet the necessary requirements. Opposition to the new guilds continued for years.

On the death of Queen Anne of Denmark in 1619 the borough reverted to the Crown. Charles I succeeded to the throne in 1625 and by 1628 he was facing increasing debts, in particular to the City of London. To alleviate the problem he granted various manors to the London Corporation including that of Leeds. It was not the first time the capital had been involved in the ownership of other estates. In 1613 during the period known as the Plantations, London had taken over responsibility in Ireland for the Ulster town of Derry and its surrounding county: hence the Irish Society changed the name to Londonderry.

Nicholas Raynton and Arnold Child, one a lawyer, the other the Master of the Haberdashers' Company, were despatched to Leeds to draw up an inventory of London's new acquisition. It describes the houses as 'verie thick and close compacted' and commented on the 'verie faire church built after a Cathedrall structure'. Economically the town had much to offer: the coal mines at Woodhouse and Knostrop were worth £100, the office of bailiff was valued at £70 and the weighing of wool and tallow produced some £30 along with entry fines of £139. It appears that the surveyors 'could learne little of the tenants' in the borough who appeared somewhat reluctant in furnishing the details required by Raynton and Child.

Now, however, a wealthy and influential group of Leeds citizens saw a golden opportunity. In 1629 they purchased the manor from London, for £2,710 8s. 10d., giving the capital a huge profit of about eighty per cent but, more important for Leeds, bringing the control of the whole manor into the hands of local people. Although Richard Sykes was identified as the sole purchaser, in fact a group, comprising William Skelton, William Marshall, Henry Watkinson, John Wade and Richard Symson, was also involved. Several of them were burgesses or assistants of the new corporation. In 1655, a more formal arrangement was established, giving the corporation itself greater control of the town.

Charles's economic problems did not disappear, but, thanks to the various strategies worked out by Ingram of Temple Newsam and other financiers, for eleven years he avoided the need to summon Parliament to ask for financial help. One of the most effective money-raising expedients he employed was that of ship money and this he turned to in 1634. Ship money was a levy at first imposed on coastal towns but the following year the king also targeted inland counties. John Hampden famously objected to the principle but failed in his attempt to stop it, and in November 1638 Leeds found itself facing the demand. It was not the first time in its history that it had been so approached. During the 1590s when the threat of Spanish invasion still hung over Elizabeth's England, Leeds, in connection with Kingston-upon-Hull, Halifax and Wakefield, was asked to provide a proportion of the expense for fitting out a ship of war to face the Spaniards. Now a new writ appeared demanding £70 from the corporation to fit out, 'one shippe of fower hundred and fiftye tunne . . . to be furnished with men, tackle, munition, victual and other necessaryes for the safeguard of the seas and defence of the realme'.

Discontent with Charles continued to grow throughout the 1630s. Taxes imposed without Parliamentary approval, arguments over the place of ritual in Church ceremonies, the abolition of episcopacy, for the Puritan element felt there was no place in the Church of England for bishops, and the king's adamant belief in the Divine Right of Kings all contributed to provoking the bloody events which followed. For years historians have disputed what the exact causes of the Civil War were, but what is not in dispute is that England was plunged into a bitter conflict between Royalists and Parliamentarians, Cavaliers and Roundheads. It was a contest in which the people of Leeds would find themselves unhappily involved as the struggle intensified.

It could not have occurred at a worse time for Leeds. Its economic fortunes were rapidly improving as trade expanded and the new corporation had been quick to encourage the town's development. For £700 it purchased the control of the markets, fairs and common oven from Sir Arthur Ingram. By 1639, it could boast of its new Moot Hall, Grammar School, Harrison's almshouses, and a workhouse opened on Lady Lane between 1636 and 1637. The following year it acquired the patronage of the new St John's Church. However, its request for the right of having its own Member of Parliament was denied. Nevertheless, Leeds was a burgeoning town with great hopes for the future. Civil war could do nothing but impede its progress and disrupt its trade.

The North generally supported the king. The exception was the Puritan clothing districts. Leeds, Bradford, Halifax and the smaller clothing towns of the West Riding raised loans for and made contributions to Lord Fairfax's Parliamentary army. But, as in any civil war, even these communities were divided. In Leeds merchants and clothiers, Anglicans and Puritans found themselves on opposing sides with the leading merchants tending to be Royalist sympathisers. But the disruption of war affected all the luckless people of the land. Sir Thomas Fairfax, a Parliamentary commander, wrote to his father on 9 January 1642/1643* describing the effects the conflict was having specifically on Leeds and Wakefield: 'All trade and provisions are stopped, so that people in these Clothing towns are not able to subsist.'

On 29 October 1642, Leeds fell to a Royalist force commanded by Sir William Savile. He then made an abortive attack on Bradford but was forced back by Sir Thomas Fairfax. After raising volunteers in

---

* In the Old Style Julian calendar it was 1642. The year began on 25 March until 1752 when the Gregorian calendar was introduced and New Year's Day became 1 January.

Halifax and Bradford, Fairfax turned his attention to Leeds. On Monday 23 January 1643 he advanced towards the town. Meanwhile Savile had organised his defences. A trench two yards wide had been dug from Harrison's church at the top of Briggate as far as the river and a six-foot high palisade erected. A second trench was dug across the tenter ground between Swinegate and the river. Two cannons had been positioned in Briggate, one strategically placed to command the bridge. The bridge at Kirkstall had also been destroyed to delay the Parliamentary army's advance. Savile's defending force was made up of 1,500 foot and 500 cavalry and dragoons.

Fairfax decided to split his command. He ordered Captain Mildmay, with about thirty musketeers and 1,000 clubmen, to move south of the river to Hunslet Moor where they could launch an attack on Leeds bridge itself. Fairfax himself, with 1,000 clubmen, 1,000 musketeers supported by six troops of horse and three companies of dragoons under the command of Sir Henry Fowles, crossed the Aire at Apperley Bridge and then moved down to Woodhouse Moor. Here the attacking force regrouped and commended 'the cause to God by prayer'.

After an attempt to persuade the Royalists to surrender, the fighting commenced at about one o'clock. With Jonathan Scholefield, the Minister of Croston Chapel, Halifax, urging the Parliamentary troops forward, the army advanced driven on by religious zeal and singing the sixty-fourth psalm: 'Let God arise and his enemies shall be scattered'. An eye-witness known as Crompton, recalled how 'bullets flew about our ears as thicke as haile'. Fairfax himself gave a graphic description in his *Journal* of how the Royalist cannoneers came under fire and his force went about their task 'furiously sword in hand'. The decisive moment came when the attackers south of the river raked the trench with a devastating fire and drove the defenders back.

Some 500 prisoners were taken but were released on swearing never to take up arms against Parliament again. It was a useful ploy that had been adopted when Chichester had been captured and seriously affected Royalist recruitment. Savile, along with Henry Robinson, the Royalist vicar, managed to ford the river to escape but about forty were killed in the engagement. The Parish Church register laconically records, 'Eleven soldiers slain, buried 24 January, ten unpaid for.'

Lord Ferdinando Fairfax, who commanded the Parliamentarian forces in Yorkshire and was Thomas's father, reported the success of the attack to Parliament. The following Monday both Houses heard his comments: 'God hath blessed my sonne and these small forces with good success against the enemy.' He reported on the 500 prisoners taken and the fact that his son had restrained the army from pillaging the town.

But the Parliamentarians did not have things all their own way. Lord Fairfax, hoping to regroup his forces at Leeds, deployed his son Thomas to undertake a distracting manoeuvre on 30 March in the Sherburn and Tadcaster area. The feint succeeded and the main body of Parliamentary troops reached Leeds safely but Thomas and his troops were caught out. Goring's Royalists swooped down on the unsuspecting Parliamentarian force at Seacroft. Casualties were heavy and some 800 of Sir Thomas's men were captured and taken to York. Fairfax himself successfully fought his way to Leeds but his force had been routed.

Meanwhile, Queen Henrietta had landed at Bridlington with arms for Charles's troops. On 3 April she wrote to her husband: 'Our army marches tomorrow to put an end to Fairfax's excellency.' At Pontefract she found her enemy had gone and thus she turned her attention to Leeds. On 9 April she was delighted to report that 'our army is gone to Leeds, and at this time are beating down the town.' It was in fact an exaggeration and by 23 April the queen revised her comments to say it had been decided to besiege the town. But the bombardment by cannon produced no effect. A council of war was held with General Goring. The queen and the newer commanders were in favour of an assault on Leeds but the counsel of the more experienced senior officers held sway and the Royalists decided to make a strategic withdrawal to Wakefield. Nevertheless, skirmishes continued in the Leeds area with three fatalities in Hunslet at Robert Williamson's house during April; nine more were killed in the district in June, twelve in July. But in June 1643, at the Battle of Adwalton Moor at Drighlington just west of Leeds, the Earl of Newcastle's Royalist army was triumphant.

The balance of power in the West Riding had radically altered and now Lord Fairfax determined to withdraw his troops quickly from Leeds to Hull before Newcastle's force could cut off his retreat. In the chaos of the withdrawal, some Royalist prisoners in the town broke free and seized the arms and ammunition there. After just over five months Leeds was a Royalist base once more. But it was not to last.

On 7 April 1644 Sir Thomas retook the town and Major-General Carter was appointed military governor. For the people of Leeds it seemed to matter little which army was in occupation. Shortages of food, the destruction of property, requisitions from the different armies garrisoned in the town and the severe dislocation of trade were the grim realities that civil war imposed on the townsfolk. Parliament was petitioned to help those whose homes had been plundered or had property destroyed. But such difficulties were nothing compared to when Nature itself took a hand in the town's fortunes. Once more it was to prove to be a far more devastating force than any rampaging army.

The inhabitants of Leeds and its out-townships were no strangers to bubonic plague. Century after century it had taken its toll on the inhabitants of the district. As recently as 1631 it had struck again in the West Riding, this time in Beeston and Holbeck. Rumours circulated that it had surfaced again in Leeds in August 1644, and on 11 March 1645 Alice Musgrave was buried. There was no doubt on this occasion about the cause of death. It was bubonic plague. The day after she was interred Major-General Carter received news of further deaths. The infection spread rapidly. Marsh Lane, the Calls, Lower Briggate and Mill Hill were all affected but the area to be worst devastated was Vicar Lane, the street where Alice had lived and died.

Eventually action was taken although the nineteenth-century Leeds historian, Edward Parsons, claims that according to the parish register 131 died 'before the plague was recognised'; in his view, 'a reckless and scandalous neglect of the necessities and wretchedness of the poor'. In fact some charitable help was forthcoming to the poor amounting to £339 18s. 9½d. Other steps taken included transferring the market to the more open area of Woodhouse Moor. Searchers were appointed to identify potential sufferers and those suspected of contracting the disease were moved to special cabins erected on Quarry Hill and their homes then sealed. The infection was most virulent in the overcrowded, squalid, insanitary areas of the poor but it was not solely confined to these, and it soon spread to the more open districts and the surrounding out-townships.

Over 300 died in July alone. Those who could fled. Grass, it is said, grew in the silent streets; cats, dogs, even rats and mice died and birds fell dead from the skies. With the Royalist vicar still absent from the town, the Parish Church was locked. But the Puritan curate at St John's, Robert Todd, remained at his post attempting to bring some succour to the suffering population by regularly preaching on 'Hezekiah's boil'.

The epidemic raged on through the long hot summer but as winter approached it finally abated. Between Alice's death in March and Christmas Day that year, 1,325 people in the town had perished, about one-fifth of the local population. Throughout 1646 the survivors set to reviving the town's fortunes. Houses had to be fumigated, things of value washed and aired, less valuable property had to be burnt. Life was beginning to return to some degree of normality, for the defeat of King Charles at Naseby in 1645 had signalled the beginning of the end to the Civil War.

In May 1646 Charles eluded the Parliamentary army surrounding his capital at Oxford and fled north. He rode to the Scottish army at Newark and surrendered. Parliament furiously demanded that he be handed over. The Scots refused and moved their army northwards. But the king's negotiations with his captors were fruitless. At Newcastle he was handed back to the English and the Parliamentary Commissioners escorted him south.

In February 1647 they arrived in Leeds and immediately rode to the Headrow and commandeered Thomas Metcalfe's new house, Red Hall, which had recently been built there. They felt it a suitable lodging for their royal prisoner. To their utter fury, however, many of the local public still held onto the old superstition that a touch of the king's person could cure scrofula, or the 'king's evil', a swelling of the tubercular glands. It was a belief that could be traced back to Edward the Confessor, and Charles, with his sincere belief in the divine attributes of monarchs, was happy to concur with the idea. On 9 February the infuriated commissioners, anxious to play down the king's 'divine powers', issued a declaration to the effect that, 'all persons whatsoever, which are diseased, not to presume hereafter to repair unto the court . . . upon pain of being punished severely for their intrusion – Dated at Leeds 9 February'.

They were also instructed to identify anyone who spoke to the king. According to legend, John Harrison ignored the warning and presented Charles with a tankard filled with gold coins. Another legend tells how a maidservant in the house offered her clothes that the king might escape disguised as a woman and hide in her friend's house down Land's Lane. From here, she suggested, he could make for the safety of France. Charles was grateful but refused.

Parliament now imposed its will on the nation. Royalist sympathisers were sought out and heavily fined. Leeds Royalists were removed from the corporation and, contrary to the stipulations of the charter, newcomers were admitted. John Harrison was accused of being a supporter of the king. It was claimed he had fled Leeds when Fairfax captured it but returned when the Royalists retook the town.

He was committed for trial at York in 1649 and had his appeal heard in London in 1651. The accusation was that he had supplied the king's troops with a couple of horses and of being 'an obstructor of the common good at Leedes . . . an enemy to godly ministers'. He argued that he had acted under duress and added that he had equally supplied the Parliamentary army with a horse, arms and money. He was condemned as a 'merit-monger', and found guilty. There was no prison sentence as he was considered too ill and too old to serve one but he was fined a hefty

£464 18s. Contrary to popular belief he did not die in poverty. When he died in 1656 aged seventy-seven, he left endowments for his family and friends. It was typical of the man who had been such a great benefactor of Leeds that he also made provision 'for the relief of such who as by the frowns of the world should unhappily be reduced to poverty'.

In 1653, Cromwell dissolved Parliament and on 1 June 1654, writs were issued for a new election. The forthcoming Parliament would be different from previous ones. Rotten and pocket boroughs were abolished and their seats redistributed. For the first time Irish and Scottish members were elected to Westminster. Adam Baynes of Knostrop, a captain in General Lambert's Parliamentary army, lobbied for Leeds to be granted one of the redistributed seats. The general feeling in the town, which supported Baynes as its candidate, was summed up by one John Walker writing to Alderman John Thwaites. Baynes, he declared, 'is in a present capacity to doe us good'. Baynes was duly elected and Leeds could proudly boast its first MP. However, his opportunity to fulfil Walker's hope to 'doe us good' never really materialised, although he did pay some attention to the needs of the cloth industry. The first Parliament of the Protectorate proved itself to be both stubborn and argumentative. When it refused to co-operate with Cromwell, the Lord Protector dissolved it on the earliest date the law permitted, 22 January 1655. It had failed to pass a single act.

On 10 July 1656 a second election was announced. Once again Baynes was returned as the member for Leeds but only after defeating Francis Allanson for the seat. However, when Richard Cromwell succeeded his father in 1658, the town lost its member and remained unrepresented until the Reform Bill of 1832.

The years of Cromwell's Protectorate saw severe restrictions imposed upon the people of England. Adultery was punishable by death; drunkenness, swearing and gambling became illegal; Christmas celebrations were condemned and 25 December became a fast day. Easter, Whitsuntide and other festivals were outlawed. Strict observance of the Sabbath was essential and work of any kind was prohibited on that day, as was travelling, unless it was to church. Even dancing around a maypole was frowned upon.

Captain John Pickering of Woodkirk was a local justice who held quarter sessions at Pontefract, Wakefield and Leeds. In 1657 he was in Moot Hall, Briggate and the cases he jotted down in his notebook clearly show that the severe restrictions imposed upon the rest of the people of England equally applied to Leeds and the West Riding:

> Thomas Wilcocke of Chidswell . . . one pphane curse in a feilde att

Rothwell . . . Christopher Smith . . . being drunke at Alverthorpe . . . John Batty, Milner of Alverthorpe . . . Grinding Corne . . . upon 16th instant being Lord's Day and also doing worldly labour . . . Fornication . . . Ann Dobson of Olton . . . sent by me to the house of Correction . . . Henery Cockill of Woodlsworth, husbandman . . . travelling from Woodlsworth to Hunslet upon . . . Lds day.

Not surprisingly when Charles II landed at Dover on 25 May 1660 there were many in the nation who rejoiced that the austere days of Puritan domination were over. Maypoles once again appeared and celebrations were held across the country. Steps were taken to restore the displaced Royalists to their positions on the Corporation in Leeds and the wealthier merchants now petitioned the king to hold an enquiry into the present system of government in the town. They urged that a new charter should be granted.

On 2 November 1661 King Charles conceded their wish and a new charter was implemented. The principal townsman was now to be entitled 'mayor' and elected annually. The twelve aldermen and twenty-four assistants who made up the council were appointed for life, unless they were 'removed from their offices . . . for their evil behaviour or evil carriage'. In addition a recorder and town clerk were also appointed for life. Again the council was empowered to regulate trade in the town and to hold quarter sessions. These were now to be conducted principally by the Leeds aldermen acting as magistrates rather than justices from outside the borough.

The first mayor was Thomas Danby. His coat-of-arms included three silver mullets and these star-shaped objects were then incorporated into the Leeds arms. Now a new generation of influential Leeds families came to the fore and sat on the council: the Wades, Hickes, Busfeilds, Killingbeckes, Ivesons and Fentons.

The borough was to be divided into six wards with individuals specifically appointed to take care of the poor. On 26 March 1662 the first bye-law was passed by the new council. It strictly forbade anyone to interrupt another member who was already speaking on pain of a fine. In November the council identified the trades that had to form guilds in the town, among them clothworkers, mercers, grocers, drapers, carpenters, bricklayers and tailors.

But if most Leeds people relished the greater freedoms now enjoyed in the new reign, there existed in the town and its out-townships, as in the rest of the country, those who still harboured republican sympathies and hankered after the devout days of Puritan supremacy. Each month it seemed new conspiracies to overthrow Charles surfaced in one place or another. But the authorities in Yorkshire grew particularly concerned about various reports surfacing that suggested a planned rising in the county, scheduled for October 1663.

They knew that republican supporters had been forced to abort an attempt in August and now proposed to mount a new protest in the autumn. The conspiracy originated in Harrogate and Knaresborough but soon spread across the North. Its object was, 'to re-establish a gospel ministry and magistracy; to restore the Long Parliament; to relieve themselves from the excise of all subsidies; to reform all orders of and degrees of men, especially lawyers and clergy'. On the night of 12 October insurgents gathered in Westmorland but the rising there proved to be ineffectual. A larger contingent from the West Riding gathered in Farnley Wood near Leeds. Allegations were later made that the real men who hatched the plot were Sir John Armitage of Kirklees and John Peoples of Dewsbury, but it was left to Captain Thomas Oates, an old republican officer and now a Morley schoolteacher, to accept the role of the ringleader. In an act of dramatic defiance he drew his sword and flung away his scabbard. But acts of bravado are no substitute for effective and discreet planning. In fact the authorities were well aware of what was afoot and the militia was ready to move in. Edward Parsons, the Leeds historian, suggests that the plot was the work of *agents provocateurs*. Whoever was behind it, within forty-five minutes the farce was over.

In all, forty-four were arrested in the North and a special winter assize was established in York. Many of the accused viewed the proceedings with a disdain that bordered on insolence. Peregrine Corney went so far as to tell the judge that in such a cause he valued his life no more than his pocket handkerchief. Oates and twenty of his supporters were found guilty. On 19 January 1664 three of them, Robert Atkins, John Errington and Henry Watson, were taken to Chapeltown Moor to be executed. A Tuesday was deliberately chosen, for being market day it ensured a large crowd would gather to witness the event.

Having committed treason they were hanged, drawn and quartered. Their decapitated heads were then taken to Briggate and skewered on the spikes of Moot Hall, a gruesome warning to any future revolutionaries of the price they would pay for insurrection.

There were other macabre events in the years that followed which attracted equally large crowds. Some 30,000 gathered on Holbeck Moor to see the execution of Holroyd, a brutal local killer, in 1682. No doubt it was a more frivolous crowd which assembled at Quarry Hill's ducking stool in 1694 to witness the ducking of Anne Saule, a woman of 'lewd behaviour'. But whereas these, like other public punishments, had only local implications, the execution of the Farnley plotters gave the king an opportunity he welcomed. He used the episode as an excuse to introduce the Conventicle Act which punished any non-Anglican worshippers.

Charles also introduced the Hearth Tax, sometimes called the Chimney Tax. The parish constable was instructed to compile a list of house-holders and the number of hearths they had in their homes. The lists were then given to the local justices and twice a year, at Michaelmas and on Lady Day, townsfolk had to pay two shillings per hearth unless they were exempted because of poverty. The returns are an invaluable source to Leeds historians, helping them piece together a picture of what the town was like at the time.

It appears that in the latter years of the seventeenth century the pop-ulation of Leeds was approximately between 6,000 and 7,000 with another 3,000 making up the out-townships. The largest villages, Hunslet and Holbeck, had only some 100 to 150 dwellings in each. In Leeds itself about two-fifths of the population lived in houses with only one hearth. These were the homes of servants, labourers and the like. Craftsmen, shopkeepers and others of a similar ilk could boast homes with two or three hearths and these again accounted for two-fifths of the town. A further one-fifth, the wealthier merchants, clothiers, pro-fessionals and gentry, lived in houses of considerable size. Haddon's house in Briggate had eleven hearths, Simpson's house on the Headrow, ten. Many of these better homes were sited in these two thoroughfares but as the century progressed wealthier Leeds folk purchased properties in fashionable Boar Lane or in the open country near St John's Church. Few, however, could equal the home of Robert Kitchingman, a Leeds merchant, whose mansion at Chapeltown consisted of sixty rooms along with gardens and pleasure grounds.

One of the best sources for understanding what life was like in sev-enteenth-century Leeds during the reigns of Charles II, James II, and William and Mary is undoubtedly the writings of Ralph Thoresby. He was born and lived in Kirkgate in a large timber-built house that boasted five hearths, according to the Hearth Tax list of 1672. As a businessman he was not a success but as a historian and antiquarian he can rightly be called the 'Father of Leeds History'.* In 1693 he compiled the West Riding section of Camden's *Britannia* and four years later was made a Fellow of the Royal Society. He also created a museum of coins, medals,

---

* Appropriately enough, the principal historical society in Leeds, founded in 1889 and devoted to the history of the city, is known as the Thoresby Society.

geological specimens, books, manuscripts and historical curiosities like the abbot of Kirkstall's stirrup. Over the years scores of people came to his home to view his collection.

However, his real contribution to Leeds history is his various publications. In 1715 he published *Ducatus Leodiensis*, the first history of Leeds, and the result of years of research. In 1724 he produced his *Vicaria Leodiensis*, a history of the Vicars of Leeds. Equally valuable to Leeds historians is Thoresby's diary which he kept for most of his life. Although much of it appears rather dull, simply recording the themes of numerous sermons he heard, it does at times give an insight into life in Leeds in those years.

He mentions the horse-racing held on Chapeltown Moor and a Chapel Allerton butcher, Edward 'Harefoot' Preston, a noted 'footman' whose races attracted a considerable number of large bets. Hunting was also a popular pastime with the gentry. Thoresby tried it for the first time in January 1681 and then observed 'Next to hawking I like hunting worst.' He appeared to find a fascination with the unusual and bizarre:

> June 1683 – Went to see a most wonderful woman, but about two feet long . . . is said to have no bone in her, though I suppose a mistake.

> November 1683 – Abroad at Alderman Sykes's; went to see a man (one Sam Fry of Dorsetshire) eat brimstone, lead, bees-wax, sealing wax, pitch, rosin, blazing hot . . . he walked on a red hot bar of iron.

Thoresby also recalls the extremely severe winter of 1684 which gripped the greater part of Europe for months. The sea froze and the bitter weather took a heavy toll of fish, birds and deer. In London the Thames froze and carts and coaches drove across the frozen river. In Leeds tents and booths were erected on the frozen Aire, ox-roasting and sports were held on it and in January Thoresby walked, 'from the Mills below the Old Church, all up the main river, under the bridge to about the upper dam, the like continued frost having not been known, or scarce heard of in these parts'.

But the Leeds Thoresby knew was a growing town with improving facilities. In 1677 a new grammar school had opened for the children of Wortley and in 1692 a library had been added to Leeds Grammar School by Geoffrey Lawson for the use of adults. Already in 1655 a new prison had been built in Kirkgate opposite the common oven. By all accounts it was a forbidding place of five or six rooms with unglazed windows and no sewer.

There were numerous medicinal spas in Leeds and the surrounding districts including those at Quarry Hill, Gipton, Woodhouse Carr, Camp Road, Burley Road, Meanwood, and several in Holbeck. But

6. Ralph Thoresby
Ralph Thoresby (1658-1725); the Father of Leeds History. A great antiquarian after whom the Leeds premier local-history society is named. His diary gives a fascinating insight into life in the town at the end of the seventeenth and beginning of the eighteenth centuries.

Leeds itself had no adequate water supply. In 1694 the engineer George Sorocold of Derby was employed to establish one. Water was pumped from the River Aire to a small reservoir near St John's Church and then fed through lead pipes to various houses in the town.

The greatest steps forward, however, were in transport. If Leeds was to prosper an improved transport system was essential. Strings of pack-horses and lumbering wagons carried raw materials to Leeds and fin-ished cloth out of the town. Already Leeds was fifth in providing sta-bling accommodation in Yorkshire. For the export markets cloth was carried to York, Selby, Tadcaster and Knottingley and then in sloops and keels to Hull. Considerable sums were spent on repairing the existing roads but it was not until the next century that new roads began to radiate from the town. The cloth market was held on Leeds Bridge itself with the dyed or mixed cloths being displayed on the parapets, but the increased volume of traffic forced the Corporation to move it from the bridge to Briggate itself in 1684.

The major advance in transport, however, was the resurrection of an idea that had been considered in 1621 and 1625. In 1679, William Pickering, a cloth merchant and mayor, attempted to revive a scheme to make the Aire and Calder rivers navigable and overcome the handicap of the vagaries of varying water levels. His hope was that cloth could then be transported regularly and directly from Leeds to Hull and thence to London, or the markets of Europe. He received little support and it was not until the mid-1690s that the scheme once more attracted attention.

The matter was raised in Parliament but opposition came from the coal interests of Newcastle and Sunderland as well as the ports of York, Selby and Tadcaster. The bill was counted out. The following year, 1699, an agreement was reached with a Pontefract MP to allow him to carry his coal on the waterway free if the act were passed. He successfully piloted it through the Commons and in November 1700 the waterway from the West Riding to the east coast, the Aire and Calder Navigation, was finally opened. Economically, Leeds was growing and well might Celia Fiennes write after her visit to the town that it was 'esteemed the wealthyest town of its bigness in the Country'.

It achieved its success despite the undercurrent of political intrigues and religious bigotry which divided the country. Charles grew more and more dissatisfied with the independence that many of the country's boroughs now embraced. He embarked upon a strategy to rescind the existing charters held by certain towns and replace them with charters giving him greater control.

Leeds received the Privy Council's instruction in May 1680. The Corporation had to guarantee that its members conformed to the Corporation Act and consequently had taken the oath of allegiance and received the sacraments of the Church of England. The Mayor sent his assurance that all was well but on 17 October 1684 a royal writ, known as Quo Warranto, was issued against the Corporation of Leeds. Mayor Ibbetson was instructed to surrender the Charter of the Borough to the king. On 24 December 1684 Leeds received its third charter and, as expected, this gave greater power to the Crown. The new mayor was Gervase Neville, a Holbeck man whose father had been a Royalist quartermaster-general during the Civil War.

Underlying the political machinations of the reign, the sore of religious bigotry continued to fester. Then in March 1672, Charles announced his Declaration of Indulgence. From now on Nonconformists were allowed to build themselves places of worship, imprisoned Quakers were to be freed and Roman Catholics entitled to worship in their own homes. In Leeds the first Dissenting meeting-house in the North was built at Mill Hill by the Presbyterians but the freedom was not to last. Protestant Nonconformist ministers were grudging in their gratitude fearing it was simply a ploy to reinstate Popery. Parliament declared the indulgence illegal and forced the king to withdraw it.

7. Mill Hill Chapel
Mill Hill Presbyterian Chapel; the first Nonconformist meeting house in Leeds was built in what is now City Square between 1672 and 1674. Here it is seen after major refurbishment in the eighteenth century. The present chapel replaced this one in 1848.

After the Restoration persecution of the Quakers or the Friends of the Truth had continued in Leeds, as elsewhere. Meetings were broken up and the participants arrested. Daniel Thackery of Holbeck was sent to Wakefield's House of Correction 'for witnessing the Kingdom of God within'. On 18 November 1683 William Rooke, the mayor, committed fifty-two Quaker men and women to be confined in Moot Hall. For four days they languished in one single unheated room, suffering from the severe weather before being marshalled off to York Castle.

Thoresby sympathised with their plight. On seeing a group of them being hurried down the street *en route* for York, he could not help remarking on the predicament of these 'poor deluded Quakers'. Even

Thoresby himself was not above suspicion being as he was a prominent member of the Mill Hill congregation. That same year he, too, was accused of attending a 'factious and seditious conventicle' or prayer meeting in Hunslet. At the Quarter Sessions he was supported by two lawyers and his defence was sufficient to see the prosecution's case dropped; he considered that the magistrates had treated him 'civilly'.

If religion was a dominant force in life in Leeds it was equally so for the rest of the country. Fear and bigotry against anyone not of the Anglican faith continued. On his deathbed Charles II was received into the arms of the Catholic Church. His brother who succeeded him had been a Roman Catholic since the 1660s. Ignoring the bitter resentment and fears of many of his subjects that he would engineer the nation into becoming Roman Catholic again, James II's actions proceeded to fuel the fires of opposition. When James's wife produced a male heir in 1688 and a Catholic succession appeared inevitable, the Protestants William and Mary were invited to take over the throne.

William invaded in November that year but in December rumours ran rife that a Catholic Irish army was ravaging the country. In Leeds on Monday 17 December 7,000 troops gathered to defend the town. Thoresby, an eye-witness, related the events which then unfolded:

> Beeston is actually burnt, and only some escaped to bring the doleful tidings! The drums beat, the bells rang backward, the women shrieked, and some doleful consternation seized upon all persons . . . [B]lessed be God! The terror disappeared, it being a false alarm, taken from some drunken people.

On 13 February 1689 William and Mary were proclaimed king and queen in the Banqueting House in Whitehall. The next day the proclamation was made in Leeds and was followed by a general celebration. That same year the old charter of 1661 was reinstated and the Toleration Act was modified although it did not abolish the laws against Dissenters. It was particularly welcome in Leeds as between a third and a quarter of all worshippers were Nonconformists. Now they could set about building themselves places of worship. That same year the Quakers rented a house in Boar Lane and ten years later opened their purpose-built meeting-house on Water Lane. The Independents opened their chapel in Call Lane in 1691 but the Roman Catholics had to wait almost to the end of the next century before they felt able to open their place of worship.

However, the new joint reign was not destined to last long. Queen Mary died in 1694, struck down by smallpox, a disease which was an all too common occurrence in England. It carried off a thirteenth of each generation until the end of the next century. In 1700 the Thoresby household also felt its full impact when two of Ralph's daughters, Elizabeth and Ruth, caught the pernicious infection and died. A new century dawned but it had hardly begun when Thoresby and the rest of the nation found themselves facing a major political crisis.

CHAPTER FIVE

A LARGE, WEALTHY AND POPULOUS TOWN

Through the opening years of the eighteenth century people faced the spectre of a Stuart king returning to rule Britain and bringing with him the threat of Catholicism. In February 1702, the Jacobites, supporters of the exiled James Edward Stuart, the 'Old Pretender' and son of the late James II, received encouragement. William III went riding in Richmond Park. His horse stumbled on a molehill, threw him to the ground and broke his collarbone. Already weak and in poor health, the king developed a fever and on 8 March he died. Jacobites celebrated the death of the Protestant monarch and toasted 'the little man in the velvet coat'.

The news of the king's death reached Leeds on 10 March. 'What shall we now do that so great a judgement has befallen us?' Ralph Thoresby bemoaned and fervently prayed that God would prevent a 'Popish successor' coming to the English throne. He need not have worried. The 1701 Act of Settlement had ensured that only a Protestant could succeed. Three days later the council in Leeds met and resolved to proclaim Anne, the Protestant daughter of James II, as queen on the very next market day.

Ten years later Thoresby was in London with a delegation from Leeds. On 2 July 1712 the delegates were taken to Kensington and there the mayor, John Atkinson, presented a loyal address to the queen herself. Thoresby and the others had been introduced by a fellow Yorkshireman, Thomas Osborne, the Duke of Leeds. He was a shrewd politician of long standing and one of the seven men who had invited William and Mary to claim the throne of England. He assured Thoresby that he had deliberately taken the title, Duke of Leeds, because 'he was dignified with that title, it being a most considerable place for trade.' Though he may well have been using a politician's flattery, there was much truth in his observations. Leeds was indeed a 'place of considerable trade'.

Historians are fortunate in that, from the beginning of the eighteenth century, writers, artists, cartographers and poets have left behind their observations of the town. The most famous of these visitors was undoubtedly Daniel Defoe, who visited Leeds some time around 1720 and wrote:

> Leeds is a large, wealthy and populous Town, its stands on the North
> Bank of the River Aire, or rather on both sides the river, for there is a
> large suburb on the South Side of the River, and the whole is joined by
> a stately and prodigiously strong Stone Bridge . . . [T]he High-Street,
> beginning from the Bridge and running up North . . . is a large, broad,
> fair and well-built Street . . . The town of Leeds is very large, and . . .
> there are abundance of wealthy merchants in it.

The impressive houses of some of those wealthy merchants were illustrated
by John Cossins in 1726 when he compiled his *New and Exact Plan of
the Town of Leedes*. Some merchants, such as Thomas Dennison, had
built their homes on the periphery of the town, whilst others erected
theirs in the more built-up areas. Alderman William Cookson's house,
for example, stood just south of Kirkgate but its extensive gardens swept
down as far as the river. For, although buildings were concentrated
around Briggate, Boar Lane and Kirkgate, there were still numerous
open places within these areas supporting tenter frames or standing as
gardens, orchards or crofts. A bowling green was sited by what is today
Lands Lane and from there, stretching westward, only the occasional
building could be seen in what was generally a rustic landscape.
Industry was concentrated along Swinegate, the Calls, Marsh Lane and
Mabgate, whilst the banks of the River Aire had become lined with
numerous warehouses and water-powered mills.

Francis Place's engraving, *The Prospect of Leeds from the Knostrop
Road*, and used by Thoresby to illustrate his *Ducatus*, was drawn from
a position east of Leeds overlooking the river. It emphasised just how
much the town, with its population of some 6,000, was concentrated
into a relatively small area. The limits of the town proper were marked
by bar stones. North Bar stood on Vicar Lane near Lady Lane; Burley
Bar was at what is now the junction of the Headrow and Albion Street;
East Bar, sometimes known as York Bar, was by the Parish Church
boundary wall; Beeston Bar was south of the river and West Bar stood
where Boar Lane meets present-day City Square. People living within
the confines of the bars enjoyed certain privileges such as paying a tithe
of only 2d. whereas those living beyond paid 3d.

Also noticeable on Place's panorama is just how extensive the parish
of Leeds was, with rolling hills, fields and woodland stretching off to the
distant townships and hamlets where a further 5,000 people lived and
worked. At this time the population of Leeds and its surrounding districts was made up of merchants, retailers, craftsmen, gentlemen, attorneys,
doctors, apothecaries, schoolmasters, clergy, farmers and labourers,
though in those early years of the century some four-fifths of the towns-

folk were engaged in the textile trade. The parish itself covered an enormous 21,000 acres and in comparison with many English parishes was immense.

John Dyer, cleric, artist and poet, captured the bustle of mid-eighteenth-century Leeds in his poem 'The Fleece'. He remarks on the red roofs of the houses, the barges sailing up and down the Aire, trains of pack-horses picking their way through the crowded thoroughfares, lumbering waggons bringing corn into the town, soaring scaffolding round new buildings which were being erected and the constant sound of builders' hammers and axes echoing through the streets.

No place was busier than Briggate with its Tuesday and Saturday markets. Crowds milled around the street buying goods, jostling with

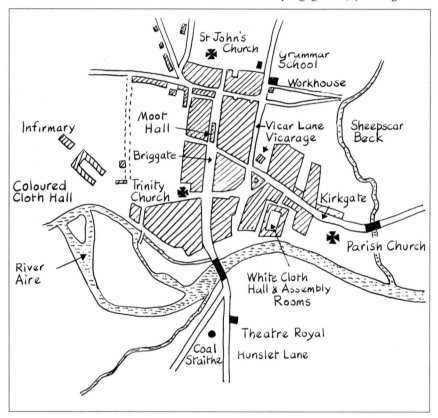

8. Leeds 1770
Note the buildings concentrated on Briggate and Kirkgate and the close proximity of the rural landscape. The Coloured Cloth Hall stands approximately where today City Square is found. Infirmary Street is now where the Infirmary was.

cattle, sheep and pigs, or listening to auctioneer Thomas Stooks plying his trade outside the King's Arms. By contrast, early on a market-day morning, trestle tables were erected in Lower Briggate where the twice-weekly cloth market was held. According to Defoe, it was 'not to be equalled in the world'. It was possible, he claimed, to see £10,000 to £20,000 of business done each morning and, ''tis all managed with the most profound silence'.

Further up Briggate were stalls where shoes, wicker baskets, wooden vessels, wanded-chairs and fruit and vegetables could be bought. Here was found the fish market and on the east side of Moot Hall the butchers' shambles. Higher up the street at the market cross poultry was for sale and beyond that was the corn market. However, for the general public, according to Thoresby, one of the most popular purchases in Briggate, and unique to Leeds, was the Brig End Shot. He explained that 'the clothier may, together with his Pot of Ale, have a Noggin O'Porage, and a Trencher of either Boil'd or Roast-Meat for Two-pence.'

Besides such observers, the Leeds historian is fortunate that two newspapers were established in the town. In 1718 John Hirst issued the weekly *Leeds Mercury*. It was known as a 'scissors and paste' newspaper because it relied heavily upon the reports contained in the London papers for its content. Its local reports initially were of little interest. In January 1723, it reported, 'From Tong, in Christmas last, Eggs were taken out of the Magpy Nest'! But gradually local news did begin to appear in greater detail. Hirst died in 1732 and James Lister took over the paper. In 1754, an active young printer, Griffith Wright, launched a competitor. Initially the *Leeds Intelligencer* proved more successful and in June 1755 was gleefully able to claim that the *Mercury* 'had died after a tedious illness'.* However, in 1765, James Bowling resurrected the paper and for the next 150 years a bitter rivalry developed between these two Leeds newspapers. The history of Leeds is graphically told in their columns: not simply in the reports they carried but in the letters readers wrote, the advertisements they displayed, and the notices they presented regarding public meetings to be called for the improvement of the town.

Many of the local inns such as the King's Arms in Briggate, the Talbot which stood on what is now Thornton's Arcade, and the White Swan in Kirkgate were used for conducting such public meetings. In

---

* In 1866 the *Leeds Intelligencer* was acquired by the Yorkshire Conservative Newspaper Company and became a daily published as the *Yorkshire Post and Leeds Intelligencer.* The *Yorkshire Post* is still being published.

THE
LEEDES INTELLIGENCER.

Printed by GRIFFITH WRIGHT, in the LOWER-HEAD-ROW

Nº I   TUESDAY, *July* 2, 1754.

The PUBLISHER's PREFACE.

WHO' from the Abundance of Materials in the public Prints, a Weekly Collection of News may be made that will answer the Printer's Intention; yet it cannot be doubted, that an Undertaking of this Kind wou'd be much more *Useful* and *Entertaining*, if it was made a Means of establishing a *public* and *friendly* Correspondence, amongst Gentlemen and Others, who have apply'd themselves with some Degree of Attention to any Branch of Science or Business in the Neighbourhood.

It is surprising to observe, and yet every thinking Man has in many Instances observ'd, from what *sinister Hints* have been produc'd the most *useful Improvements* in the several Trades and Occupations, which are the Support and Ornament of human Society. And there are perhaps but few Men of good natural Parts and Understanding, who have not form'd in their own Minds, some imperfect Schemes for the Improve-

Appearance, yet an uniform Course of Uprightness and Fidelity, of Generosity and Benevolence, which render a Tradesman a Blessing to his Country, can only be expected to be maintain'd on its true Foundation of *Conscience* and *Religion*.

The Interests of *Virtue* and *Religion* might likewise this Way be serv'd in various other Instances which are probably thought not of Importance enough, or which upon some Account or other, it seems, are thought not proper to be taken notice of from the Pulpit.

By *this public Correspondence*, some Discovery perhaps might be made of the *real Views* and *Designs* of a Body of Men lately settl'd amongst us, who are united amongst themselves, and secluded as much as may be from the rest of the World, no less by the Ties of Commerce, than by the peculiar Tenets of Religion they maintain; whether their Trade be intended for the Support and Encouragement of their religious Peculiarities ; or their Professions of Religion are made for a *cover* and *disguise* to some *artful* and *fraudulent* Designs in Trade ; in short, whether they are to be look'd upon with a jealous and watchful Eye, or deserve to be countenanc'd and encourag'd

Berlin, [Capital of Prussia] June 11. They write from Ziethen, that on the 5th Inst. about nine in the Evening, there was seen there a fiery Meteor in the Shape of a Musket, which proceeded from the Planet Venus, and ran in a direct Line towards the Earth. Several loud Claps, like the Noise of a Cannon, were heard at the same Time, which made the People apprehensive of a Storm. This Flame was succeeded by a clear white Ray, in a straight Line, and of a considerable Length, which following the Flame, and being directly under Venus as far as could be perceived, entered into that Planet, and occasioned a Smoke like that of a Chimney. The Smoke, which came away in a serpentine Form, continued visible near a Quarter of an Hour. This Meteor was also seen in this City, but we did not hear the Claps.

Hanover, [a City of Germany] June 7. Lord Berkeley and his Lady who arrived here last Monday, as also the Duke of Richmond and his Brother Lord George Lenox, are treated with particular Marks of Distinction. Yesterday these illustrious Foreigners were carried to Herrenhausen in a Phaeton belonging to the Court, drawn by six Horses ; and the Grand Jet d'Eau played for their Entertainment, for the first

9. *Leeds Intelligencer*

The first edition of the *Leeds Intelligencer* established in July 1754 by Griffith Wright. The weekly *Leeds Intelligencer* became a daily paper in 1866 and changed its title to the *Yorkshire Post* and *Leeds Intelligencer*. Today the *Yorkshire Post* is one of the most respected provincial dailies in the country.

May 1741 the mayor, recorder and aldermen of Leeds corporation called for a meeting to be held at the King's Arms in June in order to raise capital for repairing roads. Theoretically, any male in Leeds could become a member of that corporation but in reality the council was a strictly limited body. Some sixty-three per cent of it was made up of wool merchants. Twelve of the leading families between 1700 and 1780 – the Atkinsons, Blayds, Cooksons, Dennisons, Halls, Ibbetsons, Kitchingmans, Lodges, Milners, Prestons, Rookes and Wilsons – provided thirty of the seventy-three alderman appointed during those years.

The charter required twenty-four common councilmen, twelve aldermen and a mayor to make up the corporation. To replace any vacancies that occurred, the leading families on the council co-opted members. They were careful to select only those with whom they had been associated through business, and who held similar views to their own and met the criteria they considered essential to be seen as respectable townsmen. Various tactics were employed. Thoresby records how, in April 1702, Alderman Dixon and Mr Barker, 'under colour of business', asked to meet him. Thoresby saw through their devious scheme. It was 'to engage my vote for the next election of an alderman'.

The main reason for establishing the council had been to exercise control over the local woollen industry. However, as more and more cloth arriving in the town either for finishing or for sale came from the West Riding, in 1725 the county magistrates took over that responsibility. The corporation's main function became the supervision of much of the administration of the town. Its aldermen, acting as magistrates, sat in Moot Hall on a rotation basis and supervised the daily petty sessions whilst every three months they sat with the mayor and recorder at the quarter sessions.* The corporation's power was strictly limited.One of its main sources of income came from fines that were imposed when someone resigned from office. When one member, a Mr Pawson, wished to resign in July 1711, 'indecent brawlings' took place between those who wished to fine him and those who did not. Thoresby was delighted to record that in the end those wishing to impose a fine were defeated.

Although financially restricted, the corporation did undertake some improvements to the town. They were eager supporters in establishing the Aire-Calder navigation and undertook a project in 1710 'to repair and alter the Moot Hall for the conveniency of the reception of the West Riding Justices who have agreed to keep the General Quarter Sessions for the West Riding here'. Whilst the old hall was being rebuilt and enlarged the council met in Harrison's Grammar School. The new Moot Hall had butchers' shops on the ground floor and the courtroom above. In front of the building stood the stocks and pillory.

The year 1710, however, also saw Leeds cloth merchants wrong-footed by those of Wakefield who opened a covered cloth hall in their town. The attraction of being able to trade whilst being sheltered from the vagaries of the weather was obvious. The mayor of Leeds and others discussed the matter with Lord Irwin and determined to build their own covered cloth hall in Kirkgate on the site of the old hospital. Thus 1711 saw two major buildings open for business in the town: the new Moot Hall in January and the White Cloth Hall in April. Another important civic undertaking took place in 1738 with the reopening of the work-house which had closed in 1729, deeply in debt.

The general public may well have appreciated such initiatives but many had misgivings about the ruling council. Celebrations by the cor-poration members were frequently held at public expense. In July 1704, during the War of the Spanish Succession, the Duke of Marlborough defeated the combined French and Bavarian forces at the Schellenburg, a high domed hill overlooking the town of Donauwörth. In Leeds the

---

* More serious crimes were tried in York.

10. Moot Hall
Built between 1710-11, Moot Hall in Briggate was the meeting place for the corporation.
There were butchers' shops on the ground floor and a courtroom above. After years of
prevarication it was finally demolished in 1825. The statue of Queen Anne in the niche on
the front is now in Leeds City Art Gallery.

council members celebrated the victory. On such occasions the populace
would light bonfires, drink casks of ale and the town would be illuminated by thousands of candles set up in windows. Thoresby was horrified that the triumph in Bavaria had not been done 'in a more spiritual
manner' and lamented the 'misspence of both time and money'.

Not surprisingly, some viewed the council with cynicism. In April
1709, however, Thoresby was quick to point out that the entertainment
provided for the judge, Baron Price, was 'at the expense of the
Corporation, not the town, as some unworthy surmise'. But suspicion
still lingered. On 29 March 1720, John Hirst of the *Leeds Mercury* published a satirical piece in which he claimed he had appointed a journalist,
Clement Pacolet from the 'Region of the Moon', with instructions
'Never to reflect on this Corporation of Leeds, or to tell any tales of the
Aldermen thereof'. On 7 May that year the council decreed that no
more public money should be used for such celebrations 'until the
Corporac'on is out of Debt'.

But the council in the early years of the century found itself dealing with far more than local squabbles over finance as it became embroiled in the politics of the time. During Anne's reign the bitter divisions between the Whig and Tory parties dominated the scene. The Whigs were devoted to the Glorious Revolution of 1688, stood firmly behind the power of Parliament and defended civil and political liberty. The Torys' attachment was to the Crown and the Church of England and they viewed Dissenters with great suspicion.

In 1710 Godolphin's Whig Ministry was dismissed by the queen. On 12 August that year Thoresby's nephew, Richard Wilson, was convincingly elected recorder of Leeds by twenty-four votes to five. The queen refused to accept the appointment and Thoresby explained that 'scandalous' allegations had been made that 'the Corporation was desperately Whiggish'. Despite this the town claimed it remained loyal to the queen. As a demonstration of that loyalty, in 1713, Alderman William Milner paid for the erection of a white marble statue of the monarch to be placed in the niche at the front of Moot Hall.* On 12 May a vast crowd gathered to celebrate the event but such joy was soon replaced by anxiety about the future.

At half-past seven on the morning of 1 August 1714 Queen Anne died. Some Whigs in the country were concerned that the government might well ignore the Act of Settlement and proclaim the Stuart claimant as King James III. Thoresby's fear was of a 'dreaded invasion of the Pretender with an army of French and Irish' taking place. Opinions were bitterly divided in the town. One observer, the Revd Nathaniel Hough, remarked that Leeds was 'deeply tinged with Jacobitism', and went on to accuse Thoresby of being 'a favourer of the Pretender's cause'.

Thoresby was not and his fears of the return of a Catholic king turned out to be groundless. The Whig Duke of Shrewsbury ensured that George, the Elector of Hanover, was speedily brought to England to claim the throne. Thoresby, who was in London at the time, rejoiced at, 'the most blessed sight of a Protestant King and Prince (whom I had a full view of) attended with the loud acclamations of the people'.

In Leeds, however, there was still a strong undercurrent of feeling in support of the Stuart cause. Many on the Tory corporation were sympathetic towards the Old Pretender whilst the new mayor, Solomon Pollard went so far as to say that repeating his oath of allegiance to George I was 'the bitterest pill' he had ever swallowed. The government

---

* The statue can still be seen in Leeds City Art Gallery.

was wary of the situation in the town and furious when it was reported that the bell-ringers at the Parish Church had apparently blatantly demonstrated their loyalty to James Edward Stuart. The ringers normally practised on Thursday evenings, but in 1715 they chose to delay their activities until Friday, 10 June, the date of the Old Pretender's birthday.

The military reacted to this act of disloyalty by parading through the streets beating a drum. A crowd gathered and a bonfire was lit. A report was sent to the Secretary of State, James Stanhope, and Pollard and others were summoned to explain the events. The fire turned out to have been no more than the work of children and the whole affair somewhat exaggerated. But suspicion still hung over the town's leaders. Alderman William Cookson was accused of covertly supporting the Jacobites. The Lord Lieutenant of the West Riding, Rich Ingram, Fifth Viscount Irwin had him arrested and the luckless alderman spent the next six months in Newgate.

Nevertheless, fears of a Jacobite invasion were justified. In November the Earl of Mar led his Jacobite army as far south as Preston. Thoresby panicked and hid his precious manuscripts for fear of civil unrest breaking out in Leeds. However, the rebellion petered out the following year and for a time the Stuart cause receded.

But an even more damaging crisis then descended on the nation which affected everybody from errand boys to earls. The South Sea Company had been set up to trade with South America. Speculators of every social class raced to invest their savings. In March 1720 John Hirst in the *Leeds Mercury* was assuring his West Riding readers that as stocks rose 'it must Redound to the Happiness of the Nation'. But six months later that happiness turned to misery when the bubble burst. Thousands were ruined. Thomas Hudson of Leeds was a typical example. Having inherited a fortune from his aunt, he invested heavily, lost every penny and spent the remainder of his days wandering around London as a barefoot lunatic. The Irwins of Temple Newsam, who had long been involved in Leeds politics, also speculated excessively and only managed to remain solvent by acquiring loans from Alderman Milner, a wealthy Leeds merchant and lord of the manor of Beeston.

The Jacobite threat had receded but not disappeared. In 1722 another attempt was made to overthrow King George. In August 1726, the anniversary of the accession of the king, church bells were rung as a demonstration of loyalty in the town and the *Leeds Mercury* reported the Revd Brooke's sermon. He railed against 'Romanists and others who were supposed to wish well to the Pretender'. But he preached before a 'slender' congregation.

The following year George I died and it was important that the people of Leeds exhibited their loyalty to the new sovereign. In June the *Mercury* reported that a procession was led by the mayor, Thomas Sawer, from his house to make the proclamation of George II. Accompanying him were the aldermen, councillors and Arthur, Sixth Viscount Irwin of Temple Newsam. The coronation itself was celebrated by a great illumination in the town, by ringing bells, burning bonfires and letting off fireworks. Henry, Seventh Viscount Irwin made an even more permanent demonstration of loyalty. Between 1738 and 1745 he had the Picture Gallery at Temple Newsam house remodelled and instructed Thomas Perritt and Joseph Rose, the plasterers, to incorporate mouldings on the ceiling of the portraits of both George I and George II.

By 1745 English forces had become heavily engaged in Europe against France and Spain during the War of the Austrian Succession. The French government determined to open a second front and encouraged Charles Edward Stuart, the Young Pretender, better known as 'Bonnie Prince Charlie', to effect an invasion of England. He landed in Scotland and organised his army. Panic swept across the country. Leeds Corporation sent a loyal address to the king condemning 'this insolent attempt to invade thy Kingdom, on behalf of a Popish Pretender'.

September saw Marshall Wade and an army of Dutch and Swiss as well as English troops ordered north. In October they arrived in Leeds *en route* for Newcastle. The following month Charles Stuart embarked on his invasion of England. He would have preferred to attack Wade in the north-east and occupy Northumberland but Lord George Murray, his Lieutenant-General, dissuaded him. Instead he advanced through Lancashire where there was a strong Tory and Catholic base.

John Wesley arrived in Leeds from the North on 5 November with news that the Young Pretender had crossed the Tweed and was heading south. Leeds folk were out celebrating Guy Fawkes Night burning bonfires, firing guns and according to Wesley's *Journal*, 'cursing & swearing, as the English manner of keeping holidays is'. Wesley immediately reported the news of the rebel's advance to the magistrates and, as word of the impending invasion spread, the streets quickly emptied.

Many Leeds people fled, others hid their valuables and hoped for better news. In December loyal supporters from the West Riding formed the 'Leeds Parliament' which urged concerted action against the rebels. Henry Ibbetson of Red Hall on the Headrow raised a corps of 100 men at his own expense. But the danger of untrained amateurs facing the Scottish invaders was recognised and wiser counsels prevailed.

However, the support Charles had hoped for in Lancashire was not forthcoming and after reaching Derby, on 6 December, he decided to return to Scotland. That same month a professional army of 13,000 foot under Marshall Wade again arrived in Leeds. The English, Dutch and Swiss force encamped for two nights between Sheepscar and Woodhouse. Contrary to popular belief, Wade Lane does not derive its name from the event. The thoroughfare was known as Waide Lane as early as 1677.

The Stuart threat was finally removed but differences continued to divide the people of Leeds. For Thoresby the Church of England offered the 'due medium betwixt the Romanists on one hand and the Separatists on the other'. But the Church of England at this time was in a parlous state. Many clergy were unpopular and though the Church played an important part in everyday life, much of its preaching lacked flair and passion. One Hunslet cleric attended a meeting of clergy at the Angel Inn in the 1750s. Ruefully he remarked, 'All clergymen and yet not one word of spiritual things among us.'

At times the Church was divisive. When Leeds's third church, Holy Trinity on Boar Lane was consecrated in August 1727, most of the pews were rented or sold and thus poorer worshippers were virtually excluded. When the incumbency of St Peter's fell vacant with the death of the vicar in 1746, a rancorous dispute ensued over his successor. The trustees were equally divided between the two candidates, Samuel Kirshaw and James Scott. After appeals to the Court of Chancery and the House of Lords, Dr Kirshaw was finally appointed.

Whilst the dispute dragged on the Archbishop appointed a locum to fulfil the duties. The Revd Fawcett was a supporter of Kirshaw and when the new vicar finally took up his position Fawcett was rewarded with the curacy of Holbeck in 1754. This, however, incensed the inhabitants of the township who flatly rejected him and graphic accounts of the dispute appeared in the columns of the *Leeds Intelligencer*. For Griffith Wright and his month-old newspaper (it first appeared on 2 July 1754), here was an ideal on-running story. Wright's reports through August and September spoke of 'a furious, frantic rabble of Holbeckers' assaulting the new incumbent, of Fawcett's vain attempts to gain entry to his chapel, and of fifty dragoons being employed to escort him. He did manage to gain entry on Sunday 15 September but that night vandals broke into the building, destroyed the Common Prayer Book and smeared human excrement on the seats. Wright's comments were acerbic: 'Let them not assume the name of CHRISTIAN . . . much less a Protestant!'

But the Church's troubles did not end there. In 1761 the incumbency at Armley became vacant. Again two candidates were to be considered to fill the vacancy, Jeremiah Dixon and Bernard Tidswell. However, when the inhabitants of Armley arrived to cast their votes, they found the churchwardens had locked the doors of the chapel and only admitted Dixon's supporters. To complicate matters, the Vicar of Leeds, Samuel Kirshaw then nominated George Metcalfe as a third candidate. For two years the issue was dragged through the courts until finally Metcalfe became the incumbent.

Two candidates were also considered for the curacy in Hunslet in 1748, Henry Crooke and William Pashley. Opinion in the township was divided so on Sunday 17 April both men were invited to preach trial sermons that day. When Pashley commenced speaking the chapel was near empty but a mob of some 300 burst in and after five minutes he was forced to withdraw. Crooke was eventually appointed.

Crooke was one of that body of Anglican clergy who claimed to be a Methodist and who hoped to reinvigorate the Church of England from within. They were led by three clergyman: the brothers John and Charles Wesley and George Whitefield. Whitefield was a passionate, brilliant speaker. In 1750 it was estimated that the crowd that gathered to hear him in Leeds amounted to some 20,000. But by then doctrinal differences had caused a rupture between Whitefield and the Wesleys.

John Wesley became the great leader of that evangelical Methodist movement, travelling 5,000 miles a year crossing and re-crossing the country to preach to vast crowds. He formed societies or 'Connexions' across the land but always insisted that members remained faithful to the Anglican Church. Nevertheless clergy were suspicious of these groups and many churches refused Methodist preachers admission. At St Peter's in Leeds, however, Wesley was welcomed and the doors of the Parish Church were always open to him.

If the vicar was accommodating, the same could not be said about some of the people of Leeds. Wesley's receptions in the town were mixed. In May 1744 he preached 'in great peace' but violence marred other gatherings. In September 1745 he was 'pelted with dirt and stones' and in February 1746 he faced a 'great mob' and was struck several times. Allegations that he was a Jacobite sympathiser were spread about. On another occasion a spurious letter appeared in the *Leeds Intelligencer* signed 'JW'. On 26 September 1758 Wesley went to the trouble of writing to the paper to deny his authorship of it. But despite these upsets Wesley still had a considerable following in the town and when he preached in St Peter's vast numbers came to hear him; as many as 1,100 formed the congregation in 1781.

Indeed, over the next century Leeds became a centre of Methodism.

It began in 1742 when a Leeds barber, William Shent, heard a stone-mason, John Nelson, preach at Armley and was converted. Shent and about fifty similarly minded individuals formed a new Methodist society in the town. In 1743, Wesley arrived in Leeds and met them at Shent's shop at the junction of Briggate and Duncan Street. The Methodists frequently held their conferences in Leeds in their new building, Boggart House, which stood where the West Yorkshire Playhouse now stands.

But there were other groups of worshippers in the town who considered themselves outside the Church of England. Wesley visited one such group when he travelled to Fulneck near Leeds in 1747 to see the newly opened Moravian Settlement. Other Dissenting groups were also now well-established in Leeds. An Independent Congregation opened the White Chapel off Hunslet Lane. In 1751 the Inghamites established a chapel at Holbeck. In 1779 the Baptists hired part of the old Assembly Rooms on Kirkgate to hold their services and carried out baptisms in the River Aire. They opened their own chapel, the Stone Chapel, two years later. The Roman Catholics finally opened their church in Lady Lane in 1790.

The Presbyterians of Mill Hill turned from orthodox Christianity to adopt the principles of Unitarianism though they never officially assumed the name. Their most famous minister was the celebrated scientist and author, Joseph Priestley. Priestley was at Mill Hill from 1767 to 1773 and here he developed a lifelong interest in chemistry. By chance he was lodged near to a brewery where he observed carbon dioxide in the fermenting vats and this led to his discovery of oxygen. The Friends meanwhile remained at their Water Lane meeting-house and in the early years of the century Joseph Tathum opened a Quaker school above the stables there.

Various other schools were also opened in the out-townships during the early years of the century, supplementing the Grammar School in Leeds and the one which already existed at Wortley. Holbeck, Beeston, Chapeltown and Woodhouse all provided some form of education. In 1705 in Leeds a charity school, the Blue Coat School, was opened for forty pauper children in the workhouse. It was intended to qualify them ultimately for a trade and as such they were expected to be employed Tuesday, Thursday and Saturday afternoons. By the end of the century a School of Industry was opened in Beezon's Yard off Briggate to prepare girls for domestic service. But for many of the poor children the only chance of an education came with the opening of the first Sunday school in Leeds in 1784.

Private education was catered for by several establishments. Mr

Mills's writing school in Briggate, Mr Castiglione's French and Italian classes, and Jane Stock and Elizabeth Caulston's boarding school for young ladies near the vicarage all catered for middle-class students. By the end of the century Richard Kemplay had opened his famous Writing Academy in St John's Place in what became Nash's Fish Restaurant.

For adult intellectual stimulation experimental philosophy classes were held in Moot Hall during 1727, and discussions could be had in coffee-houses such as Garraway's. Concerts and dances were held in the Assembly Rooms which occupied the old White Cloth Hall in Kirkgate. Leisure pursuits were provided by Richard Taylor and included billiards at his coffee-house or bowls at the green he opened daily at the bottom of Lands Lane.

Among the most popular activities which cut across social barriers was cock-fighting, usually held at the Talbot Inn. Some people condemned it: one correspondent wrote to the *Intelligencer* in February 1770 calling for an end to this barbarous sport held 'for no other purpose than to give an opportunity of making bets'. But gambling was endemic in English eighteenth-century society. In August 1725, as a forerunner to the races, a main of cocks took place at Chapeltown with stakes reaching as high as 100 guineas for the odd battle. Cricket also attracted bets. In May 1776 the married men of Leeds played the bachelors of the town for a stake of five guineas and a dinner to follow. The bachelors won by six wickets.

Gambling in Leeds, as elsewhere, produced serious major social problems and in 1754 the *Leeds Intelligencer* highlighted it as an issue in the town. Its report of 15 October urged action from the magistrates to stop 'loose idle Fellows' from playing 'Shake Cap' in Lands Lane. It went on to describe how the winner resorted to ale-houses where he ended the night in 'Revelling and Drunkenness' whilst the loser returned home penniless and 'vents his ill humours on his Wife and poor Children'.

Family violence was just one example of the brutality of a violent age. The law was equally violent and uncompromising. A notice in the *Leeds Mercury* in March 1736 left no one in any doubt that the theft of hops from Robert Hall and John Newsham's property at Nosthorpe carried with it the death penalty. In 1774, Leeds magistrates ordered Elizabeth Winterburn to be stripped naked to her waist and 'privately whipt 'til her body be Bloody'. Crimes ranged from the theft of cloth from the tenter frames, the stealing of hounds from the kennels of the Leeds Hunt, the vandalising of Richard Tottie's property on Hunslet Lane and the destruction of ten yards of parapet on Leeds Bridge.

Duelling was a rare occurrence in the town and neither the duel fought between two officers in the grounds of Kirkstall Abbey in 1775 nor the one fought by two master breeches-makers near the bowling green in Lands Lane ended with a fatality. In the latter case, unknown to the participants, the seconds had charged the pistols with powder only!

Prostitution, however, was rife and confidence tricksters such as the Clay Lads whose sphere of activity was textiles, were always to be contended with. The Improvement Act of 1755 for 'Enlightening the Streets and Lanes, and Regulating the Pavements in the Town' shows exactly the kind of lawlessness that was rife in Leeds. It was passed to 'prevent many mischiefs which might happen as well from Fires, as Burglaries, Robberies and other Outrages and Disorders'. At times disorder turned to mob violence. In 1735 the escalating price of corn led to riots breaking out across the country. In Leeds the protesters resorted to such ferocity that the military was called in and several people were killed.

As the century developed other acts of violence and political unrest would manifest themselves in Leeds as the consequences of the Industrial Revolution began to take effect. Some historians have given 1760 as the popular date when that revolution started but today most agree that it was an ongoing process rather than an event and point out how much industry already existed in Britain before 1750. The year 1760 was a convenient date for historians, however, for it saw the accession of George III. It was during his sixty years on the throne that Britain witnessed the beginning of a metamorphosis as the nation slowly moved from the rural and agrarian way of life of the eighteenth century to the urban and industrial one of the Victorian age. It saw enormous wealth generated and equally enormous social problems created. No society had ever had to face such issues before. The people of Leeds shared in that wealth but also suffered the appalling changes that the new society created.

In January 1760 John Collier, a Lancastrian schoolmaster, summed up his view of Leeds. In so doing he anticipated some of the dormant social and political problems that would eventually surface through the latter years of the century. They would determine the political agenda of the town for the next hundred years:

> Leeds is a cunning but wealthy, thriving farmer. Its merchants hunt worldly wealth, as eager as dogs pursue the hare; they have in general the pride and haughtiness of *Spanish* dons . . . the strong desire they have for yellow dirt (gold), transforms them into galley-slaves, and their servants are doubly so; the first being fastened with golden, but the latter with iron chains.

In that pursuit of worldly wealth it was patently obvious that by the mid-eighteenth century an efficient transport infrastructure was vital for the town. Raw materials had to be brought in, manufactured goods carried away and a speedy way found of carrying the increasing numbers of businessmen, salesmen and other passengers across the country. The most effective mode of travel at the time was by water and the Aire and Calder Navigation had proved invaluable in transporting goods eastwards to Hull and thus the ports of Europe and beyond. Now merchants turned their eyes westward. Over the Pennines lay the port of Liverpool and the outlet for the lucrative markets of the Americas. In fact it was not Collier's 'thriving farmer' of Leeds who saw the potential first but merchants from Bradford, Blackburn and Liverpool. They proposed to build a canal from Liverpool to the hinterland of the West Riding and it was obvious that the route should end in Leeds where it could link with the Aire and Calder Navigation. When the 1770 Act was passed it enabled the construction of a waterway that in effect connected the east and west coasts, the ports of Hull and Liverpool.

Between 1771 and 1777 John Longbotham, the engineer, managed to superintend the building of thirty miles on the Yorkshire side of the Pennines and twenty-eight on the Lancashire side. It was a slow and difficult operation with capital not always easily forthcoming for new sections and difficult engineering problems had to be overcome. When the 1,630-yard-long Foulridge tunnel was opened in June 1796, the *Mercury* explained that it had taken five years to build. It was not until 1816 that the canal was finally completed. Nevertheless, as early as 1777, Henry Hindle was offering to carry goods on the completed section from Leeds to Skipton every Wednesday afternoon, scheduled to arrive early Saturday morning. It was estimated that water transport was 200 times more efficient than transport by road.

But road travel was still essential to the growing industries of Leeds. In the early years of the century, Thoresby described some highways he travelled on as 'rougher than a ploughed field'. The roads around Leeds were little more than uneven tracks and transporting goods on them was extremely difficult at times. Attempts to compel inhabitants to contribute a day's work on the roads or to 'send sufficient persons in their stead' proved unsuccessful. As late as April 1803, the inhabitants of Hunslet were fined £450 and those of Wortley £150 for failing to keep the roads in their townships in good repair.

The severe handicap the appalling state of the roads imposed upon the merchants of Leeds was further compounded when Wakefield merchants proposed building a new road to Halifax, thus completing a trans-Pennine route. Meetings were called in Leeds at the King's Arms and Royal Oak in Briggate to appoint turnpike trustees and to apply to Parliament to be allowed to carry out improvements on roads leading from the town.

Thus over the next few years a whole series of turnpike roads radiating from Leeds were either repaired or constructed; repairing the Leeds to Selby, and Leeds to Elland roads and the making of the Leeds to Halifax road took place in 1740. Repairing the Leeds to York road came in 1750, Leeds to Boroughbridge in 1751, Leeds to Skipton in 1754 and Leeds to Sheffield in 1759. Support from the merchant and manufacturing communities was tempered by opposition from rate-payers faced with paying for the work and resentment by locals at having to pay the tolls.

Eventually resentment turned to riot and a wave of violent protests swept across the West Riding. For three days in Selby the townsfolk, urged on by the town crier, Benjamin Wordsworth, utterly destroyed the turnpike at Gowthorpe in the town. A mob from Otley and Yeadon attacked several turnpikes in that area. In June 1753 a group of rioters from Leeds destroyed the toll bar on the Leeds to Bradford road and the one at Halton. But at the turnpike bar at Harewood Bridge they received a setback. Edwin Lascelles of Harewood House had been forewarned of their approach and with his estate workers managed to repel the attack.

Troops were sent from York to patrol the troubled areas. Three men were arrested for refusing to pay tolls and held in the King's Arms, Briggate. A fourth man was arrested at Beeston toll bar but a mob rescued him. That Saturday evening the protesters swept down on Briggate, ripped up cobbles from the street and pelted the guards outside the inn. The troops finally opened fire, several of the demonstrators were killed and about fifty wounded. Most of those killed or injured were either simply shopping at the Saturday market or merely interested spectators. Nevertheless feelings ran so high that it was felt necessary to maintain a guard over the homes of both the mayor and the town's recorder for some time.

But improved roads did produce more efficient travel and in 1760 the first regular coach service between Leeds and London was established. It took four days to travel from the King's Arms in Leeds to the Swan with Two Necks in the capital. The first night was spent at the Angel, Sheffield; the second at the Blackmore's Head, Nottingham; and the third night at the Red Lion, Northampton. Improvements continued and when Royal Mail coaches began running from Leeds in 1785 it took just twenty-six hours to travel from the King's Arms to the Bull and Mouth in London.

Leeds slowly developed into a major coaching centre, boasting eighteen coaching inns. Among the more famous of these were the Old King's Arms in Briggate and New King's Arms or the Royal Hotel in Lower Briggate. This building can still be seen with its distinctive coaching arch and its stables still run underneath the street. Another coaching inn was the White Horse on Boar Lane, though initially this was more concerned with heavy goods traffic. Goods haulier firms had become established in the town and carried freight between Leeds and London, Manchester, Liverpool, Newcastle, York and Sheffield. Some services were highly specialised. In 1765 four new waggons began operating from Flamborough to Leeds designed to carry fresh fish. Not only would it mean fish could be on sale in Leeds the day after it was caught, but, according to the *Leeds Intelligencer*, the price of butchers' meat 'must fall of course'.

However, the most imaginative mode of transport which developed in the area at this time was the building of a railway or waggon-way from Charles Brandling's coal mine at Middleton to Leeds. Brandling had two apparently insurmountable problems to overcome. His competitors from Rothwell could use cheap water transport to reach the town and the roads on which he had to carry his coals were in an appalling state. Thus he determined to build a railway line on which horse drawn waggons could transport coal with relative ease.

Brandling met the Leeds authorities at the Three Legs to gain their blessing and Richard Humble, his agent, remarked that the proposal 'met with all proper encouragement'. Agreements were made with private landowners and in June 1758 Parliament granted him the right to implement his plan. It was the first Act of Parliament authorising the building of a railway ever passed and in return Brandling had to guarantee to deliver coal to Casson Close near the end of Leeds Bridge at a fixed price. On Wednesday 20 September 1758 the first coal waggon arrived at the staithe. Bells were rung, cannons were fired and, according to the *Intelligencer*, 'a general Joy appear'd in every face'. It proved an inspired idea for the Middleton Railway is still running, though not as a colliery railway.

Coal from both Middleton and Seacroft was vital to fuel the emerging mills and factories of the growing number of industries which became established in the town during the second half of the eighteenth century. For by now Leeds was not solely dependent upon the wool textile industry. There were at least 148 other distinct occupations in the town. Small firms were involved in leatherwork, chemical production, engineering, printing, brick making, building and woodworking. In 1770 a new industry made its presence felt. Richard Humble, the steward at Middleton colliery, and two brothers, John and Joshua Green, established the Leeds Pottery in Jack Lane. Within twenty years its characteristic creamware had become internationally famous.

The manufacture and sale of woollen cloth was still the dominant industry of Leeds and the surrounding districts. It was mainly carried out on the scattered slopes of the Aire valley in the townships to the west of Leeds. These principally produced mixed or coloured cloth. It was a cottage or domestic industry where the carding, spinning and weaving were carried out in weavers' cottages. But already changes to the industry were coming. Some merchants, such as James Walker, a Wortley clothier, established small factories. Walker employed more than a hundred people scribbling and fulling his cloth and he also engaged over twenty-one weavers: eleven in his factory and another ten working on his looms which he had set up in their cottages.

The cloth was then brought to Leeds for finishing and sale. Many merchants had begun taking over the finishing processes and they also saw the economic sense of creating partnerships. As the century progressed more and more such partnerships were formed in Leeds. Some of them were family firms such as the Dennisons, Bischoffs, Blayds and Oateses all eager to exploit the burgeoning textile trade. Cloth was exported to Europe initially but later the American colonies and the West Indies accounted for some 30 per cent of woollen exports from Britain. About two-thirds of the cloth sold by those merchants went through the famous cloth halls of the town. The original White Cloth Hall in Kirkgate became too small and a second was opened in 1755 in Meadow Lane, south of Leeds Bridge; three years later the sale of dyed textiles was moved from Briggate to the newly opened Mixed or Coloured Cloth Hall. It was placed approximately where the General Post Office in City Square and Cloth Hall Court now stand. As an indication of its size, it contained 1,770 stalls and its quadrangular yard was so large that newspaper reports frequently refer to 20,000 people being able to gather there.

By 1775 the need for a larger white cloth hall was apparent and this was built on land that had previously been used as a tenter ground in the Calls. A smaller cloth hall opened in the basement of the Music Hall in Albion Street in 1793. Its name, the Irregulars' Hall or Tom Paine Hall, indicated that the cloth sold there was made by unapprenticed clothiers. Just as clothiers jealously guarded their standards and refused to allow anyone who had not completed a seven-year apprenticeship to trade in the legitimate halls, so too they ensured that foreign competitors were denied any knowledge of their processes. The mayor and corporation were happy enough to entertain the King of Denmark in 1768 and the Russian ambassador in September 1773 and impress them with the qualities of Leeds cloth, but it was a different matter for George Claus of Aix-la-Chapelle.

He was arrested and taken to the Rotation Office to face the town's magistrates in January 1781. The charge was that he had in his room a machine for spinning woollen yarn neatly packed into a box and ready for despatch to London. The *Mercury* was certain he had come to Leeds with the sole intention of recruiting a Hunslet clothmaker to accompany him back to France and to acquire the plans for the construction of a scribbling machine similar the one then operating at Armley. The machine was powered by a horse and could do the work of ten men but was so designed that no spectator was able to get a clear view of its workings. Granted bail on sureties that amounted to £650, Claus disappeared the following day.

Cloth merchants had more prosaic matters than industrial espionage to command their attention and they were not alone. All the new developing industries in Leeds required credit and banking facilities. As early as 1738 Benjamin Worsdale of the Upper Headrow was offering loans on good bonds and mortgages to borrowers. But the second half of the eighteenth century saw a national trend of small country banks being established to answer the financial needs of their local merchants and farmers. Leeds was no different. In 1758 John Arthington, a linen draper, and John Lodge, an eminent London merchant, set up the Lodge and Arthington Bank. They took on another partner, Thomas Broadbent and then in 1770, John Beckett joined them. The Becketts became the leading banking family in the town and the bank itself was ultimately known as Beckett's Bank. When a second bank opened on Boar Lane in 1777, Beckett's became known colloquially as The Old Bank, and the new bank, somewhat unoriginally, the Leeds New Bank. A third bank, Wright and Hemingway's opened in 1792 at the bottom of Briggate.

Banks played no part in the lives of the working classes. To them poverty was a constant threat and fluctuations in trade frequently meant that the poorest inhabitants of Leeds regularly became dependent upon charity. Their pastimes were often brutal. Cock-fighting and bull baiting were ever popular with the last baiting recorded in the area as late as the 1820s at Lower Wortley, where the area is still known as the Bull Ring. Bare-fist fights also attracted vast numbers of spectators. In January

1780 the *Mercury* reported on one such crowd which gathered in Holbeck to watch a 'severe battle' in which Lucas of Mabgate battered an Irish cropper into submission for two guineas.

The food of the labouring classes contrasted markedly with that of the middle classes. Drinking tea appears to have been almost the only common factor – the rest of their foods differed widely. The lower orders' diet was usually restricted to porridge, oatcakes and occasionally boiled beef or mutton supplemented with ale. The middle classes enjoyed a much richer and more varied diet. Fish courses included salmon, trout and herrings; roast beef, legs of mutton, pork steaks and a variety of game formed the regular meat dishes; and asparagus, carrots, cauliflowers and stewed cucumber were popular vegetables. Tea, coffee, chocolate and a range of wines were drunk.

Many of the wealthier classes were eager to acquire both cultural and intellectual stimulation. The eighteenth century is often referred to as the Age of Enlightenment and though historians disagree about the extent to which it can be applied in England, there was certainly an eagerness in the country for acquiring knowledge. However, even as late as 1817, the *Leeds Directory* claimed that unless the arts specifically related to commerce or manufacturing, they received little support in Leeds and it went on to remark 'still less do literary pursuits engage the attention of the individual'.

A small philosophical society was formed in the town and met between 1783 and 1786, whilst in 1792 a Music Hall was opened in Albion Street where concerts were performed, public readings carried out and exhibitions held. Improvements to the quality of life in Leeds continued through the century and within the space of just ten years four major institutions were established in the town, two of which are still contributing to the well-being of its people today.

By the mid-eighteenth century there were those middle class men in Leeds who were eager to extend their education. Unable to acquire extensive libraries like Irwin's at Temple Newsam or Lascelles's at Harewood House, they embarked upon setting up their own library in the town. At that time the only other library was Lawson's Library in the Grammar School. In August 1768 a meeting was called at Mr Myers's newsroom in Briggate and in November the *Leeds Intelligencer* announced the formation of the Leeds Circulating Library. Its membership was made up of prominent townsmen, many of whom were Unitarians. It was Joseph Priestley, their minister at Mill Hill Chapel, who was one of the prime movers in setting up the institution and then acting as its first secretary. The Leeds Library opened at 'the sign of the

Dial' behind a booksellers at Kirkgate-end on 1 November 1768. Forty years later it eventually moved to its present premises on Commercial Street and is the oldest surviving example of a subscription library left in England. A second library, the Leeds New Subscription Library, was founded in 1793.

The new Assembly Rooms were opened when it was agreed that the original rooms in Kirkgate were found to be 'incommodius'. It was proposed that the new building should be erected on the north side of the White Cloth Hall in the Calls. On the evening of Monday 9 June 1777 the building was officially opened with a minuet by Sir George Savile and Lady Effingham and the *Mercury* reported, 'The appearance of Ladies and Gentlemen on the occasion was more brilliant than ever remembered.' It was an elegant, well-furnished place which served the social hierarchy of Leeds for the rest of the century and still stands today.

The third contribution to the Leeds cultural scene was not favourably received by everyone. In March 1771 Tate Wilkinson opened the Leeds Theatre, sometimes known as the Theatre Royal, on Hunslet Lane. Through the years strolling players had frequently played in Leeds at various venues and generated different responses. In June 1722, Thoresby lamented the presence in the town of 'a company of players' for six to eight weeks 'which has seduced many'. Troupes, however, continued to arrive in Leeds and perform in the concert room at the Rose and Crown Inn or, from 1767, at the New Concert Room which had opened on Vicar Lane. Despite competition and downright opposition, Wilkinson went ahead, opened his theatre and brought his players to the town each summer. The programme was varied with performances ranging from Shakespearean plays in which Sarah Siddons performed, to topical items like the one act opera 'Bantry Bay' produced in 1797 to celebrate the failure of the French invasion of Bantry Bay in Ireland the previous year.

For many people though, theatres were considered immoral places. John Wesley went so far as to say, 'I see you have a wicked play-house in Leeds,' and two of the actresses who originally made their name at the Leeds Theatre helped to fuel such criticism. Perdita Robinson became the mistress of the future George IV whilst Mrs Jordan was involved with the future William IV to the extent that she bore him ten children. It was significant that in April 1822, when the coronation of King George IV was re-enacted at the theatre, it was performed before the evening's normal performance so that those who did not approve of plays could leave early.

The fourth institution the town acquired in those short years and, according to the *Intelligencer*, ' "dedicated to Christian charity" was open'd to the great joy of every benevolent heart . . . [T]he lower ranks of the people testified their gratitude by the ringing of bells'. They were celebrating the opening of Leeds General Infirmary. In 1767 Leeds had no hospital as such. Mrs Potter's Hospital in Wade Lane and John Harrison's Hospital by St John's Church simply catered for the needy. In June that year a meeting was called at the New Inn to consider the provision of a Leeds Infirmary 'for the Relief of the Sick and Hurt Poor within this Parish'. It was eventually resolved that it should cater for more than the parishioners of Leeds and thus was named 'the General Infirmary at Leeds'.

It opened in temporary premises, a Mr Wood's house in Kirkgate, but in March 1771 moved to its purpose-built structure on Infirmary Street. Originally two storeys high, the building had to be extended as demand increased. John Howard, the penal reformer, was much impressed with it when he visited the town. Funding came from a variety of sources: public subscriptions were given annually; individuals made personal contributions, such as the MP Henry Lascelles who donated 100 guineas in 1796 and Samuel Elam from Rhode Island who sent 5 guineas a year later; ministers such as Joseph Priestly preached to their congregations and the collections were passed on to the hospital, as were fines for non-attendance at drill sessions of the Leeds Volunteers. But no fund-raising event ever quite matched that of William Hey who charged the public to witness the dissection of the body of the executed murderer Mary Bateman in 1809. Hey made a profit for the Infirmary of £80 14s.

Hey was one of the men instrumental in setting up the hospital and became its senior surgeon in 1773. Blind in one eye from an early age and crippled in his early forties to the extent that he needed a crutch, he nevertheless became one of the dominant and most respected figures in Leeds. He was elected a Fellow of the Royal Society and twice fulfilled the role of mayor of the town. He died in 1819. His classic Georgian house is now the Law Society offices on Albion Place.

Improvements were being made to middle-class housing generally. From the late 1770s to the 1790s merchants began to build their homes away from their warehouses and finishing shops, and an area to the west of Leeds provided the sites for Park Square, Park Place, Park Row, East Parade and South Parade.

The 1770s should have been a time for commercial advancement and cultural progress in the town but events 3,000 miles away would soon bring a halt to the escalating success of the Leeds manufacturers. The thirteen American colonies were a major market for West Riding traders. In 1763 Grenville's Stamp Act was passed as a means of raising revenue from the colonists to pay for the cost of defending them during the recent Seven Years' War with France. They bitterly resented the imposition and trade with the mother country suffered. Leeds merchants petitioned the government, claiming that it was a great hardship to the Americans and pointed out the adverse effects the tax was having on trade.

By 1775 the colonists were in a state of rebellion. A letter arrived in Leeds from a trading house in Philadelphia which the *Intelligencer* printed to enable it to reach a wider audience. Its writer was emphatic: 'I don't believe all the force Great Britain can send will reduce this country to accept of dishonourable terms . . . [T]hey may destroy our cities and trade, but they will never conquer this country.' Opinion in Leeds became divided. In October another Leeds petition urged an end to hostilities which should be brought about 'by mild and lenient measures'. In December the town had organised a subscription to raise funds to help the widows and orphans of British soldiers killed in the conflict. The following year the *Intelligencer* reported that recruits from the West Riding were eagerly joining the colours 'to bring the ungrateful colonists to their duty' and it stressed that trade in the area was generally 'brisk'. Others disagreed. Tradesmen in Woodhouse, Armley, Hunslet and Holbeck drew attention to the fact that 'the distresses of the labouring Poor are very much increased'.

The divisions within the town were becoming more noticeable. In January 1777 the war seemed to be going well for Britain, and in Leeds bonfires were lit, large quantities of ale were drunk and candles set up in windows to illuminate the town. But there were those who refused to celebrate and had their darkened windows smashed. The celebrating inhabitants of Holbeck went so far as to burn the effigies of George Washington and Benjamin Franklin before the greatest crowd the township had ever seen. But France and then Spain entered the war supporting the colonists. The British government itself was divided and the effects on the West Riding textile trade were now abundantly clear.

By 1779 James Bowling addressed the issue in the *Mercury* demanding to know what the war was truly about: 'It is not surely for America, for that is gone forever. It is not for our trade, for we have none, at least worth our keeping.' Bowling continued his criticism, to the annoyance of government supporters in Leeds, and ultimately paid the price. The

Leeds Mercury of 21 December 1833 explained that the pressure brought to bear on him by the authorities contributed to his decision to sell up in 1795; though why Bowling took so long to make up his mind was not made clear.

The continued depression in trade affected everyone and spirits in the town were hardly lifted in February 1780 when the press-gang was reported to be scouring the streets of Leeds. The market closed earlier than usual and people refused to go out after dark. Such dangers finally passed when the war came to an end three years later and Leeds could once more face the future with hope. The town was about to embark upon a period of rapid economic expansion brought about by men of flair, imagination, enormous energy and exceptional skill.

In the wool textile world none was more exceptional than Benjamin Gott. He was born of a wealthy middle-class family in 1762 and eventually became the junior partner of Wormald and Fountaine, woollen merchants. In 1790 Gott found himself the sole head of the firm and embarked upon an imaginative scheme to concentrate all the processes of wool cloth manufacture under one roof. No such grandiose scheme had been conceived before in the woollen industry. He bought sixteen acres of land called Bean Ing to the west of the town. It was a well-chosen site and stood by both the river and the newly built canal. Here he had his massive Park Mills erected. It is now the site of the *Yorkshire Post* building. By 1797 his workforce of 1,200 was producing 4,000 broadcloths a year. Five other manufacturers also operated in the building, paying Gott a rent.

He extended his operation by buying Armley Mills in 1800, now the home of the Industrial Museum, and later added to his empire by purchasing Burley Mills. As his prime object was the sale of cloth he still also drew on the produce of local clothiers. He exported his finished product to the Americas, the Far East and Europe and was a major supplier of blankets and uniforms to the British Army. In today's terms he became a multi-millionaire. He bought an estate at Armley where he built a classical-style mansion which contained works of art by Caravaggio, Poussin and Reynolds. He was an avid supporter of Leeds charities, one of the founders of the Leeds Philosophical and Literary Society and the Mechanics' Institute and was mayor of Leeds in 1799. Gott was a Tory.

The other great textile entrepreneur in Leeds was a Whig. In 1788, in partnership with Fenton and Dearlove, John Marshall set up a flax mill at Adel. But the site was inadequate for his needs and in 1792 he moved the business to Water Lane adjacent to the newly built Leeds and

Liverpool Canal. Here, with two new partners, Benjamin and Thomas Benyon, he saw his business begin to thrive to the extent that it employed a workforce of 1,000 and Leeds became the principal centre of the British flax industry.

The flax used was both grown locally and imported from the Baltic. Like Gott, Marshall too became one of the pillars of early nineteenth-century Leeds society, becoming MP for Yorkshire in 1826. His most famous monument is the last of the mills he had erected in Holbeck between 1838 and 1840. Its façade is a replica of the Ancient Egyptian Temple of Horus at Edfu and can still be seen on Water Lane. But whereas Gott had been loath to introduce new machinery into his mill, Marshall was one of the first people in the country to attempt to spin flax mechanically. This was the basis of his success and it was to the third great Leeds innovator he owed much of that success.

Matthew Murray was born in Newcastle-upon-Tyne in 1765. He was apprenticed as a mechanic or wheelwright and finished his apprenticeship in Stockton-on-Tees. With few opportunities available for a young man in the North-East, he walked sixty miles to Leeds and there found employment with John Marshall in his flax mill at Adel. When Marshall moved to Holbeck, Murray accompanied him. There he set about producing the machines Marshall needed for spinning and carding the flax. His innovations were such that he was eventually awarded a gold medal from the Society of Arts.

In 1795, he formed a partnership with Fenton and Wood and the following year the firm opened the famous Round Foundry in Holbeck. Murray was one of the great pioneers of steam power and undoubtedly his greatest fame lies in the steam locomotives he built for Brandling's Middleton Railway. Had he not died in 1826, it is probable that Murray would have played an even greater part in the development of steam railways. As far as Leeds is concerned, he is rightly recognised as the 'Father of Engineering' in the town. But his success came not without a struggle. He had to face serious competition from his Birmingham rivals Boulton and Watt, who embarked upon a campaign to damage his reputation, restrict his company's expansion, and even took to employing industrial espionage against him.

The new ideas emerging in engineering and textile production were mirrored by new ideas arising in the field of economics and politics. The French Revolution swept away the *ancien régime*, executed Louis XVI and in 1793 the fledgling republic declared war on Britain. Many intellectual and liberal-minded Whigs initially welcomed the social changes the revolution brought about but condemned the violence which followed.

The Tories and the government deplored it emphatically as a radical and destabilising attack upon civilised society and feared that in England the poorer classes might soon follow their counterparts in France and rebel.

Poverty is the harbinger of civil unrest and in Leeds it was a perennial social problem which the authorities had to contend with repeatedly. Nearly 30,000 people were now living in the town and a further 23,000 in the out-townships. The council was already finding it difficult to cope. In 1797 one author vividly captured the extent of the crisis facing Leeds.

> Cellars, Garrets and such like Places, exhibit . . . abodes of human Misery, the wretched Inhabitants are frequently found either exerting the last Efforts of Nature to support themselves . . . or languishing under the most powerful Influence of complicated Disease.

In the past the corporation had acted. On occasions underweight butter and loaves of bread were confiscated by the magistrates and distributed to the poor and fines imposed for drunkenness were used likewise. The winter of 1794–5 was exceptionally severe. A meeting at the Rotation Office discussed what steps could be taken to help the needy for it was becoming apparent that action was urgently required to 'prevent them tumultuously assembling'.

In the final years of the century public subscriptions were raised. A soup kitchen was established and in one winter alone 7,000 quarts of soup were served. Benefit clubs were founded: the Brotherly Posterior Club, the Hunslet Humane Society and the Strangers' Benevolent Society were typical. Individuals reacted: Benjamin Gott gave 530 blankets to the poor, Earl Cowper supported the poor of Potternewton and Chapel Allerton; Earl Cardigan the poor of Bramley, Farnley and Headingley; Marshall and Fenton's and Murray and Wood's helped the poor of Holbeck.

But a series of poor harvests dramatically drove up the price of corn. Severe shortages developed. Sowden of Leeds Mill was investigated for raising the price of corn and so strong was local feeling that farmers and corn dealers coming to Leeds had to be given protection. In 1795 the labourers in Leeds petitioned the Home Secretary, claiming that the corn dealers had monopolised the market and 'sell it to the poor at thare owne price'. Five years later Sarah Stephenson, a local miller, was forced to admit she was still doing it.

In January 1796 miners at Middleton went on strike, adding to the suffering of the inhabitants. The following year rioters in Beeston and Holbeck attacked Johnson's mill as a protest against the use of machinery there. The government was so concerned at the outbreak of violence that the Home Secretary, the Duke of Portland, asked for a report from the mayor. Meanwhile the abortive landing of a small French force in

Pembrokeshire, though soon overwhelmed, precipitated a run on gold. In Leeds, merchants, gentry and the principal inhabitants of the town called meetings to show public support for the banks and offered to take the new £1 banknotes in place of golden guineas.

Leeds was a 'hot bed of sedition' according to the London paper the *Evening Mail*, though it based its judgement on the fact that Grey, one of the mutineers at the Nore, had come from the town. Nevertheless, seditious papers and pamphlets were being distributed in the area. The radical writings of Tom Paine could be found in the homes of numerous Leeds cloth-dressers and the Bramley Corresponding Society was in contact with Thomas Hardy's more famous London Corresponding Society, in order to exchange ideas about Parliamentary Reform.

There were also those in Leeds who deplored such radical protests. In Briggate, an effigy of Tom Paine was burnt and the crowd patriotically sang 'God Save the King'. Britain was, after all, at war and subscriptions were raised across the country to support it. The workers at Gott and Fountaine's raised £95 between them and some 60,000 spectators turned up on Chapeltown Moor in May 1795 to witness the arrival of the Leeds Volunteers and other corps from West Riding towns to partake in the manoeuvres there. When news of Nelson's victory over the French fleet at Aboukir Bay reached Leeds, the town celebrated with an illumination and the local banks opened appeals to collect for the widows and orphans the battle left in its wake.

But the war divided Leeds. Petitions from the manufacturers urging peace were despatched to Westminster claiming that trade was being seriously hampered. Compounding this in 1801 was a contagious fever which swept through the town. For the Whigs and Dissenters in Leeds things could not be worse. In 1785 Griffith Wright had finally retired and his son, Thomas, took over the *Leeds Intelligencer*. Under him it became the leading Tory newspaper in Yorkshire, ever ready to attack both Whigs and Dissenters. The only other newspaper, the *Leeds Mercury*, had degenerated into a weak insipid journal with a declining circulation and no definite opinions. In 1801, a young Lancastrian printer, Edward Baines, with the support of his Whig and Dissenter friends, bought the *Mercury* and over the years turned it into the most influential provincial newspaper in Britain.

In October that year Bonaparte offered to cease hostilities, Lord Hawkesbury, the future Lord Liverpool, signed the Preliminary Peace Treaty, and the nation celebrated. The autumn streets of Leeds were illuminated, sheep were roasted whole and 'copious libations of brown stout' were drunk in the out-townships. But it was a joy that would not last.

CHAPTER SIX

FACTORIES, FEVERS and FACTIONS

In 1801, after eight years of war it was not surprising that the peace celebrations cut across party lines, social divisions and religious differences
in Leeds. It was, however, only a temporary relief for the inhabitants of
the town. Soon war with all its brutal devastation would once again
sweep across the continent and leave in its wake, in Leeds as elsewhere,
economic distress and appalling destitution. Compounding those evils
were regular outbreaks of disease brought about by rapid and unhealthy
urban growth. And even when silence fell on the battlefields of Europe
the eternal problems of the town's insanitary environment and abject
poverty returned time and again to challenge the townsfolk of Leeds.

Responsibility to find solutions to these problems generally fell on
the shoulders of the middle classes, irrespective of their political align-
ment or religious commitment. That duty was summed up in 1819 by
the *Leeds Mercury*: 'Whenever a plan is proposed for the benefit of the
lower orders of society, we feel ourselves bound in duty to them, to look
at it with a scrutinising eye'. In Leeds it fell upon the principal inhabitants of the town: people such as Christopher Beckett, the Tory banker
and magistrate; John Marshall and Benjamin Gott, the Whig and Tory
textile manufacturers; Griffith Wright Junior, who had succeeded his
father as proprietor of the Tory *Leeds Intelligencer*, and Edward Baines,
owner of the Whig *Leeds Mercury*; James Bischoff, a Whig wool merchant, Ralph Markland, a Tory corn merchant, William Hey, the Tory
surgeon of Leeds Infirmary, and William Tottie, a Whig solicitor.

It was they and others like them who urged the mayor of the day to
call public meetings to address whatever current problem was besetting
the town and raise subscriptions when economic depressions reduced
thousands to near starvation levels. Their responsibilities extended
beyond economic help. When the poor of the town failed to take advantage
of free inoculations against smallpox in 1805, it was those civic-minded
individuals who were urged to form an association that could disseminate
the value of the treatment to the lower classes.

Previously, in 1801, that same group had acted when a virulent fever
swept through Leeds. Hundreds died. Many of the fatalities came from
the squalid two-storey back-to-backs and cellar dwellings which were

crammed into the working-class areas of the Bank, Marsh Lane and Quarry Hill. To ease the problem Disney Thorp, one of the physicians at the Infirmary, published a booklet on *Hints and Observations Relative to the Prevention of Contagious Fevers*. But Leeds Infirmary itself did not cater for people suffering from infectious diseases. Demands were made for a fever hospital to be established in the town. Once more the middle classes rallied to the call, raised adequate funds and between 1802 and 1804 the House of Recovery, with room for fifty patients, was built on Vicar Lane. Other hospitals were to follow: the Leeds General Eye and Ear Infirmary was opened in 1821 and the Lying-in-Hospital in 1824. That same year, as part of the House of Recovery, a Public Dispensary began treating the poor of Leeds and in 1828 moved to its own premises on North Street.

Peace with Napoleon, however, was not due to last. On Wednesday 18 May 1803, the British government declared war on France. A meeting at the Rotation Office in July expressed loyal support to the king and another was called in August. It was intended to re-form the Leeds Volunteers, a body of men like the Home Guard of the Second World War, who underwent military training in their spare time. Just twenty men turned up! The *Mercury* claimed that Leeds was 'within an ace of being eternally disgraced' but the town's face was saved when, a week later, more than a thousand volunteers came forward. They were grouped into two battalions of infantry under Colonel Lloyd and two troops of Volunteer Cavalry under Captain Rhodes. Their equipment and uniforms were supplied by the people of Leeds with the exception of the Quakers. They objected to war in principle and gave £1,400 to Leeds Infirmary instead.

The threat of an impending French invasion hung heavily over the nation. To give advance warning of such an event a series of beacons was placed across the country. The Leeds beacon was positioned high above the town on Seacroft Moor Top. But the threat soon receded. By the end of the summer of 1805 Napoleon had moved his army from the coast towards central Europe to confront the Austrians and in October, off Cape Trafalgar, England's supremacy of the sea was assured. It was a costly victory. Nelson was shot and a further 1,690 British sailors killed or wounded. In Leeds a month later Maillardet's exhibition of automata at the Music Hall in Albion Street raised £30 for the widows and orphans of the men who had fallen alongside their admiral.

The suffering war inflicted was not restricted to active servicemen. With the exception of men like Gott who supplied the army with blankets and greatcoats, the seemingly endless conflict plunged both West Riding manufacturers and operatives into a severe economic depression. The war with France brought about a stagnation of trade as export markets dried up.* Inevitably what followed was unemployment, poverty and social discord. Feelings ran so high in Leeds that 28,628 people signed a petition urging peace.

There were others who just as passionately opposed any agreement with Napoleonic France. Though the *Mercury* stood firmly behind the peace petitioners, it offered its columns to William Hey, the respected surgeon and twice mayor of the town. He argued that 'Peace without security is both delusive and dangerous.' The *Intelligencer* was bitterly opposed to any overtures to the French and one of its correspondents was adamant that 'our only hope of safety . . . is in war.'

That safety was finally assured in June 1815. When the news of the victory at Waterloo and Napoleon's abdication reached Leeds, newspaper offices were besieged with people eager for information. The performance at the Leeds Theatre was interrupted and the historic announcement made from the stage. After two decades of almost continuous war, England was now at peace, but it was to be an uneasy peace. Poverty in the country was rampant. The symptoms of social discord and class divisions which had begun to emerge during the years of conflict accelerated in the years that followed.

Those who had work usually flocked to the market in Briggate on Saturday evenings to buy what they needed. The poor would go to redeem pledges from the local pawnbrokers. Often in winter, when poverty reached its peak, public meetings were called to produce strategies to combat the recurring problem. The year 1820 was particularly severe. Out of a population of between 30,000 and 40,000 it was estimated that at least 7,000 lived in 'abject penury and wretchedness'. Many were so desperate that they were forced to sell their chairs, tables, beds and even clothing to provide themselves with food and shelter. Demands on pawnbrokers in the town were so great that they were being forced to close at times because their funds could not keep pace with demands. To ease the problem soup, rice and salted fish were sold at reduced prices and in 1826 the Tory Pitt Club in Leeds cancelled its annual dinner and donated the proceeds to the poor.

Numerous benefit societies still operated in the town and the workhouse catered for about 150 of the old, the sick and the orphaned. Whereas the benefit societies were purely voluntary organisations, the

---

* The Anglo-American War of 1812-1815 also seriously disrupted trade.

workhouse was run by the Workhouse Board. The corporation of Leeds appointed some members of the board, the parish vestry meeting the rest. By law all ratepayers, irrespective of whether they were worshippers at the Parish Church or not, had a right to attend vestry meetings and thus non-Anglicans could have their say on appointees.

Some of the poor felt that there was nothing left for them in the West Riding. In one week in May 1817, between sixty and seventy Leeds people emigrated to the United States 'to find an asylum from want and ruin'. Destitution was never far away and in the extremely severe winter of 1820 when ice and snow gripped the streets of Leeds, the press reported that some of the poor were trying to survive on as little as seven or eight pence a week.

Inevitably some turned to crime. Children as young as eleven were sent out to steal what they could and by 1815, to try to contain the problems of theft and vandalism, a night watch was appointed in the town. Without doubt, however, the most notorious Leeds criminal of the time was the infamous Mary Bateman, the so-called 'Yorkshire Witch'. Her exploits ranged from simple confidence tricks like getting her hen to lay an egg with 'Crist [sic] is coming' on its shell, to stripping a gullible Bramley couple of all their assets and, in 1808, poisoning the wife. Mary ended up first on the gallows at York and then the dissecting table at Leeds Infirmary.

The law only allowed the bodies of executed criminals to be used for medical research and thus a ghoulish crime developed during the 1820s and early 1830s in Leeds as in other places. Newly buried bodies were dug up by the resurrectionists and despatched to medical centres for use in research. Reports began to appear in the Leeds press of such activities locally. After the body of Thomas Rothery was removed from Wortley churchyard in 1831, the inhabitants of the township took action. They decided to form a voluntary patrol, take it in turns to watch the graveyard each night and even built a small stone hut on the north-east side of the churchyard for shelter.

Though body snatching naturally offended respectable townspeople an even greater social evil did more so. Among the worst problems that poverty produced in the town was prostitution. The brutish and often inhumane society of early nineteenth-century Leeds manifested itself dramatically at the parish cross in Briggate in May 1804 where a husband sold his wife for five guineas to 'a man acquainted with her *merits*'. But for decades the problems of vice riddled streets and common lodging houses which were in reality no more than brothels were an affront to the respectable inhabitants of the town.

From 1810 numerous letters had appeared in the press on the subject and in 1813 a meeting was called to discuss the possibility of providing a female penitentiary. The establishment of a barracks in the town between 1819 and 1820 also undoubtedly led to an escalation of the problem. So it was that in 1821 the Leeds Guardian Society was finally established and a building was opened in St Peter's Square. It catered for those women such as one quoted in the *Leeds Mercury*. When asked about her life she laconically observed: 'I have no home, friends, employment or character.'

That hopelessness was mirrored by many as unemployment rose and families were reduced to near starvation levels. Resentment grew and many of the operatives in Leeds placed the blame for their situation on the new machinery that was being introduced in the mills and factories. They claimed that machines were replacing men and inevitably this resulted in mass unemployment and endless suffering. In November 1811 disturbances had broken out in Nottingham led by the infamous 'Ned Ludd' and by early 1812 Luddism had made its appearance in the West Riding.

There were those in Leeds who argued that the wars with both France and the United States, and not the newly introduced machinery, were the real cause of the disruption to trade. But it was difficult to convince men and women whose jobs had disappeared and who faced starvation. When Benjamin Gott introduced his gig mills the number of his employees dropped from over 1,000 at the beginning of the century to 756. However, his workers took some steps to avoid redundancy and for fifteen years flatly refused to operate an hydraulic press used in the finishing process. So tense was the situation that Gott placed an armed guard around his Armley home and even that did not stop his windows being broken and threatening letters being received. Meanwhile, in other Leeds districts violence also broke out. At the finishing shops of Dickenson, Carr and Shann on Water Lane £500 worth of cloth was destroyed by angry Luddite demonstrators.

But the violent outbursts were not solely the result of industrial change. Successive bad harvests culminated in 1812 with the price of wheat reaching the highest level ever recorded during the Napoleonic Wars. In August a riot over the high price of corn erupted in Briggate. It was led by a woman adopting the title of 'Lady Ludd'. Shackleton's corn mill in Holbeck was then attacked and a further demonstration took place by the river outside King's Mill. To contain the situation, in November that year the West Kent Militia and the Scots and Queen's Greys were temporarily garrisoned in Park Lane. The two Leeds papers adopted different attitudes to the situation. The *Mercury* sympathised with the suffering of the workers but categorically condemned their violence. The *Intelligencer* claimed that the Luddites were simply agitators for peace and Parliamentary Reform.

For years an ongoing campaign to reform Parliament had been under way. Few people had the vote and many towns had no representative at Westminster. Supporters of reform argued that only when such glaring injustices had been rectified could Britain progress and the suffering of the lower orders be alleviated. Opponents argued equally volubly that reform would mean the destruction of the British constitution and some feared it might presage a revolution in England as bloody and bitter as that which had occurred in France. Calls for reform had been muted during the war but when the conflict was over demand for reform slowly increased.

Compounding that demand were other pressing issues. Following the conclusion of the war in 1815 the economy of Britain was unable to absorb the near half a million men demobilised simultaneously. Unemployment was widespread and resentment was combined with anger at the price of corn being kept artificially high by the Corn Laws. Poverty and near starvation were rampant and outbreaks of violence erupted nationwide. Nothing like it had been seen in England since the Civil War. In Leeds, subscriptions were raised at the George and Dragon, Golden Fleece, Bee Hive and White Swan and some 2,000 families benefited from the beef, potatoes, soup, bread and coal provided by these collections.

The government and its Tory supporters feared that revolution would be the outcome if steps were not taken to suppress such subversives. The Whigs in Leeds argued that there was no evidence for such claims in the West Riding. Lord Liverpool's government, however, placed spies across the country to give warning of impending uprisings. But it was Edward Baines in the *Leeds Mercury* of 14 June 1817 who revealed that one spy at least in the West Riding, William Oliver, had acted as an *agent provocateur*. He had encouraged locals in the Dewsbury area to rise up whilst he remained in close contact with the authorities, reporting on the would-be insurgents' every move. The military quickly acted and arrested the participants. However, the *Mercury*'s revelation forced Lord Liverpool, the Prime Minister, into an embarrassed admission and the paper became acknowledged nationally as a newspaper to be reckoned with.

The *Intelligencer* sneered at its rival's coup and claimed that the 'cultivated' readers of the *Mercury* were no more than impoverished croppers and weavers who could only afford to buy the paper by clubbing together and paying a farthing each. For the working classes in particular newspapers were expensive. The government's tax both on paper and advertisements carried in the press forced the price up to 6d. per copy. Baines smugly admitted it was true that some of his readers did form clubs but he also pointed out that his readers included wealthy businessmen and delighted in the fact that the *Mercury*'s circulation was three or four times greater than the *Intelligencer*'s.

The bitter rivalry between the two papers continued. Though only consisting of four pages each in the century's early decades, they culled much of their news from the national newspapers and devoted two pages to advertisements. Both papers, however, also featured local news but, most important, they argued their respective political standpoints vehemently: the *Mercury* on behalf of the Whigs and Dissenters, the *Intelligencer* for the Tories and Anglicans. Indeed, the *Leeds Mercury* is recognised as the first provincial newspaper to make regular use of a weekly editorial. No issue divided both the papers and the population more than that of Parliamentary Reform.

Campaigning mass meetings estimated at up to 10,000 gathered on Hunslet Moor but opinion was divided between the reformers themselves. There were radicals like George Petre who urged a Hunslet gathering only to accept universal suffrage; the moderates argued that the vote should be restricted only to men who paid direct taxes, in effect the middle class. In July 1819 another meeting was called in Leeds, the second of four major ones to be held across the country that summer. An estimated 6,000 gathered with a large percentage of women present. The fourth such meeting was held in Manchester at St Peter's Fields. It was here the magistrates panicked and sent in the local Yeomanry. Some 400 of the crowd were injured, fifteen were killed and the bloody incident became known ever after as the 'Peterloo Massacre'.

Sidmouth, the Home Secretary, congratulated the magistrates but the Whig opposition was horrified. Some eight days after the incident a crowd of 4,000 gathered on Hunslet Moor, the band played 'Rule Britannia' and James Mann, a Leeds radical, remarked how fortunate they had been in Leeds that the local magistrates had shown a more tolerant attitude than their Manchester colleagues. In September crowds flocked into the town from the surrounding out-townships and villages and gathered in Briggate. Then, in sober procession they marched to Hunslet Moor, their single black banner proclaiming, 'We mourn for our murdered friends in Manchester.' Once on the moor, Isabella Blackburn began to read an 'Address of the Female Reformers of Leeds to Their Townsmen' but her voice was weak and it was finished by Mr Chapman, the Chairman.

A nervous government viewed the national situation with alarm and took positive steps to ensure that law and order were strictly imposed. In Leeds a cavalry barracks covering about eleven acres was erected at Buslingthorpe; the present Barrack Road runs through its old parade ground. To support that military presence a meeting was called at the Leeds Court House in January 1820 to establish the formation of a volunteer force of 300 infantry. It would serve under the command of the town recorder.

But whilst these turbulent events were unfolding industries in the town were growing and despite periods of economic stagnation most of them flourished. In the forefront were the great manufacturers like Gott and Marshall whilst Pym Nevins, J. and E. Brooke and Fisher Nixon and Co. all launched their own wool textile factories.

The industry itself relied less and less on locally reared sheep. Merino wool brought from Australia proved to be so superior to that produced in England that Benjamin Gott testified before a select committee in 1806 that in fifty years time not even servants would wear clothes made from English wool. In 1810, 167 lb. of Australian wool was imported; some fifty years later the amount had increased to 49,209,000 lb. A canal wharf and the surrounding area by Gott's mill at Armley is still known as Botany Bay, a reminder of the first shipments of wool from Australia to arrive there.

The success of Marshall's flax business saw nineteen more such businesses established in the town by 1821. And these industries themselves spawned a demand for bricks, wood, iron and above all engineering.

In the first decade of the new century Matthew Murray, along with his partners Fenton and Wood, was already supplying the engineering needs of the local textile manufacturers. By 1812 he had built the first commercially successful steam locomotive for the Middleton Railway. Based on Richard Trevethick's patent, Murray's two steam-powered engines ran on a rack or toothed rail track, designed by John Blenkinsop, the mine agent. After a test run in June 1812, the engines *Prince Regent* and *Salamanca* began operating in August that year. A year later Murray converted a captured French privateer, *L'Actif*, to steam power. It was one of the earliest seagoing steamboats and daily plied between Yarmouth and Norwich. Meanwhile the engineering industry in Leeds continued to develop and the year after Murray had set up in business, Taylor Wordsworth and Co. began operating in the same sphere. Next, in 1812, Samuel Lawson of the Hope Foundry and, fourteen years after that, Peter Fairbairn at the Wellington Foundry opened similar engineering works.

By 1820 there were some twenty firms involved in the chemical industry producing vital supplies to the textile manufacturers of Leeds and the glassmakers of Hunslet. In that same township several firms produced copperas essential for the production of dyes whilst by 1828 a leather industry had become established in the town at Rhodes and Nickol's tannery in Kirkstall Road. Richard Paley, a soap manufacturer, property developer, potash manufacturer and iron founder had seen the growing cotton industry in Lancashire and as early as 1790 had opened two cotton mills in east Leeds. By 1800 some 2,000 people were employed in about ten such factories in the town but it was not to last. Within a decade the cotton industry had all but disappeared from the area.

Servicing all these industries were numerous transport firms. Vessels sailed regularly from Leeds to London, Yarmouth, Newcastle, Manchester and York, but not without some mishaps. In 1822 the *British Queen* sank in the North Sea with all hands whilst carrying a cargo of Bramley Fall stone from the town. Steam-powered boats operated between Leeds and London from 1823.

11. Port of Leeds
The Aire and Calder Navigation and the bustling port of Leeds about 1827. Vessels regularly sailed from here to London, Yarmouth, Newcastle and other destinations. Just beyond Leeds Bridge, seen on the left, the navigation linked up with the Leeds and Liverpool Canal.

With the completion of the Leeds and Liverpool Canal in 1816 barges plied their trade along the whole length of the 128 miles between the two towns. Ten centres were established in the town for transporting goods by land to destinations as far away as London, Edinburgh, Glasgow and the south of England. The coaching industry, which had begun to grow during the late eighteenth century, saw Leeds become a major coaching centre and by 1838 some 130 coaches were either arriving or departing from the town each day.

However, the days of coaches were numbered – the advent of the railways saw to that. But coaching proprietors prolonged their days by opening up routes where there was no opposition from steam trains or began to work with the new railways. For a time passengers travelled by coach from Leeds to Derby and then by train to London. But railways had long been on the minds of Leeds people. 'Mercator's' famous letter appeared in the *Leeds Mercury* in January 1802 proposing a horse drawn waggon-way to be built between Leeds and Selby. By 1814 other correspondents suggested adapting the steam engines running from Middleton Colliery to be used on a railway which was once again proposed to run between Leeds and Selby. One estimate put the cost of construction at £300 a mile.

Six years later the proposals were given more serious consideration but the financial crisis which struck in 1825 saw the plan shelved. It was not until 1834 that Leeds was provided with its first railway line – it ran from Leeds to Selby! Others followed in a relatively short space of time as railway mania swept the country: Leeds to Derby in 1837–1840; Leeds to Bradford in 1846; Leeds to Thirsk in 1845–9; and Leeds to Manchester in 1848.

There were disadvantages in those burgeoning but unregulated industries and trades. Hours of work were long and arduous. One young Leeds milliner and dressmaker took the unusual step, for a woman at the time, of writing to the press to point out the unreasonable hours she and her colleagues were expected to work each day, in her case from 7 a.m. to 11 p.m. Apart from long hours of work the machinery used in many industries was extremely hazardous. Middleton Railway was certainly a transport boon for the colliery but within six months of its opening, thirteen years-old John Brice had been killed on the unfenced line and in 1818 George Hutchinson, a driver, was blown to pieces when the boiler of *Salamanca* exploded. The machinery, so important to the industrial growth of the town, was unguarded and dangerous. Horrendous accidents in the mills and factories were commonplace: fourteen years-old Harriet Wilson, who lived off Marsh Lane, lost both her arms when she was caught up in a machine in a local factory in December 1809.

Even after Davy's safety lamp had been introduced, mines were still places of constant danger and disaster. When a Middleton miner at Gosforth coal pit removed the top of his lamp to allow it to cool in January 1825, the explosion which followed killed twenty-four souls. The oldest to die was forty-five years-old John Liversedge, who left behind a widow and ten children. The youngest to die was John Ambler; he was five years of age.

Some of the worst child exploitation at this time in Leeds involved the climbing boys. Day after day small boys acting as chimney sweeps were sent up confined and airless chimneys to clean the flues. Despite public outrage little was done to stop the practice. A meeting was held at the Court House in Leeds in February 1818 to discuss the problem. Joseph Haddock, a master sweep who employed five such boys, four of them orphans, made a pertinent point when he asked what would his boys do for sustenance if their occupation were outlawed.

It was Haddock who was involved in one of the most appalling cases of maltreatment of one boy in 1825. Ten years-old Thomas Lee was the illegitimate son of an African woman who had recently drowned in the River Aire. Employed by Haddock, he was goaded up the chimneys by other apprentices. His knees were lacerated and when, after sweeping seven chimneys in one day, he said he was unable to climb again, he was beaten. He finally absconded and was eventually taken to the workhouse for protection and treatment. Yet despite public outcries over the years about similar cases, no positive action was taken nationally until the Chimney Sweeps Act was passed fifty years later.

That same year of 1825 saw England plunged into a major banking crisis. A speculative boom and an excess of banknotes issued by country banks as well as by the Bank of England precipitated the situation. Seventy banks stopped payment. In December a meeting in Leeds was called and the prominent members of the town signed a declaration stating their full confidence in the stability of the local banks.

Yet despite economic crises, political upheavals and social unrest, improvements were carried out in Leeds which transformed the face of the town and many of the activities in it. It was always felt by many that the way forward to a better society was through education. Joseph Lancaster, one of the pioneers of the monitorial system of teaching, came to the Music Hall in Leeds in February 1809 and explained his methods. He claimed that one teacher with the help of older pupils acting as monitors could teach up to 1,000 children. So impressed were the listeners that in January 1811 a Lancasterian school was established in Leeds for boys and later one for girls. Handicapped children in the schools it was reported, 'are generally most apt at their learning'. Two years later the Church of England opened one of its mixed National Schools just off Kirkgate. Sunday schools and dame schools also made some impact on literacy both in Leeds and the out-townships. It was a beginning but nevertheless thousands of children were still left to roam the streets of Leeds illiterate and abandoned.

In 1813 a new court-house with a small prison was opened at the junction of Park Row and what is now City Square. Here the council met, courts were held and a new Rotation Office was established where the magistrates met on a rotation basis. Its great room could hold 800 people. It was used for public meetings but if they became oversubscribed they were suspended and quickly reconvened in the nearby spacious open yard of the Coloured Cloth Hall.

June 1815 saw a newly refurbished Leeds Theatre reopened on Hunslet Lane. Press reports described its scarlet pit seats, its green boxes and gallery, its neat chandeliers 'with brilliant cut drops', and its proscenium arch surmounted with the Leeds Arms.

Three years later, in January 1818, a public meeting set up the Leeds, Skyrack and Morley Savings Bank to cater for the needs of the 'labouring and industrious' residents of the area. It subsequently opened its offices in Bank Street on market days between 12 noon and 1.30 p.m.

The following year letters appeared in the *Mercury* suggesting the formation of a Philosophical and Literary Society in the town. Di Vernon wrote pleading that the society should be open to women. It was eventually decided to form such a society but to keep it an all-male preserve. Its lectures catered for a Leeds middle class eager for knowledge and in 1826 John Marshall proposed that a university should be established in the town.* On 9 July 1819 Benjamin Gott laid the foundation stone of the Leeds Philosophical Hall in Park Row. It eventually became the first Leeds City Museum. Another society with less rigorous membership terms, the Leeds Literary Institution, was founded in 1834.

It was members of the Philosophical and Literary Society who recognised the need to offer working-class people the opportunity for self-improvement and in 1825 the Leeds Mechanics' Institute opened in a house in Park Row. That same year Moot Hall and the straggling row of buildings behind it, Middle Row, were swept away to open up Briggate and make it a thoroughfare capable of handling the increased volume of traffic in the town.

---

* The Yorkshire College of Science which eventually became the University of Leeds was not established until 1874.

The 1820s saw a plethora of public buildings being erected: the Bazaar and Shambles off Briggate between 1823 and 1825; the Fish Market in what is now Fish Street about 1824; the Central Market on Duncan Street between 1824 and 1827; South Market between Hunslet Lane and Meadow Lane between 1823 and 1824; and, between 1826 and 1829, the Leeds Commercial Buildings at the junction of Park Row and Boar Lane. Here, amid considerable opulence, Leeds businessmen could meet and consult the leading magazines and newspapers of the day, including the long-established *Leeds Mercury* and *Leeds Intelligencer*, as well as the newcomers, the *Leeds Patriot, Leeds Times, Leeds Independent* and *Leeds Gazette.** The Commercial Buildings became a focal point for the Leeds Whig-Liberal Party.

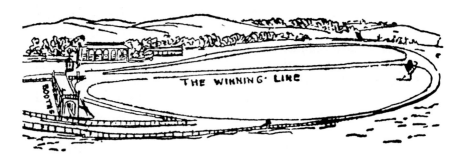

12. Leeds Racecourse
Leeds Races held at Haigh Park in the 1820s attracted crowds of up to fifty thousand. Note the Grand Stand, a 'prominent, safe and eligible erection', capable of holding a thousand spectators. The *Leeds Independent* not only supported the races but also published a series of race cards known as 'Correct Cards' from which this illustration is taken.

During those early decades of the century politics was never far from the surface of life in Leeds although cultural activities and sporting events certainly attracted attention. Leeds was able to boast that it held concerts 'inferior to no town in the kingdom, except the metropolis', whilst the Leeds Races, held annually between 1824 and 1830 at Haigh Park south of the river, could attract crowds of up to forty to fifty thousand for the Golden Tureen Race. But time and again it was politics which returned to dominate life in Leeds.

---

*   Neither the *Gazette* nor the *Independent* was long-lived. The *Patriot* was published from 1824 to 1833, and the *Leeds Times* from 1833. The *Leeds Correspondent* was not a weekly newspaper but published between 1815 and 1822 and concentrated on literary, mathematical and philosophical issues. There were several other such magazines, generally short-lived, also published in Leeds.

The Tory–Anglican community was firmly established as the ruling group on the town's council and favoured the status quo. The Whigs and Nonconformists were incensed at being so politically marginalised and unable to influence the governing body. It was left to Edward Baines to devise a strategy which wrong-footed his Tory opponents. He and his supporters did so by launching an assault through the parish vestry.

Every ratepayer, irrespective of religious belief or political affiliation, was entitled to attend the vestry meetings and take part in selecting the eighteen churchwardens. The churchwardens had the responsibility for levying a rate on the town for the running of the parish church, and for sharing with the council the administration of the Improvement Commission, the Highway Surveyors and the workhouse. It was the vestry which set up the Vagrancy Office in Vicar Lane to combat the difficulties 'vagrants, impostors and travelling beggars' repeatedly brought to the town.

In the vestry meetings the Whigs argued that greater economy should be exercised by the churchwardens. In 1818 Baines objected not to the vicar's introduction of a robed and surpliced choir, the first in England since the Reformation, but that it should be paid for by the ratepayers. In 1819 he demanded that the parish accounts should be published. Cawood, the vestry treasurer was furious and despite the vestry voting to do so, it was three years before the figures were finally made public. The Whig–Liberals' campaign of forcing a reduction in parish expenditure created such interest that when a meeting was called to appoint a new church organist, between 4,000 and 6,000 ratepayers turned up and it was necessary to hold the gathering in the yard of the nearby White Cloth Hall.

By 1827 it was agreed that every item of public expenditure should be voted on. A year later the campaign finally succeeded and the Whig–Liberals found themselves in a majority on the vestry and a considerable cutback on expenditure began.* That same year the Nonconformists in Leeds were able to celebrate the removal of what they considered to be the insulting Test and Corporation Acts which discriminated against them on account of their religious beliefs.

The question then uppermost in people's minds was whether this presaged the removal of the discrimination against Roman Catholics. Across the country, Tory Brunswick Clubs were formed in direct opposition to any such move. The Leeds Brunswick Club had as its voice the *Leeds Intelligencer* and vehemently denounced any change in the law as

---

* After 1835 no church rate was ever again levied in the town.

an all-out attempt to destroy the Church of England. The pro-Catholics had the *Leeds Mercury* as their mouthpiece. Handbills were distributed in the town by both sides and letters supporting and denouncing changes in the law appeared in the press. Patrick Brontë, writing from his windswept parsonage at Haworth, expressed his concern in the columns of the *Intelligencer* at any amendment to the law.

Feelings ran high in Leeds. A Protestant declaration claimed to have at least 1,000 signatures; the pro-Catholic faction sneered that many of the signatures were spurious. On Friday 28 November 1828 a demonstration gathered at the *Intelligencer* offices on Commercial Street and marched to the Coloured Cloth Hall yard, its banners proclaiming 'Vote Against Popery'. Some 18,000 supporters of both sides finally gathered there. John Marshall, the Yorkshire MP, acted as chairman because the mayor, Ralph Markland, had refused to do so. The crowd paid little heed to Marshall's requests for order. Speakers could hardly make themselves heard, missiles were thrown and the meeting broke up in disorder. But the following year Wellington's government acknowledged the need for change and introduced the Catholic Emancipation Bill.

However, a crisis even greater than that of the Catholic claims was about to erupt in the country and in the views of some historians bring it as close to revolution as the dark days of the Civil War. The issue was the reform of Parliament. The demands for reform had rumbled on for decades as the anomalies of the existing system were pointed out. Neither Manchester, Birmingham nor Leeds had one Member of Parliament between them. Leeds almost acquired Parliamentary representation at the end of 1819 when the voters of Grampound lost their right to have two members for 'the grossest corruption'. But Leeds's hopes came to nothing and the two Grampound seats were added to those for the county of Yorkshire.

Voting rights differed from borough to borough and denied suffrage to the vast majority of people. Middle-class Whigs were particularly incensed that it was their commercial enterprise which was generating the new wealth in the country. They argued that their stake in the country was immense yet despite that, they were being denied a say in how it was governed. Meanwhile the working classes also demanded an equal say in how the country was run.

The Leeds Radicals, led by James Mann, believed that every man should have a vote; the more moderate Whig Leeds Association led by Edward Baines, John Marshall and John Clapham argued that it should be restricted to the middle classes. The Tories were bitterly opposed to any change and the new editor of the *Leeds Intelligencer*, Robert

Perring, sneered about the Bainesocracy that now ruled in the West Riding. In 1831 the House of Lords threw out a bill to reform Parliament. Riots broke out in Nottingham, Derby and Bristol. In Leeds the effigy of the Prime Minister, the Duke of Wellington, was paraded through the streets and burnt.

Meanwhile another struggle was beginning to emerge in Leeds which would eventually dominate the nation as Leeds-born Richard Oastler, the 'Factory King', launched his campaign for factory reform. In September 1830, Oastler submitted a letter to the *Mercury* for publication. Headed 'Yorkshire Slavery', it identified the appalling conditions to which children were exposed in the mills of the West Riding.

It was not the first time that the dangerous conditions present in the local factories and mills had been brought to the public's attention. As far back as 1823 Alaric Watts, editor of the *Leeds Intelligencer*, had visited the Infirmary and published a damning account of the injured factory workers he saw there. But it was the series of Oastler's letters that launched the crusade. They placed Baines in a quandary. He abhorred the suffering reported but at the same time the people Oastler was attacking were his own manufacturing friends and supporters. When Baines's son, also called Edward, edited one of Oastler's letters, the reformer was furious and asked the *Leeds Intelligencer* to publish it in full. It gleefully did.

Charles Thackrah, a Leeds surgeon, added fuel to the controversy. Thackrah had already made a significant contribution to medicine in the town. After opening a private medical school in 1824 which the Royal College of Surgeons refused to accept, he along with other like-minded individuals set up the Leeds School of Medicine in the Dispensary on North Street. That same year, 1831, he published his classic work *The Effects of Arts, Trades and Professions . . . on Health and Longevity* and gained a national reputation. When Oastler's ally Michael Sadler, the Leeds linen merchant and Tory MP for Aldbrough, spoke in the Commons supporting the Ten Hour Bill he quoted the work at length. Thackrah well knew the problems of urban industrial life. He had spent all his working life in Leeds both as a general practitioner and poor-law doctor.

The government's Factory Commissioners have left behind graphic accounts of what they found in the town. Children of six and seven years of age were reported to be working thirteen hours a day and subject to beatings from overseers. Sarah Price stated that she worked at Marshall's mill from 5 a.m. to 9 p.m. each day when she was seven years of age. Charles Binns, another Marshall employee, testified when he was fifteen, 'We used to get beaten. They used to strap us.' Mark Best, an overlooker at the mill, admitted, 'There was a good deal of strapping at Marshall's.'

Marshall's mill reflected the harsh practices common in mills and factories of the time and its owner was held up as a *bête noire* by his enemies. But at the same time he demonstrated a sense of responsibility to his young workers by opening a school for them during working hours in 1825. By 1833 he was sending his eight to eleven years-old workers there for half of each day. His school became a national model providing not only for his own children but those of other employers in the district.

But whilst Oastler, supported by many working men and women, continued his campaign, a second parliamentary reform bill was introduced in May 1832, this time by the new Whig government of Lord Grey. The House of Lords again rejected it. Grey urged the king to appoint sufficient peers to ensure it was passed. The king refused and the Leeds True Blue Constitutional Association congratulated him. The Leeds Tories objected to the bill because it went too far, the Leeds Radicals because it did not go far enough. And thus they formed an unlikely alliance.

Those in favour of reform were furious and acted. The Whigs in Leeds called a meeting in the yard of the Coloured Cloth Hall where, it is claimed, 30,000 turned up with another 50,000 unable to gain admittance. Some of the Tory–Radicals present were manhandled and the meeting was clearly in favour of change. When it was suggested that the king was loath to act because of his wife's influence, the crowd gave three groans for the queen!

Historians still dispute how close England came to civil war in the week that followed Grey's defeat. Wellington realised the gravity of the situation and advised the king to allow the bill to be passed. So the middle classes in Leeds received the vote and prepared for a general election.

Thomas Babington Macaulay, the historian, and John Marshall Junior, the flax magnate's son were the Whig candidates. Michael Thomas Sadler, the ardent campaigner for factory reform, stood for the Tories. It was a violent election. Fighting broke out in the streets and when nomination day arrived an all-out battle was fought. The Tory–Radical supporters of Sadler arrived at the Coloured Cloth Hall yard carrying a 200-foot banner signed with 4,000 signatures. It showed half-naked children dragging themselves to Marshall's mill in a snowstorm. Chaos followed as both sets of supporters attacked each other and it was half an hour before order was restored and the Battle of the Standard was finally over.

In the election Macaulay and Marshall were victorious but Macaulay later resigned. In the 1834 by-election that followed, Edward Baines scraped home by just thirty-four votes to win for the Whig–Liberals. The Tory supporters of Sir John Beckett argued that their opponents had acted illegally and that Beckett should have been the overall winner. There was strong opposition by the working classes to the Whig–Liberals in Leeds, and the extent of the power of the Tory Party in the town was shown in the general election of 1835. Beckett turned the tables to win by 148 votes. It was an academic but significant win. Baines was returned as the second member for the borough but Leeds recorded the first victory by a Tory candidate in a newly franchised industrial town. That same year, workers in Leeds formed the first Tory operatives' club in England.

Meanwhile Oastler's campaign for factory reform was to drag on for years before the Ten Hour Bill was eventually passed in 1847. If successive governments dragged their feet over factory reform, Grey's government

13. Tunstall's Fold, Mabgate
Typical of the slum areas of Leeds, these houses by Tunstall's Fold in Mabgate posed serious health hazards in the nineteenth and early twentieth centuries. Evolving piecemeal from 1790, the different roof heights and lack of paving clearly show the haphazard manner in which such low cost properties were developed.

moved swiftly with regard to town councils. In 1835 it introduced the Municipal Reform Bill and brought to an end the closed corporation in Leeds which had existed since 1626. The Whigs, now becoming known as the Liberals, were swept to power and dominated the town for the next fifty years.

Whilst Britain was caught up in the turmoil of the Reform Bill the scourge of cholera was sweeping across the continent. It reached England in 1831 and on 26 May 1832 it appeared in Leeds. At 5 a.m. that morning, Dock, the two years-old son of an Irish family living in Blue Bell Fold in the Bank area of the town, fell ill. He died at 3 p.m. the same afternoon. The disease then ravaged the insanitary, squalid areas of the town. It raged amid the streets of back-to-back houses, factories and gas works. A cholera hospital was established in St Peter's Square but frightened locals smashed its windows and the refuge had to be moved to Saxton Lane. Of the 1,817 cases in Leeds 702 people died.

Robert Baker, the town surgeon, drew up a series of graphic reports over the following years which have become classics in the field of public health. He clearly identified the worst outbreaks as occurring in the insanitary, overcrowded slum areas of the town. Pools of stagnant water lay under doorways, and privies were 'so laden with ashes and excrementitious matter as to be unuseable'. In the Boot and Shoe Yard, a cul-de-sac of thirty-four houses, some 340 people lived. In summer when itinerant summer labourers arrived the number doubled. It took seventy-five cartloads to remove the human dung that had accumulated there. The most overcrowded area was Wellington Yard where some 773 people shared just sixty-seven houses.

The authorities were generally slow to react, however. The council failed to implement the Improvement Act of 1842 and in 1847 typhus appeared in the town. It was particularly virulent in the poor areas of the overcrowded and notorious Bank district. Six houses were identified where forty-seven people were huddled together without a bed between them. Perhaps it was not surprising that in one week five suicides occurred in the town. The infection decimated the Irish immigrant population. Five Catholic priests and a curate from the Parish Church all perished tending their flocks. Lessons were still not acted upon and in 1848 cholera returned. Once again Baker was able to show that there were no deaths in the better class areas of Park Square, Park Row and Park Place.

The 1848–9 cholera epidemic raged worst in the unhealthy narrow streets which had been developed in the previous twenty years to the west of the town and south of Park Lane. One curate from the Parish Church,

Revd E. A. Jackson, was called by an Irishwoman to visit a dying girl. He was shown into an upper room where the broken windows were stuffed with brown paper and old rags. His description of the scene was stark:

> I could at first discern nothing but what seemed a dark bundle of rags. By degrees I became conscious of a dirty cotton gown, with two legs sticking out, partly covered with some remnant of stockings, and in the extreme corner, propped up against a wall, a ghastly head; the face pallid and emaciated to the last degree, the eyes sunk, the nose sharp as before death, the lips vivid, the teeth set in convulsions. Under the dying woman was a handful of straw, and this was all there was between her and the boards on which she was laid.

The pestilence carried off some 1,674 people in Leeds itself and another 300 or more in the out-townships.

By the mid-nineteenth century Queen Victoria had begun her long, eventful reign. It was marred in the early 1840s by a series of economic crises which produced what became known as the 'Hungry Forties'. However, by the late1840s Britain's economic progress began to escalate dramatically. As her industries expanded and her export trade grew she was eventually able to claim to be 'the workshop of the world'. The rising standard of living was particularly noticeable among the middle classes – the manufacturers, merchants and shareholders of Victorian Britain.

But the major social problems of pollution, prostitution and poverty still had to be resolved. Leeds had to confront them, as did every other emerging town. 'Septimus', writing to the *Leeds Times*, spoke of the 'dark and murky cloud' which 'choked the lungs of the Leeds people'. He also denounced the apathy that his fellow townsfolk showed to 'one of the most alarming and frightful nuisances in existence'. It was more than simply a nuisance when dense fogs such as the one in December 1839 brought the town to a halt. Day after day smoke poured into the residential areas like Woodhouse Square and from 1851 the wealthier middle classes began their migration north to the more pleasant suburb of Headingley. Not surprisingly, meetings like the one called in the Music Hall in Albion Street in January 1842 were arranged to consider the problem. Some Leeds firms such as Marshalls, Murrays and Gotts had already taken steps to reduce emissions but they were in a minority. Compounding factory pollution was that produced by every fireplace in every house in Leeds. In 1824 one individual at least took a different line. In a letter to the *Mercury*, 'Philanthropist' of Chapeltown objected in principle to any public interference with pollution!

Prostitution was also still a major concern with Millgarth recognised as the red light district of Leeds. By 1840 there were some ninety-eight brothels in the town and the *Leeds Times* singled out the Ship Inn as being one of the most notorious. To combat it another voluntary institution, the Leeds Lock Hospital, was opened in York Street in 1842 to treat diseases 'the very subject of which is avoided in conversation' and in 1847 the Leeds Guardians offered help 'to unfortunate females' in their asylum in St James's Street.

The Poor Law Amendment Act of 1834 sought to address the perennial problem of poverty. Outdoor relief for the able-bodied was brought to an end. Relief for inmates in the workhouse was to be made as austere, forbidding and disagreeable as possible. The cost of implementing the Poor Law in Leeds imposed the single largest item of expenditure on the town and it was obvious by the 1840s that more outlay was required. A new workhouse was essential. The old one on Lady Lane was totally inadequate: it was overcrowded, unhygienic and immoral. A permanent noxious stench from a nearby refuse tip hung over the place and children as young as twelve had been discovered having sexual intercourse in the privies.

The Workhouse Board was made up of overseers appointed by the corporation and the vestry's trustees. The battle for power between Liberals and Tories for control of the board raged on through the 1830s. The board had refused to implement the 1834 Act arguing that it was inappropriate to Leeds and recognised that the cost of building a new workhouse would never be accepted by the ratepayers of the town. However, in 1844 part of the Act was implemented and a Board of Guardians formed.

When the Tories won the Poor Law election they decided against building a new workhouse but they did put forward a proposal to create an industrial school for 499 orphans and pauper children at Burmantofts. It would concentrate on teaching the skills they would need to prevent them from becoming burdens on society and thus the curriculum contained lessons in gardening, tailoring, shoe-making, and training for domestic service. The Moral and Industrial Training School opened in 1848. It would form part of what eventually became St James's Hospital.

The new Poor Law did not resolve the problem of poverty and reports were still appearing in the press of people literally starving to death in the streets of Leeds during the 1840s. Two such were eighty-seven years-old Irish vagrant Peter Brabson and twenty-four years-old Henry Halstead who was also 'given to intemperance'. And intemperance itself was a concern. Between 1826 and 1836 the number of alehouses in the town had doubled. To come to terms with the excessive drunkenness the Leeds Temperance Society was inaugurated in 1830.

It published it own newspaper, the *Leeds Temperance Herald*, held Temperance Festivals and organised trips to places like Castle Howard. In 1847 in a bid to attract young people before they became addicted to drink, the Revd Jabez Tunnicliff founded the Band of Hope in Leeds. Within two years more than 4,000 of the town's children aged between six and sixteen had taken the pledge. Joseph Cliff, owner of the brick-yard at Wortley went so far as to buy the Albion Inn which stood on Upper Wortley Road. He turned it into an alcohol-free house that sold tea and coffee. But it was the churches and chapels that mainly led the campaign against intemperance.

In the forefront of that battle were the Leeds Baptists, though they were ably abetted by the majority of the Nonconformist churches. Among those were the Leeds Methodists, for Methodism was the dom-inant religious force in the town and commanded the greatest support from the working classes. But Methodism in Leeds was a divided and at times factious denomination. The New Connexion broke away from the Wesleyan Methodists and then in 1828 a further rupture occurred.

Differences between worshippers came to head in the new Brunswick Chapel on Brunswick Street which opened in 1825. The building was a magnificent structure capable of housing a congregation of 2,500 in boxed pews and according to one description was 'one of the largest and most magnificent ecclesiastical buildings in the empire'. Some members of the congregation felt that the installation of an organ would make the building complete. Others vigorously objected on the grounds that to build one would be an act of middle-class pride and even popish symbolism. There were also other disputes rumbling in various Wesleyan chapels across the town. Eventually twenty-eight local preachers and 900 members left their existing places of worship to join the dis-senting Brunswickers and form the Leeds Protestant Methodists.

It was into this hotbed of Methodism that a new vicar of Leeds, Walter Farquhar Hook, arrived in 1837. In Leeds there were twice as many Nonconformists as Anglicans and the new vicar was forced to admit that, as far as Leeds was concerned, 'The *de facto* established reli-gion is Methodism.' However, a more significant fact Hook had to recognise was that in the township of Leeds there were 60,000 people of worshipping age but only 20,000 attended church or chapel. The appointment of Hook was to have a significant impact not simply upon the members of the Church of England in the town but upon its whole population. He was man of unbounded energy, who as a zealous parish priest demonstrated admirable qualities of leadership and strove end-lessly for the welfare of the working classes.

Theologically he was a moderate High Churchman and believed if services were properly performed in the Church 'right-minded people will soon learn to love her'. He determined that Leeds would have musical services as befitted a major town 'even if I have to go to prison for it', and introduced a weekly instead of a monthly communion service. During 1846 and 1847 he organised services four times daily with sermons every evening except Saturdays. He excelled as a preacher and never repeated the same sermon twice. In one he declared: '[W]hile we pray we must labour. We pray for the harvest, but we must at the same time sow the seed'. He assiduously followed his own advice.

It was patently obvious when Hook arrived in Leeds that the present old church was now inadequate. As his earnestness and zeal galvanised many of his parishioners, St Peter's was filled to capacity every Sunday and late-comers were having to be turned away. In the two years between 1837 and 1839 the number of communicants increased from about fifty to between 400 and 500. Hook initially hoped to modify the old building but it was found to be in such a poor state of repair that rebuilding became the only option.

It was an expensive operation made even more difficult as the country at the time was passing through the economic recession popularly known as the 'Hungry Forties'. Nevertheless support was forthcoming from all social quarters: there were wealthy donors like Beckett and Gott, but the poor too made their contributions. Robert Chantrell, the Leeds architect, devised schemes to reduce costs wherever possible. Some of the 'stone' vaulting of the crossing was made of wood and plaster and the 'oak' decoration on the galleries was in fact iron and plaster. But when it was opened on 2 September 1841 the *Leeds Intelligencer* was moved to remark that the church was 'one of the finest if not the finest in the kingdom'.

Another major contribution Hook made to the town was the provision of day schools. When he arrived there were just three church schools in the town. In 1839, Hook and his associates set up the Anglican Board of Education for Leeds. By raising funds locally he was able then to draw on government grants to establish more National Schools. He eventually increased the number in the town to thirty.

The 1841 census indicated that the population of Leeds had reached 88,741 and with the out-townships made a grand total of 152,054. Hook recognised that the medieval arrangement of St Peter's acting as the Parish Church for such a large population was totally inadequate. His aim was to subdivide the old parish and create new ones. It was an idea which had been mooted long before. In 1650 during the time of Cromwell's Commonwealth, a proposal had been made to divide the parish. St

John's, Hunslet, Holbeck and Beeston were to be formed into separate parishes. Farnley, Armley, Wortley and Bramley were to form a single parish, Allerton and Headingley another. But nothing came of the idea.

Hook's stated hope for Leeds was 'for every poor man to have a pastor and every poor child a school'. The Leeds Vicarage Act was given the royal assent in August 1844. It made provision for the creation of new parishes when the need arose, for the building of schools and parsonages and for an increase in the number of free pew seats.

The Nonconformists, led by the *Leeds Mercury*, bitterly attacked the Act. They were not Hook's only critics. His own churchwardens condemned him for refusing to reuse consecrated wine left over after service! And at times he was criticised on theological grounds by both the Anglo-Catholics and by the Evangelicals.

Hook believed that ritual played an important part in worship. But some incumbents went so far as to introduce confessional boxes, sprinkle holy water on the congregation and hang stations of the cross around the walls giving their churches a distinctly Roman Catholic air about them. Hook, however, never introduced a new practice or object in church unless his congregation asked for it.

At this time a new movement had originated at Oxford University known as the Oxford Movement or Tractarianism, which was dedicated to encouraging a revival of Catholic traditions within the Church of England. It was led by the Oxford academics John Keble, John Newman and Edward Pusey and generated much opposition from those Church members who feared anything which smacked of the Church of Rome. Hook had some sympathy with the early movement but took exception to the more extreme Tractarians.

In 1845 Pusey himself paid for the erection of St Saviour's Church in order to bring High Church worship into a working-class area of Leeds. It stood on Ellerby Road south-east of the Parish Church and was administered by a group of clergy who lived almost monastic lives, introduced a daily Mass and carried out practices mostly associated with Roman Catholicism. Hook was furious that his own Act had created the independence of St Saviour's parish where such practices could be followed and the Bishop of Ripon considered it 'a plague-spot in my diocese'. Both Anglican and Nonconformist clergy condemned what they saw as a move to popery. The Baptists went so far as to build a school-room in the area in 1847 and two years later the Wesleyans opened a new chapel at Richmond Hill; both had the avowed intention of counteracting what they saw as the pernicious influence of these latter-day papists.

The Roman Catholics themselves built a new church at the bottom of Cookridge Street facing down Park Row. It was dominated by a 148-foot-high spire. St Anne's was opened for worship in 1838. A presbytery and schools were built adjacent to it. Forty years later it became a cathedral when the old diocese of Beverley was divided and those of Middlesbrough and Leeds created.

It is difficult today in a more tolerant and secular age for people to grasp the passions and bitterness generated by different denominations at that time, in particular the fear of Roman Catholicism. Similarly it is equally difficult to grasp the depth of feeling regarding the sanctity of the Sabbath which became particularly noticeable in the 1840s. Feelings ran so high that Robert Perring, the long-serving editor of the *Leeds Intelligencer*, decided to launch the *Leeds Wednesday Journal*. It appeared on 6 January 1841 specifically published on a Wednesday because all the other Leeds papers, his own included, were produced on a Saturday. In remote places they were not received until the Sunday which, Perring pointed out, 'is not a day for political discussion or the amusement of light reading'. But the enterprise was not a commercial success and lasted only a matter of weeks.

Strong feelings were also generated in the town over the new Leeds Zoological and Botanical Gardens which opened in 1840. Throughout 1841 a public debate ensued in the Leeds press as to whether the gardens should be opened on a Sunday. The Sabbatarians were adamant that Sunday was a day of rest and to open the gardens would bring the 'vilest characters as well as the most frivolous, worldly and worthless' to the area. The radical *Leeds Times*, under its editor Samuel Smiles, took the view that Sunday was the only day working people could enjoy the facility and that Sabbath freedom was 'part of the great question of civil and religious liberty'. A compromise was finally reached and the venue opened from 4 p.m. to sunset. The gardens were not a success, however, and by 1848 had been sold. Their only remaining feature is the bear pit which can be seen on Cardigan Road.

Religious differences were not the only ones that divided the town. Dissatisfied with the outcome of the Reform Bill a working-class movement emerged nationally. In 1838 it drew up a charter demanding manhood suffrage, equal electoral districts, voting by ballot, annual parliaments, abolition of the property qualification for MPs, and payment of MPs. The movement became known as Chartism. In Leeds, Feargus O'Connor, a radical journalist, launched the *Northern Star* which became its national voice. Some middle-class radicals in the town, men like James Garth Marshall, Hamer Stansfeld, George Goodman and Samuel Smiles, sympathised with its aims and formed the Leeds

Parliamentary Reform Association in order for 'the improvement in our Political Institutions, and the Extension of the Franchise to the great Mass of the People by all legal and constitutional means'. In January 1841 a massive meeting was held at Marshall's new mill which attracted some 7,000 working-class and middle-class radicals from across the country. But the alliance between middle and working classes was not to last. More radical Chartists like Feargus O'Connor saw it as no more than a 'Fox and Goose Club'.

The anger of the more violent Chartists and recurrent unemployment, poverty and near starvation during the 'Hungry Forties' led to outbreaks of violence. The Leeds Police force, which had only been established in 1836, found itself facing a major crisis in August 1842 as the Plug Riots erupted. By smashing the plugs from boilers, Chartist insurgents across the North sought to bring entire factories to a standstill. Rioters stopped the mills at Farnley and Wortley and then sought reinforcements in Pudsey before attacking the mills in Armley. The Chief Constable, Edward Read, led his force armed with cutlasses and heavy batons. A further 1,200 special constables followed. A troop of the 17th Lancers under Prince George, a party of the 18th Infantry with fixed bayonets, the Royal Horse Artillery with a mounted field piece and a troop of the Ripon Yeomanry completed the detachment.

News reached Read that the insurgents had made for Holbeck and he diverted his men accordingly. The mob broke into Marshall's mill but they were unable to locate the boiler plug. The Riot Act was read and the crowd eventually dispersed. An uneasy peace hung over the town. The Freemasons of Savile Lodge No. 677 held no meetings in August, its members were engaged in keeping guard over the peace of the town and neighbourhood. Of the insurgents thirty-eight people were arrested and the Special Commission in York passed sentences which ranged from ten years deportation to being bound over to keep the peace.

For a time, however, Chartists made a more peaceful impact on the town, having a major influence in the vestry, taking control of the board of highway surveyors and for a time of the Improvement Commission. The last great year for the Chartists came in 1848. In Leeds mass demonstrations were held throughout the spring and summer at Vicar's Croft, on Woodhouse Moor and in Wellington Street. The movement gradually withered away but all of its aims, with the exception of annual parliaments, were eventually achieved.

Other issues also were dominating the attention of Leeds people. The need for a new burial ground had become essential. The privately owned Leeds General Cemetery, which had opened off Woodhouse

Lane, was only used by the Nonconformists. In 1842 the Leeds Burial Act made provision for the establishment of a public graveyard which would accommodate both Anglicans and Nonconformists and in 1845 Burmantofts Cemetery on Beckett Street was opened. Conscious of religious differences, even in death, it was divided into two with an identical chapel built in each half, one for the Anglicans and one for the Nonconformists.

Demands for a suitable jail in the town were also answered in 1847 when James Beaumont became the first inmate of the newly built

14. First photograph taken in Leeds. Philip Foster aged five posing for possibly the first photograph taken in the town. Before William Huggon opened his Photographic Portrait Gallery in Park Row to the public in 1844 he invited his local doctor's family down for a sitting. The first photograph he took was young Philip.

Borough Jail at Armley. The necessity for an improved water supply led the council in 1852 to exercise its option to take over the local water company.

Meetings were called to campaign for the repeal of the Corn Laws, to debate the respective advantages and disadvantages of state controlled education as opposed to education provided by the voluntary sector, and to urge immediate help for the people of Ireland and Scotland as the potato famine swept across the United Kingdom. The Leeds area itself lost twenty per cent of its winter harvest, but the devastation which followed in Ireland left between one million and one and a half million dead.

There were, however, lighter moments for the people of Leeds as famous visitors like George Stephenson and Charles Dickens arrived to lecture at the newly amalgamated Mechanics' Institute and Literary Institution. Some 1,300 listened to the great author despite his suffering from a 'disastrous cold'. Those who could afford it visited the newly opened Photographic Portrait Gallery at 27 Park Row. There, William Huggon would take their picture using the new daguerreotype process and supply it in a morocco case. Even colour photographs were available. Large crowds gathered to watch the balloon ascents in the Botanical Gardens or the games of knur and spell played on Woodhouse Moor for as much as £10 a stake.

Despite the seemingly eternal social and political problems facing its inhabitants, Leeds was unquestionably a thriving and successful town. In December 1844 the Leeds Stock Exchange Association was formed. Whereas in 1836 there had been only two stockbrokers in Leeds, by 1845 there were over 100. In January that year the association opened for business and, by 1847, had its own premises in Albion Street. For many years Leeds remained the only provincial town with a purpose-built stock exchange and thus it was perhaps not surprising that Henry Brougham, the one-time Whig Lord Chancellor, remarked that it was, 'one of the finest towns of the Empire, the seat of the greatest commercial community in Yorkshire'. It was then with utter chagrin that the merchants and manufacturers who made up that commercial community realised that, in Bradford, St George's Hall had been erected to meet the 'cultural needs of a business metropolis'. Leeds had no such public building. Not to be outdone, a move was launched to provide Leeds with a similar one but the plans were changed. In January 1851 the council decided to build not a public hall but a Town Hall, and one which would demonstrate to the world the pride Leeds felt in its achievements.

CHAPTER SEVEN

BECOMING A CITY

At the beginning of 1851 discussions across the town centred on more than the proposed Town Hall. For some time interest had focused on the forthcoming Great Exhibition which was to be held in Hyde Park. It was an interest that cut across class barriers. For months the inhabitants of the West Riding had been discussing the event and many working-class people from Leeds and the out-townships intended to join the 60,000 visitors who would daily visit Paxton's famous Crystal Palace. The new railways had made travel so much easier and when the entrance fee was dropped on four days a week to one shilling, visits became much more affordable. Parties left Leeds at 7.45 a.m. arriving in the capital at 5 p.m. Middle-class fears that thousands of workers descending upon the exhibition would bring chaos and outbreaks of violence proved to be groundless.

Prince Albert's brainchild was an attempt to demonstrate to the world the superiority of British industry. It was an opportunity that did not escape the attention of Leeds businessmen who were ever eager to demonstrate their commercial activities. That same year the mayor, George Goodman, called a public meeting at the Court House to form the Leeds Chamber of Commerce.* It was set up to stimulate trade by finding new markets. Moreover, it was a campaigning organisation anxious to combat dishonesty in trading and eager to win a significant reduction of restrictions on businesses in the town. It also sent delegates to view foreign exhibitions and report on technological innovations they found.

The Great Exhibition of 1851 was an ideal opportunity for British manufacturers, and of 7,000 United Kingdom exhibitors 142 came from Leeds. The town itself made a contribution of £1,600 towards the Great Exhibition and Leeds's success was recognised when a substantial number of prizes were awarded to several of its cloth manufacturers. Gott and Sons had on show examples of the cloth they regularly exported to China, America and Russia whilst John Walker and Son clearly demonstrated just how efficient Leeds industrialists were. When Queen

---

* A Leeds Chamber of Commerce had existed previously for a short time between 1785 and 1793.

Victoria opened the exhibition on Thursday 1 May 1851 a customer placed an order at the Walker's stand for 2,000 yards of crimson cloth. It was telegraphed to Leeds and, by 7 a.m. on Tuesday 6 May, the consignment was delivered in London.

It was to celebrate the civic pride the town felt in its industrial and commercial achievements that in January 1851 the council finally voted, by twenty-four votes to twelve, to build a Town Hall. Dr John Deacon summed up the mood of the town saying what Leeds needed was a 'noble magnificent palace' to vie with 'the best town halls of the Continent'. Joseph Paxton, the designer of the Crystal Palace, was consulted and various towns were visited to view their civic buildings. The site chosen was occupied by a house owned by John Blayds and at the time rented by Dr Richard Hobson. The council decided to hold a competition for the design and offered a first prize of £200. Cuthbert Brodrick, a twenty-nine years old Hull architect, was the winner and that despite the fact his mother had done her best to dissuade him from entering. She had argued that he was too young!*

In August 1853 a large crowd gathered to celebrate the laying of the foundation stone by the mayor, John Hope Shaw, but not everyone was in agreement about the building. A disagreement rumbled on for a time as to whether the new hall should have a tower or not. Work on the building was slow and disputes between Brodrick and Samuel Atack, the builder, were common. Atack eventually went bankrupt and various other contractors had to be employed. At last the Town Hall was completed but the cost had soared from an estimated £41,835 to £122,000.

The official opening by Queen Victoria was fixed for Tuesday 7 September 1858. Excitement had begun to mount in the town in the preceding weeks. John Barran's shop in Briggate was offering 'flags, banners, bannerets and flag poles in every size, colour and description'; Hyam's advertised artificial flowers and decorations; and Fenteman and Son published *An Historical Guide to Leeds and its Environs*. Her Majesty arrived in Leeds accompanied by Prince Albert the day before the opening and was met at Central Station on Wellington Street by the mayor, Peter Fairbairn, and other civic dignitaries. She was then escorted to Woodsley House, Fairbairn's home on Clarendon Road. Huge crowds lined the route; streamers, banners, flags and specially constructed arches were everywhere in profusion. Mr Trant, the chemist on Park Lane, even went to the extent of perfuming the air outside his shop!

---

* Brodrick went on to design two of Leeds's finest mid-Victorian buildings: the Leeds Institute on Cookridge Street and the elliptical Corn Exchange.

143

The small fall of rain at about 7 a.m. next morning did not dampen the enthusiasm of the vast crowds that turned out. The route Victoria and Albert were to take had been carefully planned so that they could see much of the town without catching a glimpse of Brodrick's building. First the royal procession crossed Woodhouse Moor where 32,110 Sunday school children had been gathered. Then down Woodhouse Lane it went to Briggate, on Boar Lane, Wellington Street, Park Place and finally up East Parade. At the top was a magnificent triumphal arch and once the royal couple had passed through it, there in all its glory was the Town Hall itself.

The steps of the entrance had been covered in crimson cloth. Before the building a military guard of the 22nd Regiment with band and colours had been drawn up and a vast crowd assembled. One popular song of the time summed up the scene:

> To see the thousands of spectators,
> Round about the New Town Hall,
> Butchers, bakers, hotel-waiters,
> Tinkers, tailors, snobs and all;
> Children pouting, women shouting,
> To see the sight they all do run,
> Some are busy picking pockets,
> Some do take them as they come.

The great organ thundered out the national anthem, the Bishop of Ripon said prayers, the Hallelujah Chorus was sung and the Town Clerk read the loyal address to 'good Queen Victoria'. The queen in reply praised the building as 'a work well worthy of your active industry and enterprising spirit'.

That 'active industry and enterprising spirit' which had so successfully guided Leeds to the mid-point of the century was to prove itself extremely adaptable during the latter decades of the Victorian Age. The shape of industry in Leeds was changing. From about 1850 the trades which had given Leeds its wealth and power went into decline. Worsted manufacturers relocated themselves in Bradford. The heavy woollen districts of Dewsbury and Batley found themselves no longer dependent upon Leeds as the new railways enabled then to transport goods directly to Hull, Manchester and Liverpool and the flax industry saw increased competition from Ireland and Europe.

During the years of the so-called 'Great Depression' between 1873 and 1896 overseas competitors began to challenge Britain's industrial supremacy. In fifty years the number of mills in Leeds and the out-townships fell from 102 to 74. Though Leeds was still the centre for finishing and dyeing, local dyers were slow to adopt the newer synthetic dyes and to face the challenge coming from Germany. Gott and Son, the firm synonymous with Leeds textiles, closed down in 1870. For ten years Marshall's, who at one time absorbed a tenth of all the flax imported into Britain, ran at a loss. In 1886 production ceased and the plant and premises were auctioned off. By the last decade of the century textiles ceased to be the main employer in the town.

The coal industry, however, with its 102 collieries in the townships, continued to thrive. Seams, however, in 1875 were still generally worked only to a depth of about 300 feet and output from a shaft was, on average, less than 500 tons a day. But other established industries, like engineering, leather and chemicals, developed and new ones emerged, the most predominant being footwear, printing and clothing. By the end of the century engineering and clothing would come to dominate the rest.

15. Industrial scene from Richmond Hill
Victorian Britain was said to be 'the workshop of the world'. Looking west from Richmond Hill it is clear to see that by 1885 industry totally dominated the landscape of Leeds. One of the prices paid for the wealth it generated was appalling pollution. Symbolically, the Parish Church, right-centre, is almost lost in this industrial panorama.

In 1871 there were 174 puddling furnaces to be found south of the river, most being in Hunslet. Blast furnaces were sited at Farnley and along York Road. A forge had existed at Kirkstall from about 1600 and once the Butler family took it over in 1779 it prospered. By the nineteenth century it was producing some of the finest axles in the world. The railway industry that Murray had launched in the early years of the century spawned a series of highly successful engineering offspring. As the railway boom took off, an ex-apprentice of Murray's, Charles Todd, went into partnership with James Kitson and established their Airedale

Foundry in Hunslet. Todd went on to create the Railway Foundry with John Shepherd and then, on his own, the Sun Foundry in Dewsbury Road. His successors to that company, Carrett and Marshall, produced an innovative steam road vehicle for George Salt of Saltaire which was exhibited at the 1861 Royal Show in Leeds. The press acclaimed it as the 'most remarkable locomotive ever made'. But the law took a different view when one of its later owners, Frederick Hodges of Kent, dared to travel down the road at thirty miles an hour in it!

When the Railway Foundry closed several engineers took their skills elsewhere and the firm of Manning and Wardle was established. Hudswell and Clarke had also been employed at the foundry and set up their company in 1860. Four years later John Towlerton Leather founded the Hunslet Engine Company. The locomotives produced by such firms were exported world-wide and gained these Leeds engineering companies an international reputation.

It was a reputation enhanced by other engineering firms. The Leeds Steel works which opened in 1889 became Britains' largest producer of steel tram-tracks. John Fowler, who had pioneered the use of steam power in farming, set up the Steam Plough Works in Hunslet in 1860. His steam engines were exported to the United States, pulled Prussian guns during the Franco-Prussian War and transported military stores across the South African veldt during the Boer War. Thomas Green's company on North Street churned out a variety of equipment ranging from sausage machines to tennis ball cleaners whilst its mowing machines found favour at the royal courts of Russia and Japan.

Munitions produced at Greenwood and Batley's Armley works stocked the arsenals of Japan, China, Germany and Turkey. Twenty years after the firm of Balmforth, Smith and Booth was established in 1840 it embarked upon making cranes. By 1861 Thomas Smith acquired complete control of the company and Smiths of Rodley became synonymous with crane building. Other firms were busy producing nails, bolts, screws, spades and shovels, oil cans and oil lamps. George Bray and Company specialised in making non-corrosive gas burners for street lighting, and came to dominate the national market. Haythorn Davey built pumping machines for collieries whilst at Bramley, J. and J. Binns launched an organ building industry that gave the township a world-wide reputation. Exploiting the boom in cycling which mushroomed in the 1880s, five Leeds firms began manufacturing bicycles and tricycles. Hudson and Sons based at the Airedale Bicycle Works on Park Lane claimed their 'Airedale' cycle was the cheapest on the market.

It was the diversity of the town's industries which gave it its economic strength. 'Soapy' Joe Watson, originally a skin and hide dealer in the 1830s, began manufacturing soap and by the end of the century his Whitehall Road works was producing about 500 tons a week. The development of the printing trade saw Leeds specialise in quality colour printing with Alf Cooke's Crown Point Works opening in 1872. E. J. Arnold became nationally recognised as a major school supplier who catered for the needs created by the compulsory Education Act of 1870.

For years the coarse clay at Wortley had been the basis for the local production of clay tobacco pipes but as the population escalated demand for houses soared and consequently there was an urgent need for bricks and chimney pots. Brickyards were opened in East Leeds, Holbeck, Middleton and Farnley. Joseph Cliffe at Wortley specialised in glazed sanitaryware for sewers and in 1883 his was one of six companies which amalgamated to form the Leeds Fireclay Company. A more aesthetic clay product was the faience-ware made from 1883 at Burmantofts. Its terracotta work was exported world-wide, gracing such buildings as Brazil's new Opera House at Manaos.

By 1886 thirty-three breweries were operating in the town including that of the famous Joshua Tetley. Tetley, an Armley maltster, had bought Sykes's Brewery in Hunslet in October 1822 for £409 0s.6d. In his first month he did not receive one order! Another Leeds firm that acquired a national reputation was Goodall and Backhouse the *Yorkshire Relish* manufacturers. By the 1880s they were selling some six million bottles a year. The glass bottles they used were also the product of local industries.

By the 1870s Leeds claimed to be the leading town in the kingdom with regard to the leather industry. Tanneries and skinworks were located mainly at Kirkstall, Meanwood and Buslingthorpe. Here Wilson Walker and Company had established the largest tannery in England. Much of the leather produced was used in the burgeoning boot industry. Both Stead and Simpson and Joseph Conyer and Son began life as curriers but moved on to producing ready-made boots to the extent that they were responsible for two-thirds of the Leeds output. By 1890 the ninety or so boot producers in Leeds managed a weekly output of 100,000 pairs between them. However, failure to recognise new trends like the fashion for wearing shoes saw the industry eventually fall into a decline.

But of all the new manufacturing enterprises which emerged during the latter part of the century one in particular stood out: the clothing industry. John Barran, the son of a London gunmaker, had set himself up as a clothier in Briggate but during the 1850s he saw the potential Isaac Singer's new sewing machine offered. From his small factory in Alfred Street he began to manufacture ready-to-wear garments. In 1858 he ordered a band-knife for cutting several layers of cloth at the same time and thus vastly speeded up the whole process of manufacture. Demand escalated from the more prosperous members of the working class and was further accentuated by the mass-production of uniforms, for troops during the Crimean War, for the police and for the expanding railway industry.

In 1867 Barran moved to Park Row but within ten years the firm had outgrown its premises. Then Barran commissioned Thomas Ambler to design a Moorish–Venetian style clothing factory and warehouse, St Paul's House, in Park Square. It opened in 1878 and boasts terracotta decorations and exotic minarets. It is still one of the architectural gems of the city and according to the architectural historian Patrick Nuttgens it is 'much the most entrancing and romantic of the industrial buildings' in Leeds. The firm continued to prosper and in 1888 moved to Hanover Lane where, in 1904, a further new factory was built adjoining it.

Barran had shown commendable imagination and entrepreneurial flair in developing mass-produced clothing. But an employee of Barran's also made a significant contribution. Herman Friend was a Russian Jewish immigrant employed as an outworker because Jews at the time were not allowed to work inside Barran's factory. Friend opened a workshop on the site of the old workhouse at the junction of Vicar Lane and Lady Lane. By dividing up the stages of manufacturing garments into processes such as machining, buttonhole sewing and pressing, he was able to train unskilled workers to complete just one aspect of the production efficiently and speedily.

Joseph Hepworth and Sons at their Wellington Street works also used a similar approach to that which Friend had developed for garment manufacture. At Hepworth's it was estimated it took some twenty-five to thirty hands to complete one suit of clothes. But about 1883 the company diversified when it not only produced clothes but also began selling them in its own retail shops. Other clothing companies followed the trend.

Most of the unskilled workers Friend attracted were Polish–Russian Jews fleeing from the pogroms of Eastern Europe which followed the murder Tsar Alexander II. Leeds Jewry was almost completely made up of such victims who had escaped to the west. Most landed at Hull and made their way to Leeds. The majority provided cheap labour in the industry although some arrivals were highly skilled tailors. The first Jew recorded in Leeds was Gabriel Davis who arrived in the town in the 1820s and was listed as a voter in 1832 whilst a small community of middle-class German Jews had become established in the 1840s hoping to find better prospects for trade.

148

But the new wave of immigrants came in far larger numbers. By 1891 some seventy-two per cent of the 8,000 Jews in Leeds were occupied in tailoring. They settled in the Leylands, a slum area of the town bounded by North Street and Regent Street. It was renowned for its violence and immorality but at least offered shelter at a time when many properties and workshops in Leeds were displaying the cryptic notice: 'No Jews Need Apply'.

By 1893 there were ninety-eight Jewish tailoring workshops. Many became known as notorious 'sweat shops'. Robert Sheracy, an investigative journalist for *Pearson's Magazine* visited the Leylands in 1896 as part of a series on 'The White Slaves of England'. He wrote: 'Here may be seen, in some filthy room in a dilapidated factory in the Leylands, fifty people (men, women, boys and girls), all huddled together, sewing as though for dear life . . . [t]he stench in the room, its uncleanliness, surpass description.'

Between 1851 and 1891 the population of Leeds and its out-townships more than doubled, leaping from 172,270 to 367,505. As its industries had increased so too did its retail capacity. The need for additional covered market accommodation in the 1850s led the council into agreeing to erect a covered market on the site of the old cattle market in Kirkgate. The cattle themselves were transferred to Smithfield Market, a five-acre site which was opened between Camp Road and North Street in 1855. But as the livestock trade increased, the Victoria Cattle Market, a new sixteen-acre site on Gelderd Road, opened in 1886. The importance of Leeds as a meat centre was further enhanced in 1898–9 when a new wholesale meat market and abattoir came into operation.

In May 1857 the new iron and glass Kirkgate Market was opened with forty-four shops outside and a further thirty-five inside. They traded until 9 p.m. on weekdays and 11 p.m. on Saturdays. East of the structure was an open area of 5,000 square yards where fruit and vegetables were sold at the Tuesday and Saturday markets. But as the population increased so too did demand for space. A further ninety shops were added to the site in 1875.

At least one of the stalls later achieved international importance. The Penny Bazaar opened in 1884 by Michael Marks, a Polish Jewish immigrant, had as its slogan 'Don't ask the price – it's a penny!' In 1893 he opened his first shop in Manchester and eleven years later one in Cross Arcade, Leeds. Marks went into partnership with Tom Spencer and their business proved such a success that by the time Marks died in 1907 the firm Marks and Spencer was operating sixty-one branches.

In 1898 the council, contemplating the need to widen Vicar Lane and to increase once more the covered accommodation at the market, opted for a new building. The present City Markets were opened in 1904. With its Flemish façades, Venetian domes, Burmantofts glazed brick walls and Art Nouveau decoration, it has been described by Derek Linstrum, the architectural historian, as 'one glorious salute to the new century'.

The town centre of Leeds, compared with other emerging towns of the nineteenth century, was concentrated into a relatively small area. As retailing demands increased shopkeepers found the number of outlets onto the main streets limited. The solution was directly influenced by Paynel's original development of his new town in 1207. The narrow yards off Briggate which reflected the shape of Paynel's thirteenth-century parcels of land or tofts were bought up.

Shops were then built on them but under a covered awning. Charles Thornton instituted the first Leeds arcade on the site of the Talbot Inn and yard in 1877–8 where its clock became a popular attraction. When the characters from Scott's *Ivanhoe*, Robin Hood, Friar Tuck, Richard the Lionheart and Gurth the Swineherd, started striking the bells with their fists every quarter hour crowds gathered in such numbers that the chiming had to be halted for a fortnight. Other arcades were opened. Queen's Arcade was built in 1888–9; the Grand Arcade in 1896–8; the Victoria Arcade named to commemorate the Diamond Jubilee of the Queen in 1898; and the County Arcade between 1898 and 1900. Its lavish design with marble pillars and decorated frescos, the most opulent of the Leeds arcades, was the work of Frank Matcham whose other notable buildings included the London Coliseum and the Palladium.

It was during this period of the development of the arcades that multiple shops and department stores began to appear in the town. However, the greatest retail outlets in Leeds were not owned by some enterprising entrepreneur like Charles Thornton or the Leeds Estates Company responsible for County Arcade. They were owned by a society which in turn belonged to the men and women of Leeds. For years one of the prime concerns in the town had been the selling to the public of adulterated foodstuffs by unscrupulous traders. Letters had repeatedly appeared in the Leeds press condemning the practice of selling contaminated tea or flour bulked up with plaster of Paris and lime. It was even suggested by one correspondent to the *Mercury* that adulterated food was the possible cause of the cholera epidemic that was prevalent in Leeds in 1825. There was at least one case that year of a man dying from polluted beer and in 1847 the magistrates dealt with what they said was the 'most atrocious case of adulterated flour that has been discovered in this town'. When Samuel Vickers and his wife Elizabeth mixed plaster of Paris with the flour at their shop in George Street the result was that several people needed treatment at the Dispensary.

In 1847 workers at Benyon's mill in Holbeck called a meeting at the Union Tavern to raise funds in order to erect a mill and provide their own flour 'to preserve ourselves from the invasion of covetous and merciless men in future'. Within two months 1,023 people had joined the Leeds Flour Mill Society. The society expanded into selling groceries, renamed itself the Leeds Co-operative Flour and Provision Society and in 1856 opened its first shop in Briggate. Profits were paid to all members based on the amount of money they had spent. In the next fifty years the Leeds Industrial Co-operative Society, as it came to be known, had increased its scope dramatically. As well as selling food it had expanded its business into providing clothing and fuel. It owned its own farm, boot factory, brush works, provision warehouses, joiners' workshops and builders' yards. Its coal wharf was in Neville Street and it had

16. Dewsbury Road Co-op
It was claimed that the Leeds Industrial Co-operative Society was the largest on earth. It opened its first shop in 1856 and by 1927 had a hundred stores across the city. This store on Dewsbury Road is typical, offering meat, groceries and confectionery.

151

coal depots at Wellington Bridge, Kirkstall and other railway stations. Its head store was in Albion Street and by 1896 it owned over seventy local stores in the suburbs. It had attracted 33,000 members and according to the *Yorkshire Factory Times* 'the Leeds Industrial Co-operative Society is the largest on earth.'

But the movement did not grow without it critics. Dr Hook related how, when he mentioned the society in educated circles, he was greeted with the comment 'A Co-operative Association is contrary to the principles of political economy.' These middle-class critics feared that such an organisation would set labour against capital and saw co-operative societies as part of the growing socialist, trade union and labour movement. In reality, for much of Victoria's reign, most working-class people in Leeds were moderates. The growing success of the commercial and manufacturing enterprises enabled George Goldie, the medical officer for health, to testify to the Royal Commission on Housing that the workers in them were 'all well to do people, all people earning good wages'.

There was, however, one occasion in February 1865 when working-class bitterness broke out. It had last erupted on the streets of the town during the Chartist disturbances. The catalyst which provoked it this time was not some political ideology or religious dogma but a small amount of dripping. Eliza Stafford was the cook at Henry Chorley's house in Park Square. It was general practice that when a cook had roasted a joint the dripping produced was hers to use or sell as she pleased. Chorley, a local surgeon and magistrate, took exception to the practice and had Eliza arrested for theft.

She was sentenced to a month in Armley Jail but incensed working-class demonstrators set out to embarrass Chorley as much as they could. Graffiti was scrawled on walls, abusive letters were sent to his home and doggerel ballads sung:

> *Now all you cooks and servant girls wot's very fond of 'tipping'*
> *Don't take your master's scraps of fat and boil 'em down for dripping:*
> *For if you do bear this in mind, the magistrates won't fail*
> *To try you in a private court and send you off to gaol.*

Because a large demonstration was envisaged on the day she completed her sentence, Eliza was released an hour early and smuggled away by train to her daughter's home in Scarborough.

When it realised what had happened a mob marched down to Chorley's home in Park Square. Missiles were thrown and the Leeds Police turned out in force. In the ensuing fracas George Hudson, a potter, was killed, the Chief Constable, William Bell, fell and broke his arm and another officer received a serious head wound. The mayor called for help from Bradford Police and for two troops of cavalry from York. A crowd of 2,000 then gathered outside the Town Hall but eventually was peacefully dispersed. Only five men were arrested and the magistrates, sensing the injustice which had precipitated the event, took a lenient line.

The story was graphically covered in the Leeds press but it was not just local outbursts that were featured in the Leeds newspapers. Every major issue of the day was covered, analysed and the party line urged.* Local people were fortunate that by the 1870s they had a number of papers to choose from. The *Leeds Mercury* had become a daily in 1861; the *Intelligencer* followed suit in 1866 under the new title of the *Yorkshire Post and Leeds Intelligencer.* There were two other daily papers, the *Leeds Daily News* and the *Leeds Evening Express*, and three weeklies, the *Leeds Times*, the *Leeds Express* and the *Yorkshire Independent.* Two evening papers were later launched: the *Yorkshire Evening Post*, a sister paper to the *Yorkshire Post*, in 1890 and in 1903 the *Leeds Daily News* became the *Yorkshire Evening News.*

The press fulfilled a need to keep people abreast of local and national trends and by and large many of the working classes were showing themselves to be responsible individuals, eager to learn. Their membership of the twenty-three mechanics' institutes in the town and of the various friendly, temperance, building and charitable societies emphasised the point. In 1867 the Second Reform Bill was passed and an additional 30,000 Leeds workers were granted the franchise. Most were Liberal supporters and the Liberal Party dominated both council and Parliamentary elections. It was not until November 1895, following the Conservative Party's general election landslide over a bitterly divided Liberal Party, that the Conservatives in Leeds assumed control of the council. It was their first taste of power in the town for nearly sixty years. They held that on to that position for the next nine.

William Gladstone himself was elected to represent the town in the 1880 General Election. However, he also stood for Midlothian and when elected by both constituencies chose to represent the Scottish seat. In the by-election that followed in Leeds, his son, Herbert, was returned unopposed.

In 1881 the Prime Minister, W. E. Gladstone, the Grand Old Man, visited the town as a belated thank-you to the people of Leeds for having

---

* This was not strictly true of the *Leeds Mercury.* During the 1870s the owner, Edward Baines, Jun. refused to allow any mention of theatres in the paper because he felt they were immoral places.

elected him. For a hectic two days he was caught up in a whirlwind of activities. A torchlight procession of between 250,000 and 300,000 paraded through the streets. He said it was the 'most remarkable' he had ever witnessed. He gave three speeches and witnessed four processions on Friday 7 October, and delivered three more speeches and witnessed two more processions on the Saturday – and all done whilst he was suffering from lumbago! A crowd in excess of 30,000 gathered to hear him speak in the Coloured Cloth Hall yard, and before 1,300 guests at a banquet held on the Friday he delivered one of his keynote speeches on Ireland. In it he condemned the Irish leader, the 'malicious Parnell', and went on to coin the classic and much-quoted phrase, 'The resources of civilisation are not yet exhausted'.

But for some the Liberal Party did not offer the more just society that many working-class people desired. Many of the working classes lived in poverty and were regarded by their employers 'with no more concern than their steam engines'. At least that was what the correspondent to the *Monthly News of Leeds Mechanics' Institute* wrote in 1865. By the 1880s several skilled trades had formed themselves into twenty-eight small trade unions. In an attempt to remedy the situation two men in particular, Tom Maguire, a photographer's assistant, and John Lincoln Mahon, an engineer, came to the fore and devised a double strategy. They began an active campaign to wrest power from the Liberal middle-class councillors, who up until then had represented the lower classes, and give it to the working men themselves. The second part of their campaign was to launch an assault against capitalist employers on behalf of the workers. To this end in September 1884 they formed the Leeds Branch of the Socialist Democratic Federation (SDF) with Maguire as its secretary. The party itself had been founded only three years earlier and was Britain's first Marxist political party.

But disputes within the national organisation saw William Morris, the Pre-Raphaelite poet and craftsman, lead a secession from the SDF to form the Socialist League. In Leeds a meeting was called at the Royal Sovereign Inn on Vicar lane in March 1885. It was agreed to dissolve the local SDF and form a branch of Morris's new party. Arguing for parliamentary and municipal reform the League drew great support from the trade unions. It rejected the individualism so dear to the Liberals and urged collective action. Maguire summed it up aptly: 'We working men, although divided by politics and religion, are socially one.'

A series of strikes between 1889 and 1892 followed. Strikes were not new to Leeds. Coal miners had struck in 1796, joiners and cabinet-makers in 1805, and the clothiers' strike at Stanningley in 1820 had seen the troops called out. Now in the late 1880s tailors, corporation workers, tramway employees and other trades struck in turn and then went on to form unions. The most serious of these strikes, however, was the strike by gas workers in June and July 1890.

In September 1889 the Gas Workers and General Labourers' Union petitioned the Leeds Gas Committee for improved working conditions. The committee rejected the demands and then compounded the problem by refusing to pay double time for work on Good Friday.* Relations between employers and workers deteriorated. At a mass meeting of nearly 14,000 Tom Maguire announced that they intended to 'show the Leeds Committee that the people of Leeds were their masters'. In the first week of July 1890, in an attempt to teach that lesson, Maguire and his strikers precipitated some of the worst street violence seen in nineteenth-century Britain.

The focus of the dispute was the two large gasworks on Meadow Lane and at New Wortley. As the strike began to disrupt gas supplies the *Leeds Daily News* reported, 'Last night . . . the town was in complete darkness . . . local business has been disorganised; hundreds of men and women thrown idle.' Yet despite the inconvenience to the public, contributions flowed into the strike fund, for a time at up to £100 a day. Matters reached a climax when blacklegs were brought in from Manchester and London. They were lodged in the Town Hall but when the police and a military force tried to escort them to the works violence erupted. Crowds estimated at 30,000 gathered. At Wortley missiles were hurled from the rooftops and railway bridges. The police used their batons. The following day similar scenes were duplicated at Meadow Lane where the gate to the works was destroyed. The mayor read the Riot Act and additional troops were called from York. When most of the blacklegs left the town, protesting that they had been led to believe they were to be part of a building project, not strike breaking, the committee backed down. The gas workers had registered a significant victory.

To co-ordinate the ongoing struggle for improved conditions, the Leeds Trades and Labour Council had been created. Its role was to draw together the different strands of the Labour movement and represent the interests of working people in trade unions. Engineering was one industry where disputes surfaced. Despite the fact that engineers' pay in Leeds was lower than that in most other towns and unemployment more fre-

---

* Many Leeds firms worked on Good Friday and had the Tuesday after Easter Monday as holiday.

quent, not all unions were in agreement about taking action. The Leeds Amalgamated Society of Engineers (ASE), one of the most important groups of workers, opposed demands for an eight-hour day. But a dispute erupted in 1898 when thirty-four engineering firms locked out their workers. Members of the Independent Labour Party (ILP) and the gas workers' union supported ASE members during the lock-out. When it was over large numbers of its members decided to join the ILP and take part in more positive action. But there were others who also had significant battles to fight. Among those were the womenfolk of Leeds.

Women had long played an important part in the politics of Leeds, albeit their role was that of supporting the male struggle for enfranchisement. In 1819 there already existed a group known as the Female Reformers of Leeds. But by 1841 simply demanding the vote for all men was not enough and at least one local woman, 'Laone', took it upon herself to widen the demands for women's involvement. Writing to the *Leeds Times* in March she made it abundantly clear that 'It cannot be asserted that women are indifferent to political existence . . . there are many women in England who think'. Leeds women became more active. By the 1890s the Leeds Tailoresses' Society had been formed and the initial protests of the gas strike itself had been led by local women. It was they who, on 26 June, had milled around the entrance to the Meadow Lane plant and blocked the road.

Following the defeat of John Stuart Mills's amendment to give women the vote during the debate on the Reform Bill in 1867, the London Society for Women's Suffrage was founded. Shortly afterwards similar societies of the National Society for Women's Suffrage were formed in Birmingham, Bristol, Edinburgh and Manchester. In 1871 a Leeds branch was established as a subsidiary branch of the Manchester Society and within twelve months meetings in Leeds were attended on average by 100 women. Most of those present were working-class and they ended each meeting by signing a petition demanding the vote.

In 1872 the Central Committee for Women's Suffrage was formed with the express intention of achieving votes for women. The Leeds society associated itself with the new organisation and among its committee members was Alice Cliffe Scatcherd of Leeds. Alice was the daughter of the local magistrate and brickworks owner, Joseph Cliffe. Her husband Oliver was a solicitor who accepted her belief in women's rights though what his views were on her refusal to wear a wedding ring is not known!

During the 1880s demonstrations for women's franchise took place in several towns including Manchester, Birmingham and Bradford though none were reported in Leeds. The society was reformed in 1889 as the Leeds Suffrage Society and among its leading activists were Isabella and Emily Ford of Adel. Although the women's movement in the country generally attracted middle-class women, Isabella set out to recruit young girls from the local mills to support the campaign. To co-ordinate the various women's movements the National Union of Womens' Suffrage Societies was formed in 1897 and the Leeds society joined it. These suffragists, as they were known, believed in working for change within the law.* It was not until after 1903 with the formation of the Women's Social and Political Union, dedicated to bring change about by 'deeds not words', that major demonstrations occurred in Leeds. It was only then that the militants, known as suffragettes, became really active in the town.

The third great political movement from the latter part of the nine-teenth century also manifested itself in Leeds. But unlike the labour movement and that for women's suffrage which both came to fruition in the first quarter of the twentieth century, the final solution of the Irish problem has not yet been fully resolved. Home Rule for Ireland had long been demanded by both the people of Ireland and certain English sym-pathisers. Leeds was not short of such supporters for in 1851 there were 10,333 Irish people living in the town. A small influx of Irish emigrants settling in Leeds had been noticeable for years but the effects of the Great Famine in the 1840s and the subsequent economic crises that fol-lowed led to an escalation.

Most settled in the east end of Leeds, a part of the town infamous for its squalid slum dwellings, inadequate sanitation and polluted water supplies. In the notorious Bank area a report in 1839 commented on 100 dwellings inhabited by 452 people who shared two privies. It was an area where crime and prostitution were rife; drunkenness and violence commonplace. At least fourteen per cent of cases which came before Leeds Quarter Sessions between 1851 and 1861 involved the Irish. In 1852 a third of all assaults on the police and breaches of the peace were committed by Irish individuals.

Understandably, the local population reacted to the violence and the authorities established a police station in the district. For a decade or more the immigrants remained an isolated group. Many English Catholics found their co-religionists an embarrassment, particularly when not only drunken brawling was a cause for concern, but also Irish

---

* Another society, the Leeds and Yorkshire Branch of the Women's Emancipation Union, also existed in Leeds in 1895.

Nationalism. It was the son of James Holdforth, the mayor of Leeds from 1838–9 and England's first Catholic mayor since the Reformation, who called on English Catholics to dissociate themselves from Fenian terrorism.

There already existed in the town the Leeds Home Rule Association which had premises in Kirkgate. In 1862 Father Patrick Lavelle, president of the National Brotherhood of St Patrick, a front for that secret Irish nationalist organisation the Fenians, visited Leeds. He had arrived in England, *The Times* reported, to urge 'the Catholic doctrine on the right to revolt'. The Leeds authorities kept a wary eye on the worsening situation in Ireland and its specific effect in the town. The secretary of the Leeds Fenian Society, James McCarthy, was warned about his conduct. It was alleged he had claimed he looked forward to seeing the streets 'running with Englishmen's blood'. There were reports also that an attempt had been made during the 1860s to burn down the Parish Church school. In February 1867, the abortive attack on Chester Castle to procure arms for a proposed uprising in Ireland was also supported by Leeds Fenians. One was arrested in Basinghall Street carrying a supply of cartridges.

In September that year Fenians were again active. In Manchester an attempt to free republican prisoners led to a police sergeant being killed. At Clerkenwell Prison an explosion to free others killed seven people and mutilated many more. Republicans claimed that the deaths were not assassinations but the unintentional consequence of trying to free the prisoners. They also argued that the three men ultimately hanged at Manchester had not fired the fatal shots and had simply been present at the scene of the attack. Republican sympathisers regarded them as the 'Manchester Martyrs'.

In Leeds a funeral procession was organised for Sunday 15 December 'in honour of the Irish Patriots executed at Manchester'. 'All lovers of Ireland, men and women' were urged to attend. The procession was to meet at Vicar's Croft and then proceed through the streets to St Patrick's Cemetery on York Road. Understandably, the magistrates took a dim view of the proposal fearing that it could precipitate a major outbreak of violence. Mounted special constables and a strong military presence occupied Kirkgate. Infantry, a battery of artillery and a squadron of yeomanry were held in reserve nearby. The police occupied Vicar's Croft and the situation was effectively defused. There were no more serious threats to the peace by Irish nationalists in Leeds but that did not mean they had given up the struggle for Home Rule.

They adopted more constitutional methods in striving for their political goal realising that the Irish vote could be crucial. It proved markedly so in the general election of 1885. That year the Redistribution Act had divided Leeds into five constituencies: Central, North, South, West and East. Two days before the polls opened, Charles Stewart Parnell, the leader of the Irish Home Rulers, issued a manifesto instructing all mainland Irishmen to vote against Gladstone's Liberals. The Irish in the working-class East Leeds constituency did as they were bid and the Conservative, R. Dawson, was duly elected. The Liberal government was ousted and later that year, Gladstone converted to Home Rule. Parnell switched his support to the Liberals and in the general election next year the only seat in Leeds that changed hands was that of East Leeds where the Irish vote helped return J. L. Gane, the Liberal.

Cosmo Gordon Lang, later to become Archbishop of Canterbury, arrived as a young curate in Leeds in 1890. He wrote of his first-hand experiences of the squalid East Leeds area where the Irish had settled among the poorest local inhabitants and he noted how these two communities lived: 'Some of them, especially the women in the Marsh Lane courts, were worse than beasts, for beasts are not degraded. I seem to see now their unkempt hair, their tattered clothes, their bleared eyes.' He described beggars with missing limbs who miraculously recovered them once they were out of public view and blind men who regained their sight each night. And there were the inevitable prostitutes. In 1852 there were 150 listed in the Chief Constable's Annual Report; most were servants or factory hands and worked in the sixty-five brothels in the town.

The dwellings in which the people in the area lived were mostly soulless cottages about five metres square and made up of a cellar, a living-room and a bedroom. Many of the houses were huddled in a jumble of crowded courts and unhealthy yards. Some were forced to rent cellars for their homes and these were often flooded with water and effluent from the sewers. Those who could not afford to rent a dwelling of any kind took accommodation in the local lodging houses. Overcrowding here was commonplace with both sexes sharing the same room and either sleeping two, three and sometimes five to a bed or finding a vacant place on the floor. Many places were so filthy that the council's Sub-committee on Common Lodging Houses even went to the expense of buying a dozen brushes for whitewashing. The intention was to lend them to landlords who did not have their own.

James Hole, the Leeds social reformer, deplored the vice and ignorance 'that beget inferior social conditions'. He went on to argue that improving housing conditions was 'intimately connected with other social issues'. He complained in 1865 that not a dozen new streets had been laid out in Leeds in the past thirty years whilst the *Leeds Mercury* had commented that the town looked as if it had had 'an earthquake for an architect'.

Private enterprise operating in a free market was a fundamental belief of nineteenth-century British Liberalism. Only slowly through the second half of the century did municipal ownership of pubic utilities come to be regarded as increasingly important. Regulations smacked of government interference and that, it was felt, stifled initiative. Thus although the council may have been concerned to undertake to lend whitewash brushes it was loath to act when it came to imposing building standards. The council obtained the right to issue compulsory purchase orders on sub-standard housing but enforcing regulations on builders ran contrary to the spirit of the individualism Liberals so cherished. Consequently, only three times were the provisions of the Act implemented. It was not until 1890 when typhus broke out in East Leeds that two major slum clearance schemes were finally agreed upon.

Attempts had been made in the past to improve living conditions. The lower-middle and upper-working classes formed terminating societies or building clubs which raised subscriptions from their members. The monies collected paid for the purchase of land and the erection of houses. Once every member had a house the club was then terminated. St James Street at Woodhouse was commenced in 1788 by such a building club and these societies produced the first back-to-backs in Leeds on Union Street, George Street and Ebeneezer Street. However, enthusiasm for the idea waned when unscrupulous officials sometimes disappeared with the money. One such was the secretary of the Brick Close Club off Camp Road. In 1843 he absconded to America with the funds. Permanent building societies were eventually introduced though both the Leeds and Holbeck and the Leeds Permanent Building Societies originated as terminating societies in the 1840s.

Speculative builders went on erecting street after street of back-to-backs, 'the barracks of industry' as the historians Barbara and John Hammond called them. Between 1886 and 1914 there were 57,029 new houses built in Leeds, two-thirds being back-to-backs. Most of these houses were unlike many working-class houses across the country, which backed onto a narrow passageway separating the rows of houses. Leeds back-to-backs literally backed up against the house behind. They were in effect half a house with one dwelling facing onto one street and the other onto the street behind.

A bye-law of 1866 insisted that new houses should have a privy and ashpit yard or midden for every eight houses, though some more enlightened builders provided one ashpit and two privies for every three or four dwellings. One fireplace with an oven was the means of cooking and one tap provided cold water. By the 1880s some houses were being built with set-pots, small copper boilers set in brick, which could be used for heating water. Their separate chimneys were perched above the guttering away from the main chimney stack. Washing had to be hung across the street to dry and slopping out had to be carried out each morning. Milk, meat and butter were stored in the coolest place at the top of the cellar steps, known locally as the 'cellar-head'.

More sophisticated versions were later built with attics, double fronts and individual privies. For many who lived in them the intimate contact with local neighbours and the heat drawn from adjacent houses at the side and the back made them appealing.

Already a migration of the middle classes had begun to the more pleasant areas north of Leeds where they hoped to escape the noisy and smoked-filled atmosphere of the town centre. By 1871 about half the upper middle classes had moved to the north-west. The suburbs of Headingley, Potternewton, Burley, Roundhay and Adel were slowly developing with their villas and mansions providing homes for wealthy merchants and successful professionals.

If the council had been reluctant to act positively regarding inferior housing, it did respond to the population explosion in Leeds and its out-townships which reached 172,270 by the 1850s and placed enormous demands upon the infrastructure of the town.* The need for an improved water supply and sewerage system were paramount.

In 1852 the council took over the local private water company. It was the beginning of the municipal ownership of pubic utilities. However, it refused to establish reservoirs as it had been advised and opted to draw water directly from the River Wharfe. The benefits of the improved supply were soon recognised; in 1842 only ten per cent of houses had mains water, but by the 1860s some ninety-five per cent were so supplied. But pollution of the Wharfe supply became intolerable and the Leeds Waterworks Act of 1867 offered a solution by enabling the council to build reservoirs during the 1870s at Linley Wood, Swinsty and Fewston.

Insanitary living conditions had repeatedly seen the town suffer from outbreaks of fevers, often with the most devastating results. Yet it

---

* The 1851 census shows Leeds itself with a population of 101,343. The largest out-township was Hunslet with 19,466.

was only when the cholera epidemic of 1848 had wreaked its havoc that the council took the first hesitant steps to improve things. The days of the night soil men had to be brought to an end and a suitable system of drainage introduced. By 1855 just over fifteen miles of sewers had been constructed. For the next nineteen years raw sewage was deposited into the River Aire just below Thorpe Mill Pool. Little wonder William Osburn, a member of the Leeds Philosophical Society, remarked:

> *The AIRE below is double dyed and damned;*
> *The Air above, with lurid smoke is crammed.*

And not surprisingly the owners of land below Thorpe Mill took out an injunction against the council. In 1872 twenty-six acres of land were purchased from the Temple Newsam estate at Knostrop and the town's first sewage purification works was built. As an indication of the improvements brought about, in 1856 only 1,005 houses had water closets; in 1889 the number had risen to 27,990.

The benefits of a free-enterprise economy are lost to the general public when cartels are allowed to operate. By the 1850s two Leeds companies monopolised the gas supply of the town. The first, the Leeds Gaslight Company, had been established in 1818 with the remit to light 'streets, highways . . . shops, inns, taverns, private houses and manu-factories'. Its critics complained it was 'a profane way of dissipating God's darkness', and John Kaye, in a letter to the *Mercury*, expressed his concern about the effects of gas on public health. Nevertheless public interest slowly grew and by 1820 there were some 250 lamps operating in the town.

In 1835 a competitor arrived in the guise of the Leeds New Gas Company. It erected works in Meadow Lane and then at New Wortley. But it was a bogus competitor, for the two companies operated a cartel by fixing prices and making considerable profits. The prospect of taking over the gas supply began to appeal to the council. It already consumed large amounts of gas itself and it would enable it to provide cheaper fuel to the Leeds public. Initially objections were raised in the press, the vestry and the council itself but by 1868 feelings had changed.

Apart from supplying cheaper fuel another positive advantage was that by taking over the companies the council would then have complete control over the highways. Already the corporation had taken on the responsibility of the highway surveyors and was buying out the bridge and turnpike trusts. As the gas companies frequently needed to dig up roads either to lay or repair pipes, buying out the companies was a logical step to ensure that the council itself determined all policy regarding control of the queen's highways. In 1870, at a cost of £763,245, the council took over control of the gas supplies to the town.

In 1881 Newcastle-upon-Tyne installed five lamp-standards on its streets. They were the first in Britain to use electricity. Two years later Leeds council gave permission for its Electric Lighting Committee to carry out experiments. After six years the committee felt confident enough to recommend that the council should obtain plant to light town centre properties. It stressed that the corporation would be able to supply customers at half the cost that a private company would. But the technology involved in providing electric lighting was still new and the council erred on the side of caution. They rejected the idea.

April 1891 saw permission granted to the small Yorkshire House-to-House Electricity Company to establish a works on Whitehall Road and provide the town's supply. The *Leeds Mercury* which had been a vociferous critic of the council's proposal to take over the gas companies now reversed its view and condemned the corporation for failing to accept what was 'essentially a municipal responsibility'. The council's decision not to be involved proved an expensive mistake. It finally decided to take over the company in 1895 but by the terms of the Board of Trade order which allowed the company to be set up, the corporation was obliged to pay compensation above the market price of £63,011.

The council had been hesitant to take on responsibility for running public utilities and accept what some termed 'municipal socialism'. It was, then, surprising that those same councillors showed such a determination to provide the town with an infrastructure that would benefit the people of Victorian Leeds and one which has lasted into the twenty-first century. The foundations of the town's art galleries, libraries, museums, parks, transport and education services were all laid down in the latter part of the nineteenth century by the very men who had shown such reluctance to take on board civic involvement in housing, water, gas and electricity supplies. In some cases the initiative for this was taken by the council itself, in others it encouraged private enterprise.

Crucial to the growing needs of the town was an efficient transport system. As early as 1818 James Sykes was running his *Woodpecker* coach on a route that ran through the townships west of Leeds and ended at the Talbot Inn, Briggate. By 1836 a coach ran every Tuesday and Saturday between the Cardigan Arms, Bramley and the Griffin, Leeds to accommodate those wishing to attend the twice-weekly market. Within a year of the coming of the railway to Leeds in 1834, a horse-bus service began to operate from the offices of the Leeds and Selby Railway Company in Kirkgate to Marsh Lane station. But it was on Monday 25

June 1838 that John Wood began his omnibus service five times a day between Headingley and Leeds and heralded the introduction of the real public transport system for the town. By 1860 regular services were operating to Chapeltown, Kirkstall and Hunslet and less frequently to Whitkirk, Meanwood, Wortley and Roundhay. An abortive attempt to introduce steam-powered road vehicles in the town had been made years before when the Leeds Steam Carriage Company had been formed in 1830. However, there appears no record of it ever having operated.

But a revolution in public transport was on hand. Horse-drawn tramways opened in London and Liverpool in 1869–70. Horses pulling a vehicle on smooth rails could pull one twice the size of one on an uneven road surface. Between 1871 and 1874, the Leeds Tramways Company, private operators with council approval, opened five routes from Leeds: to Far Headingley, Chapeltown, Hunslet, Kirkstall and Marsh Lane. The first route, Boar Lane to Headingly came into service on Saturday 16 September 1871. Routes to the working-class areas of Wortley and Meanwood Road followed in 1878–9. By 1900 fifty-eight route miles of track criss-crossed the town, and over 27,000,000 passengers were carried annually.

The 1880s saw steam trams begin to supplement horse trams. But an engineer's report looking into alternative transport systems for the town felt that steam trams polluted the atmosphere, that horse trams caused excessive wear and tear on the roads and that the gradients on the highways were often too steep for the animals. His solution was the introduction of electrified routes. Opponents claimed it was a 'step into the unknown' and that the wires were an ugly death trap. But the scheme went ahead. On Thursday 29 October 1891 the first electric tramway using an overhead wire system came into service between Sheepscar and Roundhay. It was the first such system in Europe.

In 1894 the corporation took over the network. Cheaper fares were introduced and services increased. Most routes ran trams every ten minutes and by the beginning of the twentieth century operated from 4.30 a.m. until half-past midnight. One of the most significant changes the tramway system brought about was that the routes extended beyond the built-up areas of the town. Thus people were able to migrate to the suburbs and commute to work. In 1889 workmen's fares were introduced. At the same time private omnibuses ran to a variety of termini which included Armley, Burmantofts, Dewsbury Road, Halton, Whitkirk, Hyde Park, Roundhay, and Shadwell.

Perhaps the most lasting contribution and the most valuable that the Victorian middle classes made to the people of Leeds was an effective education system. In January 1826 John Marshall, president of the Leeds Philosophical and Literary Society, had proposed the opening of a university in Leeds without much success but in 1825 adult education for the working classes had already taken a major step forward with the opening of the first Mechanics' Institute, later the Leeds Institute. Hopes for a higher education foundation in the town languished for several decades.

It was becoming obvious that to keep abreast of developing technologies Leeds businesses needed, in the words of Thomas Nussey, a prominent local businessman, 'skilled workmen of the highest class'. To this end in 1869 two other members of the Nussey family, Henry and Arthur, established a technical school.

In 1868 James Kitson, head of the Leeds engineering firm, had submitted a proposal for a central college to be opened to cater for the West Riding. Other enthusiasts were forthcoming. One group, the Conversation Club which had been founded in Leeds in 1849 and formed the Yorkshire Board of Education, encouraged science in day schools and set up evening classes. Now it turned its attention to Kitson's proposal.

In 1874 the Yorkshire College of Science opened in temporary premises in Cookridge Street with the object of promoting the education of men and women. It would specialise in sciences and arts that were particularly relevant to manufacturing, mining, engineering and agriculture, all industries strongly established in Yorkshire. But the extension of the subjects offered in other academic areas saw it change its name to the Yorkshire College. Financial support from the Clothworkers' Company and others enabled the college to move to the present university site off Woodhouse Lane. Its new buildings were opened in 1877.

The Medical School in Leeds, which had started life in a backroom at the Dispensary in 1835, amalgamated with the College in 1884. It was a significant move for only three years later, on 3 November 1887, the Yorkshire College became a partner with Manchester's Owens College and the Liverpool College to form Victoria University. Leeds was now a university college with faculties of Medicine, and Science and Technology and one for Arts in the making. In 1903 both Manchester and Liverpool were granted university status in their own right. Then on 25 April 1904 the Privy Council granted a charter and the Yorkshire College became the University of Leeds.

Education of children in Leeds had begun as far back as 1341 and the Leeds Grammar School dates its foundation from 1552. By the eighteenth century several of the out-townships had their charity or free schools and Sunday schools also played an important role in spreading literacy in the town. Factory schools made some provision – the first school inspectors were factory inspectors – and Marshall's school based at his Holbeck mill was particularly effective. Day schooling was provided by the different denominations and a further sixty evening schools helped to complete the work of the day schools. For those who could not pay the odd coppers for attending these places, free schools were available. There were two ragged schools, two industrial schools and schools attached to the Leeds and Hunslet workhouses offering help. Even so there were still over 21,000 children not being catered for and James Hole was correct when he deplored the fact that in Leeds 'large masses are yet steeped in the grossest ignorance'.

The middle classes were more favourably catered for. Numerous small academies had been established in the town in the preceding fifty years. In January 1870 the Leeds Parish Church Middle Class school opened it doors in Basinghall Street. It was a mixed school offering sciences and languages with the intention of preparing its pupils for commercial and professional careers. In 1875 members of the Leeds Ladies' Educational Association and the Yorkshire Ladies' Council for Education felt that there was still a need for more provision of high class education for girls in the town. In 1875 the Leeds Girls' Grammar School Company was formed but within a month changed its name to the Leeds Girls' High School Company Limited. In September the following year it opened a school in rented property at St James's Lodge, Woodhouse Lane. By the beginning of the twentieth century the governors were concerned about the deterioration of the area. A move was agreed upon and by 1907 the school was settling into its present premises. Meanwhile the Leeds Grammar School had moved from Harrison's building in the centre of town to the edge of Woodhouse Moor and a more healthy environment. Work began on the new building in 1858 and in 1863 a chapel was added.

Hole's concern for the education of the vast majority was shared by many others. The old arguments that only voluntary bodies should provide education were recognised now to be spurious. To prepare children for the new industrialised and increasingly democratic society that was emerging in nineteenth-century Britain, state involvement was felt to be essential. In 1870 a milestone was reached when the Education Act was passed and opened the door to compulsory and eventually free education by authorising the creation of school boards. Leeds Council was not slow in responding to the new provision. It was well aware that of the 48,787 children of school age in the town only 27,329 were actually being catered for, and one in three of those were habitually absent.

At the beginning of November Whitehall contacted the mayor asking him to arrange an election of such a board. The fear in Leeds was that political and religious factions would dominate its work and the *Mercury* urged its readers to 'sink their personal differences'. On election day, Monday 28 November, voters arrived at polling stations to cast their votes for the fifteen board members. There were 45,000 people eligible to vote and a significant 30,000 fulfilled that duty. Even more significant was the fact that for the first time some women had the right to vote on local issues and did so in large numbers. The *Mercury* once again had a comment to make and sniffed superciliously, 'It was somewhat amusing to observe the air of satisfaction on their faces.' On 30 November the result was declared; eight Liberals and seven Conservatives made up the first Leeds School Board with Sir Andrew Fairbairn elected as chairman.

It established thirteen schools in temporary premises, hiring local Sunday schools and public halls and by August 1873 its first purpose-built school was ready for opening; it was Bewerley Street. That same year four evening schools and seven science and art classes were also opened. In 1882 the board then decided to go ahead with a new and adventurous plan. To cater for the brightest children in the town it was decided to open a higher grade school. Once again bitter differences surfaced. Questions were raised as to whether the council had the right to embark upon such a policy when it was supposedly only responsible for providing elementary education. Others saw a higher grade school in Leeds as a direct challenge to the Grammar School and the Leeds Church Middle Class School.

However, the School Board, divided as it was on the issue, decided to go ahead. Fees would be charged but some scholarships were made available. The Central Higher Grade School opened in temporary premises in 1885; the boys in Oxford Place Chapel and the girls in the newly built School Board Offices. The school's new premises on Woodhouse Lane opened in 1889.

Just as the council provided education at evening classes it also recognised that the reduction of working hours and the closing of mills on Saturday afternoons provided far more leisure time than was ever before available. The demand for leisure activities and the increase in wages among working people giving them more to spend was not lost on local entrepreneurs.

The latter years of the nineteenth century saw the number of theatres in Leeds increase dramatically. The Theatre Royal opened in 1876 on the site of the Royal Amphitheatre which had been gutted by fire that same year; the Grand Theatre opened in Briggate in 1878; the Coliseum in Cookridge Street in 1885 and the Empire Palace Theatre in 1898. The most famous is probably the City Varieties which grew out of the singing room of the eighteenth-century White Horse coaching inn.* Rebuilt in 1865, it changed its name in 1894, and claims that in the latter years of the century to have been graced by Edward, Prince of Wales, on his incognito visits to see his favourite Lily Langtry.

Culturally Leeds had long had a reputation for music but it was not until 1858 and the opening of the Town Hall that it became a recognised festival town. Its first festival was held the day after Queen Victoria had performed the opening ceremony of the building. Reports claimed that the concert was excellent, though running as it did from 8 p.m. until midnight was, according to the *Leeds Times*, 'much too long'. Bitter squabbles between the Choral and the Leeds Madrigal and Motet Society brought an hiatus in 1861 but in 1874 the idea of music festivals in the town was tried again and triennial festivals are still an important part in the cultural life of Leeds.

The year 1889 saw two innovations introduced into the town, one cultural, the other sporting. In May that year Colonel Edmund Wilson had called for the establishment of a society dedicated to preserving the history of Leeds and the Leeds Historical and Antiquarian Society was founded. At its first meeting in July it was proposed that a more imaginative title should be used and that the new association should be named after Leeds's first historian. Thus was born The Thoresby Society. It is still flourishing today.

The rapidly increasing interest in sport was also seen as an opportunity to provide Leeds and district with what was hoped would become the greatest sporting venue in the world. In 1888 the Clarendon Estate came on the market. In January 1889, under the chairmanship of Lord Hawke, the Leeds Cricket, Football and Athletic Company bought lot 17a. It was to be turned into a sporting arena the like of which had never been seen before. Cricket, lawn tennis, bowls, athletics, cycling, Rugby Union,** and, for a short time, Association Football were provided. In May 1890 the cricket ground was opened when Leeds played Scarborough. A more surprising fact, however, is that in September that

---

* It hosted the popular BBC TV programme *The Good Old Days* from 1953 to 1983.

** When Scotland defeated England in an international in 1893 the 30,000 crowd was the biggest for any Rugby Union match in the country to that date.

year the Australians played a North of England XI there and thus played cricket at Headingley before Yorkshire ever did! Apart from watching sporting activities people were encouraged to partake in them. By the end of the century the council had provided six swimming baths. They were well used. The council report for 1889–90 shows that in that year 343,347 had taken advantage of the facility. Equally important was the provision of parks and recreation grounds. By 1870 Leeds could boast only two such areas, at Woodhouse Moor and Bramley. But in 1871 thanks to the foresight of John Barran, then mayor, the town purchased part of the Nicholson estate for £127,000. Roundhay Park was to become one of Leeds's greatest assets, yet at the time Barran was condemned for wasting public money and caricatured as the buyer of a white elephant. Only when the newly opened tram route to Roundhay made it available to the vast majority of the population did the people of Leeds realise what a valuable asset they had really acquired. By 1900 Leeds was second only to Liverpool in providing open public spaces.

Another invaluable acquisition for Leeds came in the shape of a gift from Colonel North. When the Countess of Cardigan sold the abbey at Kirkstall, Colonel North bought it and presented it to the corporation in 1890.

The council continued its policy of providing leisure facilities which included cricket and football pitches, bowling greens, rowing on Waterloo Lake and, for the green-fingered, allotments at Burley and Harehills. It also did its best to improve the quality of people's lives by providing bandstands in various parks and enriching the environment in those parks with flowers and plants.

One of the first steps taken by the council in their policy of social enrichment linked education and leisure. It did so through the provision of public libraries. In 1870 a librarian was appointed to Leeds and in April that year branch libraries were opened in Holbeck and Hunslet. When asked why these locations had been chosen, John Barran succinctly summed up the thinking that lay behind the decision: it was 'where the masses lived'. In order to introduce the scheme as quickly as possible temporary premises were used; these included fourteen schools and a police station. By 1901 eight purpose-built libraries had been opened.

Within a year of opening its first branch libraries, the Central Lending and Reference Libraries began operating from the premises previously occupied by the old Leeds Infirmary on Infirmary Street. It had long been felt that the original building dating back to 1771 had outlived its usefulness as a hospital. New demands were being made upon the medical profession and new ideas circulated.

During the 1840s a trend had grown nationally to provide specialist women's hospitals and in 1853 a hospital for women in Leeds was opened in temporary premises in East Parade. The Hospital for Women at Leeds moved to its purpose-built site on Woodbine Place in 1860. Seven years later the Dispensary moved to new premises in North Street and after a damning report had been published on the House of Recovery, a new fever hospital was instituted at Seacroft in 1893. The old workhouse on Lady Lane, condemned for so long, was finally replaced with one on Beckett Street in 1861 and to cater for its inmates a hospital, the Leeds Union Infirmary, was built on the same site in 1874. By 1902 the children at the Industrial School there had been removed to a new home in Roundhay and the old building became part of the workhouse infirmary.

The Leeds General Infirmary was also destined to move from its home on Infirmary Street. A new site was found on Great George Street. Advised by Florence Nightingale on the medical requirements, Sir George Gilbert Scott was chosen as the architect. On 19 May 1868 the Prince of Wales opened the new building. The patients had still to be moved in and a National Exhibition of Works of Art was held to celebrate the event in the new Infirmary. Over 3,000 drawings, paintings and decorative art objects were put on display.

From the early part of the century privately owned works of art had been exhibited to the public in Leeds but now the Library Committee took on the responsibility for providing a public art gallery. In 1888 it opened one in the newly erected Municipal Buildings which also included the new premises for the Central and Reference Libraries. In 1892 it claimed over 198,000 visitors had viewed its exhibits.

Leeds also produced its own artists of some note. Phil May became one of Britain's greatest cartoonists and caricaturists. His work, often used in *Punch* at the turn of the century, brought a new simplicity of line drawing to the art form. May lived in Wallace Street, New Wortley. By a coincidence John Atkinson Grimshaw had previously lived in the same street for a short time. Grimshaw exhibited two paintings at the Infirmary opening in 1868 and both showed his growing interest in atmospheric effects. His paintings of nocturnal scenes with silver moonlight drifting across the landscape, of gaslights glistening on rain-soaked pavements or suburban lanes and leafless trees on wintry afternoons have made him one of the most sought after northern painters of his age. A third Leeds man was also to demonstrate a fascination with mists and moods. Frank Meadow Sutcliffe, son of the Leeds artist Thomas Sutcliffe, was born at Headingley but moved to Whitby where, in the last decades of the nineteenth century, he specialised as a photographer of the North Yorkshire Moors and of life around Whitby harbour. His work gained him an international reputation.

17. Still from Louis le Prince film of Leeds Bridge
Leeds Bridge, October 1888 and a piece of cinema history. Louis le Prince, a pioneer of cinematography filmed this from the window of a building on the south-east corner of Leeds Bridge. The pedestrians crossing the river from Briggate little realised that they were appearing in one of the world's earliest moving pictures.

But it was another photographer based in Leeds who made one of the greatest breakthroughs in photography. Louis Aimé Augustin Le Prince married a Leeds woman from Roundhay and set up in the town as a photographer. In 1885 he patented the first motion picture film process. He took some of the earliest moving film ever shot in his in-laws' garden at Roundhay and in October 1888 he filmed traffic and pedestrians crossing Leeds Bridge.* In 1890 Le Prince set off to Paris

---

* A few seconds of this film can still be scene at the Leeds Industrial Museum.

with a new projector hoping to get commercial backing for his ideas. He never arrived. Neither his body nor his equipment were ever found and the mystery of his disappearance is still unsolved

Le Prince's legacy of moving pictures became just one of the innovations that had transformed society during the previous hundred years. Most of those changes had taken place whilst a diminutive queen ruled Britain and an empire on which the sun never set. Leeds had changed beyond all recognition. When the first census in Britain had been conducted in 1801 the population of Leeds with the out-townships stood at 53,276. Now in 1901 Leeds and the out-townships had coalesced almost into one amorphous whole with a population of 428,968. It was one of the largest urban areas in the kingdom and in 1893 became a city. Four years later in June 1897 the chief magistrate became a lord mayor.

On New Year's Eve 1900 special watch night services were held in Leeds churches to celebrate the beginning of the twentieth century. In a matter of weeks those same congregations would gather to mourn the passing of the queen. At 6.30 on the evening of Tuesday 22 January 1901 Queen Victoria died. At exactly 7pm the news reached Leeds. Within minutes a special edition of the *Yorkshire Evening Post* was available on the streets announcing the end of the Victorian Age.

CHAPTER EIGHT

A VERY INTOLERABLE PLACE AND A WONDERFUL TRANSFORMATION

Shortly after 6 p.m. on the evening of Sunday 1 June 1902 a telegram arrived in Leeds announcing the end of the Second Boer War. The three years-old bloody conflict in South Africa was finally over. More than 21,000 British troops had perished in it, many of whom came from Yorkshire regiments. Two Leeds men, Sergeant Alfred Atkinson and Private Charles Wood, were awarded the Victoria Cross for bravery. The few people in Leeds with telephones placed the operators of the town's telephone exchange under great pressure as they quickly spread the news that peace had been announced. But the vast majority of the population had to wait for the special edition of the *Yorkshire Evening Post* which was rushed onto the streets as soon as sufficient newsboys could be found to hawk the paper. Editions were ferried to the suburbs by tram and by 10.30 that evening almost everyone in the city was celebrating.

Now Leeds, like the rest of the country, could look forward to a period of peace and prosperity. Britain's empire, the largest the world had ever seen, stood at its zenith and even news that a Leeds missionary, Charles Robinson, had been butchered during the Boxer Rebellion in China hardly shook the belief in Britain's pre-eminent place among the nations of the world.

There were those in Leeds for whom the years leading up to the First World War were years of affluence and success. For the first decade and a half of the century major economic slumps in the town were avoided and a general prosperity was enjoyed. For others, however, it was a period of struggle. Short-time working for some between 1906 and 1910 coupled to price rises meant that in real terms wages were often lower than they had been in the 1890s. Insecurity and poverty led to an ongoing struggle between labour and management, between socialism and capitalism. It was a conflict which manifested itself time and again in the years immediately preceding the Great War. Socially, culturally and politically Leeds was a divided city and yet for the first time the working and middle classes found themselves more and more undergoing shared experiences in the newly provided art gallery, libraries, parks and sporting venues.

George Bernard Shaw, on a visit to the West Riding, saw Leeds as no more than a northern provincial town and with his usual acerbic wit passed his flippant observations about it: 'Leeds as it exists is a very intolerable place . . . a place that no decent individual ought to live in.'

Leeds traders naturally disagreed and by 1909 could claim, 'No city in England can boast a more wonderful transformation.' The civic pride in its vaunting was understandable and in some ways justified but it would take the rest of the twentieth century, with input from both public and private enterprises, to effect a truly major transformation of the city.

Nevertheless, plans were afoot by the last decade of the nineteenth century to ensure that visitors pouring into Leeds were given a good first impression of the town. It was acknowledged that travellers arriving at the station were hardly impressed with the sight of the dilapidated old Coloured Cloth Hall, now used for sports and exhibitions or the equally ramshackle Quebec Buildings which jostled alongside it. By 1893 the council had conceived a plan to create an impressive square outside the station and the new designation of the town as a city gave it its name: City Square. In 1889 the council bought the Cloth Hall which it then demolished and replaced with a new General Post Office seven years later.

Whilst Colonel Thomas Walter Harding, a local industrialist, was on holiday in Italy, he whiled his time away dreaming up what he felt should be the content of the new square. Not satisfied with the proposal to erect a public lavatory or tramway waiting room there, Harding proposed turning the square into a work of art filled with statuary which he would personally finance. He commissioned William Bakewell to commit his bold imaginative concept to paper and design for him a place, as he said, that would put 'decorative art works among the people'. The council saw the merit in the scheme and approved.

On Wednesday 16 September 1903 Harding formally presented his gift to Leeds at a crowded ceremony. The square – it was never a true square – comprised a circular balustrade surmounted with eight electric-torch-bearing nymphs sculptured by Alfred Drury. Four, standing proud and upright, are called Morn; the other four, resting their weary heads on their shoulders, are known as Even. Four men who had contributed to the success of the city were also placed on pedestals. The statues of Dr Hook and Joseph Priestley were paid for by Harding himself; Councillor Boston contributed John Harrison and Richard Wainwright paid for James Watt, the pioneer of steam power. Originally a statue of Ralph Thoresby had been proposed but Wainwright argued that it was Watt's steam engines which had powered the mills of early industrial Leeds and laid the basis of its present wealth. The centrepiece was an equestrian bronze statue of Edward, the Black Prince, by Sir Thomas Brock.

Why Edward was chosen has never been satisfactorily explained. He had no connection with Leeds and the suggestion that his father brought Flemish weavers to England is tenuous in the extreme. Nevertheless, as an equestrian statue it is considered by some to be excelled only by Verrochio's statue of Bartolommeo Colleoni in Venice. It may well be that the choice did no more than simply reflect Harding's own interest in medieval history. Local wits, however, were soon to comment that it pointed to new arrivals from the station and emphatically warned them they should get out of the town whilst they still could!

But many did come and stayed. There were the famous like Colonel William F. Cody, better known as Buffalo Bill, whose Wild West Show and Congress of Rough Riders in 1903 played to packed houses on Cardigan Fields. Royalty also came in the guise of Edward VII and Queen Alexandra who arrived in July 1908 to open the new university buildings. Thousands flocked to see the royal party as it drove through the city's flag-bedecked and flower-festooned streets. It was the first visit to Leeds by an English king since Charles I had arrived as a Parliamentarian captive.

And thousands of ordinary folk arrived every week in Leeds city centre. They came from the industrial towns of the West Riding, from the scattered villages and market towns of North Yorkshire and from the city's own suburbs where 'going to Leeds' or 'to town' was a common expression, despite the fact they were already part of the city. The attraction which brought people to Leeds was the same that had attracted people for centuries: to buy goods of every description from the multiplicity of shops which had been opened there and from the thriving market that had functioned since the Middle Ages.

Boar Lane, Duncan Street, Vicar Lane and Briggate were packed with a multitude of retail outlets. Owners of property on Commercial Street modernised their premises and the newly opened arcades were unique attractions to the weekly shoppers. The Scottish pioneer in multiple grocery stores, Thomas Lipton, opened his first English store in the town in 1881. Others followed. Michael Marks, who began trading in Leeds Market and who was so influenced by Woolworth's marketing strategies, opened his first shop in Leeds outside the market in Cross Arcade in 1904. In 1912 Woolworth's itself arrived in the town and opened their fifth British store on the Headrow before moving to Briggate in 1928.

It was the time of the growth of great department stores. Snowden

Schofield came from Liverpool and opened a shop in May 1901 on the corner of Victoria Arcade. Within five years he had expanded into several other shops and then doubled the size of his floor space by moving into Red Hall next door. Hitchen's, originally a hatters in Kirkgate, expanded into a major store. Another high-class store, Marshall and Snelgrove of Oxford Street, London, opened at the junction of Bond Street and Park Row, whilst the Leeds Industrial Co-operative Society's store in Albion Street was already a well-established institution.

The attractions Leeds offered in those heady Edwardian days were many and varied. Kendall's in Briggate sold draperies; Denby and Spinks in Albion Street carpets and floor coverings; Archibald Ramsdens in Park Row pianos. Motorcycles and bicycles were available from Greenwood's on the Headrow. Saxone supplied footwear and its site at the junction of Briggate and Boar Lane became almost as famous a meeting place as 'under t'clock at Dysons', the jewellers in Lower Briggate. There was a range of theatres to choose from and newly opened cinemas like the 600-seat Rialto in Briggate

Numerous pubs and inns were available: the Old George in Lower Briggate, made famous by Charlotte Brontë in *Jane Eyre*, and the Turk's Head, known locally as Whitelock's and which became the artistic centre of the town and home of the Leeds Savage Club, were but two. For tee-totallers there were temperance hotels such as Trevelyan's on Boar Lane. Also on Boar Lane was Fairburn's White Horse Restaurant with the company owning a second restaurant, the City, in Briggate. Miss Greetham's Imperial Café operated on Commercial Street. Those venturing further afield by tram to Kirkstall Abbey could stroll round the ruins, listen to the musicians on the bandstand and in winter skate on a specially flooded area. Skating was popular in Leeds. When the Upper Lake in Roundhay Park froze in 1910 the corporation provided flares around its perimeter so that people could skate at night.

Providing these services was a vast workforce of some 208,000. Gas, water and electricity supplies had to be maintained. Local government officers were required to administer the council departments. Professional and commercial expertise was equally essential in a developing city even though its physical boundaries did not expand until 1912. But manufacturing still played a vital part in the local economy with engineering, clothing, footwear and textiles dominating the industrial scene. A small percentage of workers was still employed in agriculture with growing rhubarb, known locally as 'tusky', a local speciality.

John Barran and Sons still dominated the ready-made clothing market with a staff of 1,500 and a reputation which attracted visitors from

Japan, China, India, Brazil, the United States, Canada and South Africa and included, among other famous dignitaries, the Shah of Persia. Engineering firms such as the Monk Bridge Iron and Steel Works, which produced axles, boiler plates, bars and steel tyres, and Clayton's of Hunslet which specialised in gasholders for the home and export markets, were to the fore. Petty and Sons had become a leading colour and lithographic printer in a town which for over a century had enjoyed a reputation for printing.

Unemployment, however, was still a problem at times whilst those in employment made demands for better working conditions and improved pay. Disputes led to bitterness and bitterness at times led to outbreaks of violence. Already there was a groundswell of support in the town for the emerging labour movement. In the autumn of 1887 Tom Maguire had a written a handbill in which he claimed that definite steps had been taken to create what he called, 'a Socialist Labour Party in Leeds'. In 1892 the East Hunslet Independent Labour Club was formed and in November that same year the Leeds Independent Labour Party was established. In January the following year Keir Hardie founded the national Independent Labour Party (ILP) in a deliberate attempt to gain working-class representatives at Westminster who would no longer be reliant upon the Liberals. But the Leeds ILP lacked political muscle because of its refusal to co-operate with the Leeds Trades and Labour Council and with other labour organisations in the town.

In February 1900 the Labour Representation Committee, the forerunner of the Labour Party, was formed and the Leeds Trades and Labour Council agreed to affiliate to it. Its hope was that the new committee would work with the Liberals to achieve social justice. However, the Leeds branch of the ILP exerted pressure on the newly established Leeds LRC to break its Liberal association and urged it to draw into its fold both trade union and other socialist groups. It thus unified the new labour movement in the town and significantly excluded any further links with the Liberal Party.

The agenda offered by the new local labour movement was based on reform and socialism. Its strategy was aimed specifically at breaking the power of the Liberals in the city. Many of the working classes, however, had been and still were dedicated Liberal supporters. In parliamentary elections, despite concerted efforts by Labour, the Liberals consistently held South Leeds. In West Leeds, always a stronghold of Liberalism, Labour never even bothered contesting the seat before 1914.

But in East Leeds in the general election of 1906 it was a different story. Here the Liberals decided not to submit a candidate in the hope that James O'Grady of the Labour Party would be successful against the Conservatives. To that extent the ploy worked and O'Grady went on to represent the constituency until 1924. The Liberals hoped that many Labour supporters would see the way forward to greater social and economic improvement by supporting them. For so long their party had, after all, been the party of the working man but now the fledgling Labour Party challenged its position.

The town's Liberals were furious when they realised that Leeds socialists refused to reciprocate the local agreement that had allowed O'Grady's election in East Leeds. Labour candidates opposed Liberals whenever the opportunity arose. The Labour strategy began to succeed. In 1903 it returned its first town councillor. By 1909 the Leeds labour movement was able to boast 11,232 members made up of trade unionists, socialist clubs, ILP members and women's groups.

In the municipal election of 1907 the Conservatives and Liberals actually formed an alliance in the Armley and Wortley wards of West Leeds, to combat the Labour threat. From 1913 the Tory Alderman, Charles Wilson, regularly proposed alliances with the Liberals against socialist candidates at local elections, though in fact such coalitions never materialised.

Two men in particular dominated their parties in Leeds during this time. W. L. Jackson of the Conservatives, later ennobled to become the first Baron Allerton, and the Liberal, James Kitson, the first Baron Airedale. But if the Labour Party could claim no peers in Leeds its power was growing and from its one seat on the council in 1903 it had secured fourteen councillors and two aldermen by the time the First World War began, only two less than the Liberals.

For the Conservatives the rancour between the Liberal and Labour parties proved beneficial. Building on their success in capturing the council in 1895, the party went on to hold the reins of power for most of the years up to the end of the Second World War. But parliamentary elections in the borough presented a very different picture. After H. S. Cautley's success in East Leeds during the famous 'Khaki' election of 1900 no Conservative was returned for a Leeds constituency until 1918.

For long periods up to 1914, however, the Labour Party did not attract the support that its two leaders in Leeds, Tom Maguire and John Mahon, had hoped for back in the 1890s. Maguire died a disillusioned man in 1895 and Mahon, as a leader, proved to be both quarrelsome and devious. Nevertheless the party was growing in strength and in October 1911 added to its assets a newspaper, the *Leeds and District Weekly Citizen*. Meanwhile the Liberals failed to attract support from

Labour supporters. Their stand during the corporation strike of 1913 showed clearly where their sympathies lay when they gave their support to the Conservative councillors rather than the strikers.

The years immediately preceding the First World War saw repeated industrial disputes rocking the country as workers struck for higher wages. It was not only the workers who struck, for towards the end of the long hot summer of 1911, a strange phenomenon occurred in the country. Seemingly in imitation of their elders, a spate of strikes by pupils in council schools erupted across the nation. They began in Llanelly in September but quickly spread. From Sunderland to Southampton school strikes were reported and within days they manifested themselves in the West Riding. Outbreaks occurred in Bradford, Halifax, Sheffield and Leeds.

In Leeds, for a brief time, hundreds of pupils refused to attend school. The *Yorkshire Post* sneered that it was no more than 'truancy by another name'. Nevertheless Burley Road, Belle Vue Road, St Simon's in Ventnor Street, Sacred Heart, Burley Lawn and Upper Wortley schools were all affected. One of the ringleaders explained their demands to the *Yorkshire Evening News*: 'Shorter haars, noa hoam lessons and a penny a week for t'monitors'. The *Evening Post* loftily observed 'Ideals are very good things even for schoolboys, but discipline is much better.' Eli Howe, the headmaster at Upper Wortley agreed. One story, probably apocryphal, tells how he brought the ringleaders into his office the day after the strike and announced, 'Yesterday you struck, today I strike!'

But a strike culture had gripped Britain and in 1913 three strikes all but paralysed Leeds. In June corporation workers struck, in October carters, and then from 11 December until 14 January 1914 corporation workers struck again. The Conservative leader, Charles Wilson, took a determined stance against the unions and established a special committee to deal with the deteriorating situation. Three Conservatives and two Liberals formed it but no Labour representatives were invited to join despite the fact that the party had only two seats less than the Liberals on the council. After the June strike of corporation workers the interim settlement that followed proved unsatisfactory. The workers argued that the cost of living was rising and they had had no increase in pay for some years. Council leaders claimed the workers were seeking a 'privileged position' whilst the *Yorkshire Post* condemned them as 'anarchical' and 'hotheads'.

On 11 December 3,000 council workers struck. Electricity and gas supplies were halted. Streets were plunged into darkness. Thousands of workers were thrown onto short-time working as the mills and factories which were so dependent upon gas ground to a halt. Trams stopped running two days later. Tons of stagnant refuse gathered in the streets. The situation rapidly deteriorated. As the strike dragged on violence erupted when non-union labour was brought in to keep essential services running. Demonstrators were scattered by mounted police and strikers arrested for intimidating non-union workers. Bombs were planted at the Electric Power Station at Crown Point on 6 January 1914 and the following day at Harewood Barracks. No one was killed in the explosions but demands on the police necessitated each officer being employed on twelve-hour shifts every day.

But the 'five intolerant Pharoes' (*sic*), as the *Weekly Citizen* referred to the Special Committee, were successful and the strikers defeated. However, the strike itself did have one positive effect: it shook the council out of its complacency and forced it to modernise itself.

Not only men were engaged in the Labour struggle. Over a third of adult women in Leeds went out to work even though many working men were critical of working wives. Isabella Ford of Adel Grange pioneered women's trade unionism in the city and in 1903 went on to make political history. When she attended the Labour Representation Committee conference at the Co-operative Hall in Newcastle that year she was the first and only female delegate among 250 males. Apart from her interest in the Labour Party and trade unionism she was deeply involved in the campaign for women's suffrage.

At the beginning of the twentieth century the women's movement generally was gaining momentum. Isabella was active in the moderate and non-violent National Union of Women's Suffrage Societies (NUWSS) and acted as secretary to the Leeds Women's Suffrage Society. But it was becoming increasingly clear to many women that the moderate policy of the NUWSS was making little headway to enfranchise women. In 1903, Emmeline and Christabel Pankhurst formed the Women's Social and Political Union (WSPU), an organisation which believed that only by militant and sometimes violent action would change be brought about. As Adela Pankhurst wrote to the *Yorkshire Post*, the aim of the WSPU was to gain 'power for women to help the helpless' but it was another newspaper, the *Daily Mail*, which first described them as 'suffragettes' to distinguish them from the more moderate 'suffragists'.

Suffragette meetings on Hunslet and Woodhouse Moors often attracted crowds of up to 100,000. One such meeting was held on 26 July 1908 when a procession with bands playing and banners flying left Victoria Square in front of the Town Hall and made its way to Woodhouse Moor. There ten platforms had been erected from which various speakers addressed the crowd. But the highlight of the demonstration came when Mrs Pankhurst herself spoke. Groups of spectators had also gathered expecting that violence might break out but they were disappointed. The press commented that the proceedings were 'remarkably orderly'.

It was not always the case and violence did break out in the town at various suffragette gatherings. When Prime Minster Herbert Asquith arrived in Leeds to address a major meeting at the Coliseum in Cookridge Street women had been deliberately excluded. The organisers feared they would persistently disrupt proceedings. The suffragettes did not wait for the Coliseum; even as he descended from the train the booming voice of one suffragette, a Mrs Jennie Baines, challenged the Prime Minister. The crowd then followed him to Cookridge Street and Mrs Baines threatened to fight her way into the building. The police then moved in, arrested her and four others and charged them with unlawful assembly and inciting riot and sedition. For that they served a six-week prison sentence in Armley Jail.*

Suffragette action became even more violent and many people deeply resented the militancy. At Holbeck Feast an effigy of Mrs Pankhurst was stood on a gallows with a noose round its neck and when anyone hit a bullseye, the effigy was plunged through a trapdoor to the cheers of the watching crowd. But militant action continued. In 1913, Emily Davison famously threw herself under the king's horse during the Epsom Derby whilst that same year Leonora Cohen of Leeds made her way to the Tower of London. There she smashed the glass of the Crown Jewels' case. She was imprisoned in Armley and went on hunger strike but her weak heart prevented her from being force fed. Having a weak heart did not appear to affect her unduly. She lived to be 105! However, the following year the suffragette struggle was soon to be abruptly curtailed as an even greater confrontation swept aside every other issue.

On 4 August 1914 Britain declared war on Germany. Historians still dispute the underlying causes of the First World War but what is certain is that in the subsequent four years the world was to witness the bloodiest conflict mankind had ever seen. Initially many people were euphoric about Britain's gallant stand to avenge the German invasion of neutral Belgium. In Leeds the Conservative and Liberal parties agreed to support the government's plan to enrol five million in the armed forces. To

---

* Originally Armley housed both men and women prisoners.

that end a decorated recruiting tram clanged its way round the city with its indicator clearly showing its destination – 'Berlin'! The Leeds City Tramways band played from its open top and a recruiting sergeant on board urged local lads to 'take the King's shilling'. Performances at the Empire and Hippodrome theatres were interrupted to encourage enlistment and at Elland Road at the end of the Leeds City versus Fulham match volunteers were invited onto the pitch. As they came forward the crowd sang 'It's a long way to Tipperary'. The recruiting office in Hanover Square was crowded day after day but it was badly sited and later transferred to City Square.

Over 5,000 Leeds men had volunteered by September including 1,275 in the Leeds Pals, the 15th Battalion of the West Yorkshire Regiment and most famous of the city battalions. The city also provided two other battalions for the West Yorkshires: the 8th Battalion, the Leeds Rifles and the 17th Battalion, the Leeds Bantams, specially raised to cater for men of restricted height.

Most believed that the war would be over by Christmas. For fun they hung the Kaiser in effigy at the local feasts but the enthusiasm was not shared by everyone. The *Leeds Weekly Citizen* saw that ahead loomed 'a war of dimensions unprecedented'. There were those who objected to war in principle. Quakers such as Edmund Harvey, one of the most respected Liberals in Leeds, whose conscience refused to allow him to fight, instead involved himself in relief work at the front. The Labour Party in Leeds also included a large number of pacifists and it decided not to support the Conservative and Liberal recruiting initiative as a party but to allow individuals to act as their conscience dictated.

Leeds was swiftly put on a war footing. Aliens in the city were arrested and then interned. Boy Scouts were employed to guard reservoirs. School children like those at Green Lane Elementary School dug up fields to turn them into allotments and collected eggs to be given to military hospitals. Special constables kept nightly watch from the Town Hall for air attacks by Zeppelins. Street lights were dimmed. In 1916 British Summer Time was introduced and the following year came food rationing with the Art Gallery being turned into the Food Office. Public houses reduced their hours of opening and beer was watered down. The Leeds clothing industry came into its own, working twenty-four hours a day to produce uniforms. The National Area Clothing Department was set up in Swinegate. And women in the city, as they did all over the country, demonstrated that they were capable of taking on the jobs their menfolk left behind, be it delivering coal, running the trams or working in munitions factories.

Such factories were established in Armley, Hunslet and Newlay with existing engineering firms modifying their traditional output to produce shells, cartridges and fuses. Sopwith Camel aircraft were constructed on Roundhay Road. At Barnbow in East Leeds 400 acres of farmland were requisitioned between Garforth and Cross Gates and a munitions factory set up to house 16,000 workers employed in making shells. It would eventually ship out over 500,000 tons of ammunition to the armed forces. But shell making was a dangerous business. Three times fatal explosions occurred at the site; on 5 December 1915, just after the night shift had started, thirty-five women were killed in the first of those accidents.

The war had its impact on the city. The hundreds of men in khaki bustling through the streets gave the impression that it had become a garrison town. Searchlights probed the night sky for any Zeppelin attacks although in reality the nearest any German airship came to Leeds was Collingham. But soon the euphoria that the war had generated evaporated as its true cost in human terms sank home.

Within a matter of weeks the decisive first Battle of the Marne was fought. The Allies succeeded in halting the rapid enemy advance and for the Germans hope of a speedy victory was ended. But the Allied success was at a fearful cost. The first convoy of eighty wounded British troops from the battle arrived in Leeds on 17 September. They were taken to Beckett Park Teacher Training College which had been requisitioned as a military hospital. Other hospitals were established at Temple Newsam House, Chapel Allerton and the East Leeds War Hospital in the work-house on Beckett Street where the Leeds Union Infirmary was part of the site.* Casualties continued to arrive in the city from the war zone at all times of day and night. They were often mud bespattered and riddled with lice and local people were soon well aware of the terrible price being paid in the trenches on the Western Front. But if any single day were to symbolise to the people of Leeds the full extent of the horror of that bloody conflict it was Saturday 1 July 1916.

On that bright summer Saturday people in Leeds read in the *Yorkshire Evening Post* of the great offensive launched that morning along a twenty-mile stretch of the River Somme to break through the German lines. The West Yorkshires, including the Leeds Pals, charged the enemy machineguns just west of the village of Serre. The special Sunday edition of the paper stressed that the Allies' attack had been 'satisfactory'.

---

* Not to be confused with Leeds General Infirmary. The pauper inmates were moved to Hunslet Union Workhouse and never returned. The hospital continued functioning after the war and eventually became known as St James's.

It was only at the end of the week that the full extent of the catastrophe was realised as the casualty lists were released. The British recorded 57,000 casualties on the first day of the Battle of the Somme. Some 900 Leeds Pals had charged the enemy at 7.30 a.m. that Saturday morning. By evening when roll call was carried out just seventeen answered their names. It was estimated that on that first day of July every street in Leeds had lost at least one man. It was a disaster summed up succinctly by Private Hollingworth of 'D' Company who simply commented, 'Have we won then? Cos, if we've won, God help us if we lose!'

The Battle of the Somme dragged on from July to November and cost the British Army alone 400,000 lives. One man who did live to tell the tale, however, was Sergeant Fred McNess of the Scots Guards and a native of Bramley. Severely wounded in the battle in September, he continued to lead his men, as the official citation said, 'with the greatest dash in the face of heavy shell and machine-gun fire'. For his bravery he was awarded the Victoria Cross as were five more Leeds men during that war. Another Leeds war hero, probably the most famous from the city, was Geoffrey Studdert Kennedy better known as 'Woodbine Willie'. An army chaplain from Leeds, he was awarded the Military Cross for tending the wounded under fire at Messines Ridge in 1917.

Not always were the heroes so recognised. An infuriated correspondent to the *Yorkshire Post* writing in October 1914 complained that about a dozen wounded soldiers leaving Beckett Park Military Hospital boarded a tram three-quarters of an hour after the free travel time had lapsed. They were not allowed to travel free and, having no money, the conductor had no option but to take their names and addresses so they could be charged later. It was council policy! 'Headingley', the pseudonym the writer used, was incensed at such a lack of understanding and railed that it was 'a disgrace to our city'.

On 11 November 1918 the guns fell silent and the armistice was announced. In Leeds jubilation broke out in the streets, bonfires were lit and fireworks set off. But for the troops returning piecemeal to the city over the following months there was no triumphant reception. Some 82,000 men had left the city to take up arms. The Leeds Roll of Honour recorded 9,640 who never came back.

Prime Minister David Lloyd George had declared that Britain should now become 'a country fit for heroes to live in'. But for many of those returning troops life was never the same again. Now a common sight on the streets of the city was that of maimed or shell-shocked veterans. Less noticeable were those suffering mental strain like Fred Abrams, a Leeds council school teacher. He had left for the front just a

18. Back-to-backs
Between the wars almost three quarters of the population of Leeds lived in back-to-backs. This view of Little London seen from Camp Road is typical of such housing. Note the washing hanging in the street and smoke pollution, the ever present blight of Leeds, scarring the landscape. This photograph was taken as late as 1968.

month after the war began and returned to teach at Queen's Road School four years later in 1918. His health was ruined and the Army Medical Board finally gave him a certificate of absence for 'Nervous Exhaustion'.

Compounding readjustment to civilian life for those returning troops was the deadly outbreak of influenza which swept the world and reached England by the autumn of 1918. By 16 October John Gaunt, the headmaster of Whingate Elementary School, noted in the school log-book that 'Signs of Influenza are appearing, especially in Standard IVa.' Eight days later half the children of the school of over 400 were absent. The Education Committee closed Leeds schools two days early for half-term and opened them two and a half weeks later. In all during the winter of 1918–19 some 150,000 English people perished from the virus and the world-wide toll was greater than the total war deaths of all countries in the recent conflict. There were also other problems that beset both the returning ex-servicemen and the rest of the population, for ahead lay years of economic crises and political volatility. Two of those political forces, Communism and anti-Semitism, had become noticeable in Leeds even before the war was over. They would return again in force twenty years later.

In March 1917 the first Russian Revolution broke out.* Following strikes and riots in Petrograd, the Russian Parliament, the Duma, forced the Tzar to abdicate and a Provisional Government headed by Alexander Kerensky was formed. In June 1917 a Socialist convention was called in Leeds by the ILP and the British Socialist Party to express solidarity with the Russian people and, it was hoped, to inaugurate a British revolution. The Cabinet, fearing its subversive tendency, considered banning the assembly but eventually decided to allow it to go ahead. Leeds City Council took more positive steps. It cancelled the convention's booking of the Albert Hall, the circular hall in the Mechanics' Institute, and the police banned the public meeting which had been arranged to be held in Victoria Square. Hoteliers were encouraged to refuse bookings for the 1,150 delegates who were due to arrive and thus most were forced to make alternative arrangements and stay in private accommodation.

The Coliseum in Cookridge Street, however, was made available for the Sunday meeting and here some of the luminaries of the British Labour movement gathered: Ramsay MacDonald, Philip Snowden, Herbert Morrison, Ernest Bevin and the philosopher Bertrand Russell. Leeds sent two delegates, D. B. Foster and Bertha Quinn. The Leeds Convention was critical of the war, congratulated the Russians on their revolution and frightened the establishment by urging local bodies to co-ordinate working-class activity. However, its revolutionary fervour evaporated when Lenin's October Revolution overthrew the more moderate Kerensky and the Russians signed a separate peace treaty with Germany.

But within months of the convention gathering in Leeds an ugly outburst of anti-Semitism scarred the city streets. In June 1917 street fighting broke out between Christian and Jewish youths. The disturbance soon developed into a vicious riot involving pit workers and older men. Jewish properties in the Leylands area were vandalised and looted. The *Yorkshire Post* insisted that the Jews had in no way provoked the incident and many people remarked that over 2,000 Jews had patriotically

---

* It was known as the February Revolution because Russia still used the Julian Calendar.

enlisted during the war. But anti-Semitism was only one of the social and political issues which confronted Leeds people in the years which followed the Great War.

The majority of those Leeds people, somewhere in the region of seventy per cent, lived in endless rows of back-to-back houses. Many of those homes were substandard and one report claimed that thirty per cent of them were unfit for human habitation. Pollution from mills, factories and the chimneys of every home blackened the buildings and hung like a pall over the city with fog frequently bringing it to a standstill.

The most common fear people had was that they would die in the workhouse or that 'galloping consumption' would strike someone in the family. The fear of consumption or tuberculosis in those days was even greater than that of cancer. Another concern was that their children might develop rickets, for a regular daily sight on the city streets was that of people hobbling by with bowed, distorted and twisted legs. The cause was vitamin deficiency. The diet of Leeds working-class people left much to be desired.

Cheap cuts of meat with vegetables and potatoes, cheap fruit, black pudding, tripe, kippers, fish and chips and pikelets were popular. Egg and bacon on a Sunday morning was a rare treat. The staple diet was bread: bread and dripping, bread and butter, or bread and jam – people rarely had bread, butter and jam together. Some favoured Nestlés milk spread on bread, sometimes sugar was sprinkled on it. Poorer people often dissolved an Oxo in hot water to make a gravy and bread was then dunked in it. Chicken was a rare luxury often reserved for people who were seriously ill. Charitable action was taken at times to ease the poverty. When economic problems were inherent, as they were in 1904, some children were fed at school by the Leeds Children's Relief Fund and in 1921 miners at Wortley and Farnley provided free meals for children in the William IV public house.

To combat the poor nutrition generally in the town the local authority issued a mixture of cod liver oil and malt to necessitous children at schools and from September 1929 those children whose parents were prepared to pay 5d. a week could be supplied with a third of a pint of milk a day. An effort was made to reduce the high rate of child mortality in the country when the Babies' Welcome Movement was launched. In addition to saving lives, it gave advice and training to mothers and stressed the need for the prevention of disease. The first Babies' Welcome in Leeds was opened in Ellerby Lane in 1909. By the mid-1920s, some fifty per cent of the children in the city came under the influence of the movement. It was held in such high esteem that in 1928 when Armley Babies' Welcome was opened the Princess Royal was invited to carry out the ceremony.

Social progress for families was slowly being made but one cause of poverty was excessive drinking and gambling. Though gambling away from racecourses was illegal bookmakers operated from various places in the town, often with the connivance of the local police. Bookies' runners were frequently used to pick up bets in public houses or on street corners and then take them to lay off at the bookie's premises.

Working-class areas always had a large number of public houses concentrated in them. On the half-mile stretch of Wellington Road eight pubs and a working men's club could be found. Temperance societies, the Salvation Army and local chapels in particular sought to combat the problem but drink was deeply entrenched in the culture of many working-class men. Women's drinking did not usually present a problem but few landlords went to the extent of the one at the New Inn on Tong Road who insisted that if women wished to drink on a Sunday they should wear a hat! For men it was a different matter. At the beginning of the century it was common for groups of men to club together for several weeks and then take a 'Cobblers' Monday', a day off work, to drink away everything they had saved.

Poverty was commonplace. Leeds working-class people did not use cheques or pay bills monthly. Few people had bank accounts and many people were suspicious of banks for they were deemed to be for the middle classes, an attitude which reflected the 'them and us' culture so prevalent in the first half of the century in the city. Workers were paid weekly and paid for things weekly, usually on Friday pay day. Clothes and household goods could be purchased on the 'never-never' and paid off each week. Furniture was available from Smart's in Briggate: 'Furnish today without delay; easier to pay Smart's four year way.' Food and everyday items could be had 'on tick' from local corner shops, the Co-op, the butcher's or the newsagent's.

Friday was also the day goods were redeemed from the local pawnbroker's, which would in all probability be returned the following Monday morning. Relief for the poorest came in the form of grocery and clothing coupons that could be redeemed at specific shops. Unfortunately, some of the clothes issued quickly found their way into local pawnshops. To offset this, when the *Yorkshire Evening Post* and the Leeds Education Committee launched their 'Boots for the Bairns' charity three small holes were punched into the top of the footwear. Local pawnbrokers gave a guarantee not to accept as pledges any footwear with the telltale holes.

Saving for Christmas or holidays was carried out in 'diddle-'em clubs', and there were also chocolate clubs and scent clubs. The club money was collected each week by a street collector as was that owed to the rent man, the coal man, the milk man and the man who collected money to be used to pay forthcoming doctor's bills. Some local pubs and clubs set up weekly funds to pay for yearly visits to the Rugby League Cup Final at Wembley.

Self-help was essential and many self-help societies were established over the years. Weekly contributions were paid to help offset the problems caused by sickness and death. Some, such as the Odd Fellows Society in Leeds, which was founded in 1857, were sophisticated, well-organised societies. Others were simple organisations often formed by the regulars in a local public house.

In the home, too, self-help rather than relying on professional and expensive medical help was used where possible. Bread poultices were used to treat carbuncles, grated raw potato for burns, cabbage water drunk to prevent rheumatism, and to clear wheezy chests children were encouraged to inhale the fumes from hot tar being used to repair roads. For toothache, tooth tincture was applied but if a tooth needed extraction the local chemist or druggist would carry it out, sitting the patient down on a chair in the middle of his shop. Some tougher souls were even known to pull out their own teeth! Even in death self-help was apparent. Many people had their winding sheet carefully set aside and when they died a local woman who specialised in 'laying-out' was called in to prepare the corpse for the undertaker.

Numerous memoirs have been written recapturing the spirit of life in the back-to-back communities of pre-Second World War Leeds. Reference is frequently made to the tingle-aireys or barrel organs that were trundled round the streets, to gypsies selling pegs, to rag and bone men with jaded ponies pulling carts, to the fish man selling kippers 'as'll set your chimney back alight', and the Kleeneze man offering a variety of brushes and cleaning materials. Romantics dwell on the camaraderie born of a unifying poverty: of home-baked bread cakes cooling by open doors, of men sitting on the doorsteps on balmy summer evenings exchanging gossip with neighbours, of housewives swilling the pavements outside their houses and hanging washing across the street, and of children wearing their new clothes bought only every Whitsuntide.

But there was a grim forbidding downside to that life. Social investigators claimed that in the first decade of the twentieth century a third of the nation lived below subsistence level. Between the wars poverty was endemic and visits from the Means Test man commonplace. He was empowered to order a family to sell whatever he determined was not essential before aid was granted. Relief was given to the needy by the local poor law unions either in their own homes or in the workhouse and relatives were liable to make a contribution towards their upkeep. Early in the century the Hunslet Union announced that their cure for pauperism was to focus on the children of the poor. To this end special homes were built away from the workhouse where it was hoped more positive social attitudes could be developed. Other poor law unions followed suit.

That hardship was further intensified by the 'slump' which haunted the nation throughout the 1920s and 1930s. One in ten of the working population was then unemployed. The peak of the Depression was reached between 1932 and 1933 when three million people were on the dole. Ironically those in work were better off than they had ever been. But for those who endured the distress that unemployment generated no better description of the Thirties was ever coined than 'the black years, the devil's decade'.

In Leeds unemployment fluctuated. It declined after the high it reached at the end of the Great War until 1927, then between 1929 and 1931 it doubled. By 1937 it hovered around 17,000 and showed signs of increasing in the years immediately preceding the Second World War. Some efforts were made by the council to create jobs. It introduced a direct labour unemployment relief scheme, which was not a new idea. In 1906 the Leeds to Rodley tram-track was laid by unemployed men. During the 1920s the idea was adopted again and work commenced on an ambitious project to build a ring road round the city and to create a series of arterial roads in the town. Unemployed labour was used for those as it was in the 1930s for the building of the Civic Hall. Backed by the Unemployment Grants Committee the construction of the new building was undertaken by a workforce of whom ninety per cent came from the unemployment register. In all some 34,000 were employed in the city in approved unemployment relief schemes.

But not all could be accommodated and some fell through the net. Charities helped where they could and three churchmen came to the fore in Leeds each making a significant contribution to alleviating the suffering in the city. One man recognised the pressing need to help that unfortunate economic underclass. He was the Revd Percy Don Robins who arrived in the city in 1930 as the Vicar of St George's. By the end of that year he had turned the crypt of the church, in his words 'a derelict rubbish heap', into a sanctuary for the poor and the homeless. There food, shelter and help of every kind was made available. He went on to provide a rest home for women and children and for eighteen years assiduously campaigned for those in need with Christian compassion and boundless energy.

Another minister, J. G. Sutherland – no one ever called him James Gunn – also reacted positively to the suffering he saw around him. For thirty-three years he laboured at his Belgrave Central Church in New Briggate where he established a crèche for working mothers, and opened a chiropody clinic, a surgery where psychiatric help was forthcoming and a legal bureau. Next to the chapel he created his 'Children's Palace' which contained a nursery, youth hall and an ante-natal clinic. But he is best remembered for his 'Never Seen the Sea Fund' which gave an opportunity to youngsters from the grim slum areas of the city to witness for the first time the heaving North Sea at Scarborough.

One of the most pressing immediate social problems the authorities faced after the First World War was the number of substandard houses in the city. Seventy per cent of the houses in Leeds were back-to-backs and the general consensus was that without a through flow of air they were unhealthy. In 1909 an Act of Parliament forbade any further building of them but Leeds City Council found a loophole in the law and allowed the building of back-to-backs to continue in the town until 1937.

It was another Leeds churchman who was to play a leading role in urging action from the council. In 1927 the Revd Charles Jenkinson became the Vicar of the combined parishes of St John and St Barnabas in Holbeck. Much of Holbeck was slum property. Jenkinson was furious that Leeds lagged behind other cities in its slum clearance programme and published a pamphlet, *Sentimentality or Commonsense*, revealing that fact.

The Conservative Party now in control of the city put forward a modest proposal to demolish 3,000 houses over a five-year period. The Labour and Liberal opposition urged greater action and Jenkinson, now a Labour councillor, put forward a counterproposal for demolishing 3,000 houses in one year and dramatically increasing the number in subsequent years. Its opponents designated the plan the 'Red Ruin' but the difference between the parties was not the principle of clearance but the pace at which it was to be carried out.

Already council estates had been built at Hawksworth, Wyther Park, Meanwood, Cross Gates, Middleton and York Road as a result of the 1919 Housing Act. By 1930 some 7,000 houses had been erected. The achievement certainly made its impact on the housing shortage in Leeds but it made little impact in providing alternative accommodation for slum dwellers. One reason was that even the cheapest council rents were only affordable by the wealthier working-class and lower-middle-class tenants.

When Labour gained control of the council in 1933 Jenkinson became the Housing Committee chairman. He introduced a differential rent scheme to aid poorer people to take advantage of new council houses and move out of their slum neighbourhoods. It was bitterly opposed by both the Conservative lobby and those council house tenants who found themselves paying more for their homes than other people. Nevertheless, other huge estates mushroomed across the city: Gipton, Seacroft, Sandford, Halton Moor and Belle Isle all appeared in the 1930s.

However, there were disadvantages to slum clearance. Some Leeds landlords, realising their properties had been condemned, refused to maintain them in a fit state whilst tenants were still occupying them. Letters appeared the *Yorkshire Evening News* condemning the practice and a graphic report appeared in its columns describing the situation its reporter found. Another problem was that many of the new council tenants moving to these estates soon found that they were not everything they had hoped for. Originally living near the city centre people were used to having shops, cinemas and other amenities on their doorstep. Now they found no such facilities on hand in their new neighbourhood. Middleton was a classic example where the new estate was literally cut off from the rest of Leeds by a wood. Isolated and in a strange environment many resented the move and juvenile vandalism became a cause for concern.

Jenkinson's most imaginative housing development of the inter-war years was unquestionably the building of Quarry Hill Flats, the biggest block of council flats in Europe. Built between 1935 and 1941 they were based on the Karl-Marx-Hof development in Vienna which included homes and public facilities combined on a single site. Quarry Hill covered an area of twenty-six acres on which would be built 938 flats for over 3,000 people. Also provided were a laundry, shops, a Garchey waste disposal system in every flat, five playgrounds and a nursery. Only eighteen per cent of the site was built on in order to provide areas for fresh air and relaxation.

The Mopin system of construction, used light steel frames and the concrete facing slabs employed were cheaper than traditional brick and dispensed with the need for skilled labour. Many people, however, preferred to live in council houses rather than flats and tenants of Quarry Hill disagree about just how satisfactory the revolutionary accommodation was. Unfortunately some of the buildings were never erected, the landscape areas deteriorated into expanses of waste and in less than forty years the flats themselves were demolished.

Whilst the corporation was busy overseeing the provision of homes for the working classes private developers were occupied in building

19. Quarry Hill Flats
Charles Jenkinson's imaginative housing development was built between 1935 and 1941.
It was the biggest block of council flats in Europe. Unfortunately it did not prove to be the
success its supporters had hoped. The West Yorkshire Playhouse and the offices of the
Department of Health and Social Security now cover the site.

middle-class semi-detached and detached houses in the suburbs. The middle-class population drift to the north had begun in earnest after the 1850s in order for people to escape from the polluted and noisome city centre. During the inter-war years it accelerated. New developments at Adel, Alwoodley, Gledhow, Headingley, Moortown, Oakwood, Roundhay and Weetwood were undertaken. In all about 36,000 private houses were built in the city at this time.

By the end of the nineteenth century, thanks to improved rail services, places beyond the city boundaries had become popular with those who wanted, and could afford, to live in a more rural setting. Ben Rhydding, Ilkley and Harrogate became popular commuter bases. Semi-detached and good-class terrace houses were built at Pool-in-Wharfedale, Weeton and Scholes. Developments occurred at Horsforth, Cross Gates and Garforth.

The main factor that made such rural locations possible as dormitory suburbs were the improved rail and bus transport services. The new housing estates saw tram routes being built to Cross Gates in 1924, Middleton in 1925, and Gipton in 1936 but buses were cheaper to operate and bus routes were opened to service most corporation estates. Trolley buses began operating on a few routes from 1911. But in the old borough of Leeds trams still carried the bulk of passengers until 1959.

The expansion of the use of buses on the road was mirrored by an increase in both private and commercial vehicles. Roundhay Road showed almost a twelvefold increase between 1903 and 1933. Dangers to pedestrians consequently increased and a Safety First Council was set up in the city to monitor the problem. The police, too, found themselves having to divert more officers from criminal investigations to traffic duty. In an attempt to ease the demands on manpower, automatic traffic signals known as robots were installed to control the movement of vehicles. The first automatic signals ever used in Britain appeared on the streets of Wolverhampton in November 1927 but by March 1928 similar signals had been installed at the junction of Park Row and Bond Street in Leeds.

The development of transport revolutionised life in the twentieth century. Improved rail and bus services opened up the nearby Yorkshire Dales and the county's increasingly popular seaside resorts of Scarborough, Bridlington and Filey. Equally popular with Leeds people were the Lancastrian resorts of Blackpool and Morecambe. But if trips by charabancs became the norm between the wars, the future was seen in aviation.

In October 1928 the Air Ministry urged larger councils to develop local aerodromes. The following year the search began for a suitable location which would serve both Leeds and Bradford. A site was suggested at Whinmoor to the east of Leeds but was understandably rejected by Bradford. However, an airfield had already been established at Yeadon to the north of both towns. In 1931 the Leeds and Bradford Joint Aerodrome Committee took it over and two years later the Air Ministry granted it a full commercial licence. Scheduled commercial flights began in April 1935 to Newcastle, Edinburgh and Heston, one of London's four airports. In 1939 Yeadon airport was requisitioned by the Air Ministry and, after some deliberation when the war ended, in 1956 both councils decided to retain it, anticipating the increasing demand in air travel that escalated during the latter part of the century.

Though he never lived to see the plan come to fruition, among the great supporters of the scheme was Sir Charles Wilson. Wilson replaced John Gordon as Conservative leader in Leeds in 1904. He was a dynamic individual with a rare gift for political machination. With the exception of 1911–12 he led the council from 1907 to 1928. Despite having an outright majority during only three of those years, it was Wilson's brand of Conservatism which dominated council policy. The Conservatives went on to be the largest party on the council for the years up to 1945, with the exception of 1928, and from 1933 to 1935 when Labour gained control.

Wilson's dream, so it was said, was for Leeds to control everything from the Pennines to the North Sea. In 1912 Shadwell, Roundhay, part of Cross Gates and Seacroft were added to the city. Middleton was absorbed in 1919 and in 1922 a joint venture by Leeds and Bradford was launched to add 17,000 more acres and an additional population of 48,000 people to both towns. But Wilson's policy of municipal imperialism infuriated the threatened local authorities. In 1921 an enquiry was set up to investigate the plan and when asked what the people of Leeds thought of the proposal Wilson replied somewhat disdainfully, 'I am Leeds.' In May 1922 the Leeds Corporation Bill was debated in the House of Commons and to the relief of Pudsey and Farsley MPs rejected it.

Wilson, however, carried on regardless. Adel voluntarily became part of the city in 1924 and in 1927 a further bill for expansion was presented in Parliament. Alwoodley, Temple Newsam, Eccup and part of Austhorpe were then added. After his death in 1930 expansion continued and in 1937 parts of the borough of Pudsey, and the parishes of Arthington, Austhorpe, Barwick-in-Elmete, Swillington and Wigton were absorbed. In twenty-five years, Leeds had grown by seventy-five per cent.

Sir Charles represented the Central constituency of Leeds in Parliament from 1923 to 1929. During that time the nation had to face the crisis of the General Strike of 1926. In 1925 the Trades Union Congress (TUC) promised that if necessary it would call a general strike in order to support the miners who at the time were in dispute with the coal owners. When the pit managements locked out the colliers on 30 April 1926 the TUC called for a general strike to commence on 4 May. The government, however, was well prepared and Prime Minster Stanley Baldwin called on middle-class volunteers to come forward to help maintain vital services. Captain Hacking from the Home Office was appointed civil commissioner to Leeds. Alderman Sir Charles Wilson called a special meeting of the council, the Leeds Volunteer Services Committee was formed and special constables were called up. Of the 10,000 strike-breakers who volunteered to help in Leeds about 2,000 were actually used.

The enlistment of sixty police officers on special tram duty enabled about 150 of the city's trams to continue operating. However, some trams were attacked and serious riots broke out in Duncan Street, Vicar Lane and outside the municipal tram depot at Swinegate. Several men and women were arrested but the *Yorkshire Post* insisted that picketing was 'by and large peaceful'.

20. The 'Sultan of Leeds' Sir Charles Wilson dominated Leeds politics during the interwar years to the extent that he was able to claim, 'I am Leeds'. It was said that his vision was to see the city stretch from the Pennines to the North Sea.

If Sir Charles Wilson was the most prominent politician in Leeds between the wars, the leading industrialist was Montague Burton. A Lithuanian Jewish refugee, he established his retailing business in Sheffield in 1900 but realising the potential of wholesale bespoke tailoring he moved to Leeds in 1909. By the time the First World War commenced he had made the city his base, at first producing military uniforms but then, when the war ended, going on to produce bespoke suits. In 1920–1 he opened his Hudson Road factory which would eventually employ 16,000 people and the year 1925 saw his firm become the largest and most popular clothing company in Europe.

His genius manifested itself in the efficient way he organised production. Not only did it mean an order taken one week could be supplied seven days later but it also held costs to a level which enabled working-class people to afford his clothes. Production soared to 100,000 garments a week and it was estimated that Burton's supplied a fifth of the clothing worn by all British males. His retailing outlets quickly spread across the country rising from forty in 1919 to 595 in 1939. His factory became not only a focal point for good productive practices but also an exemplar of good practice in staff relations. Rest rooms, medical, optical and dental services were available; the staff canteen boasted it could serve 2,000 cups of tea in five minutes and seat in all 8,000 workers. Perhaps the greatest testament to him was that years after his death many of the workers who knew him affectionately described him simply as 'a gentleman'.

By the outbreak of war 10,500 were employed at Hudson Road and a further 6,000 at three factories in Lancashire. Other firms too realised the potential. Price's on Kirkstall Road, Hepworth's, John Collier and Jackson the Tailors each competed in the burgeoning market. Generally bespoke tailoring stimulated the economy of Leeds and specifically offered employment for female seamstresses.

Tailoring employed twice as many workers as any other single industry but the pattern of a diversified economy that had been noticeable in Leeds in the past continued. A random selection of such industries in the 1920s and 1930s includes general engineering, furniture manufacture, bread and biscuit making, brewing, ferro-concrete construction, hair-dressing appliance making, button making, camera making, coach building, soap manufacture, brush making and the making of umbrellas. Some companies became household names: Crabtree's for printing presses; William Moorhouse and Sons for jam-making; Thorne's for toffees. Leeds-based British Fish Canners produced four-fifths of the nation's consumption of brisling and sardines and Waddington's became internationally famous for its playing cards, jigsaws and the board game 'Monopoly'. Kershaw's on Harehills Lane specialised in lenses and catered for the growing film industry by building cinematograph projectors for cinemas.

The heyday of cinema occurred during the 1920s and 1930s but cinemas had been operating in Leeds a decade before that. Moving pictures were originally shown in marquees at the local feasts but in 1905 the old Coliseum concert hall was converted to show films and became the first full-time cinema in Leeds. In 1938 it changed its name to the Gaumont. In 1907 the Assembly Rooms, originally used for variety performances, was similarly converted. As the cinema became more and more popular in the years up to the end of the First World War a host of new picture houses was established, including two of the few cinemas still operating in the city today. The Hyde Park was opened in 1914 and the Lounge at Headingley two years later.

By the 1930s almost every month brought a new cinema opening somewhere in the town. Some, like the Ritz on Vicar Lane which opened in 1934, the Regal at Cross Gates in 1936 and boasting the largest theatre car park in the country, the Kingsway at Moortown in 1937, the Clock on Roundhay Road in 1938, and the Rex at Beeston in 1939, were opulent picture palaces designed to take people out of their everyday humdrum existence and allow them to enjoy a few hours of escapism in a luxurious setting. But the most magnificent of all was the Paramount built in 1932 at the corner of Briggate and the Headrow and known as the 'Wonder Theatre of the North'. In 1940 it changed its name to the Odeon.

Going to 'the pictures' was a weekly, sometimes twice-weekly pursuit. Although the main city-centre cinemas showed newly released films for a week or more, cinemas in the suburbs showed older films, changing their programme twice a week, usually on Mondays and Thursdays. By 1939 Leeds had sixty-eight cinemas in operation. Cinema going was relatively cheap and its growing popularity tolled the death knell for many live theatres across the country.

In Leeds the Queens Theatre on Meadow Road, like the Coliseum before it, gave up the struggle in 1923 and became a cinema. The Empire in Briggate dallied with films when it showed Charlie Chaplin's first talkie *City Lights* but with the demise of the Hippodrome in 1933 it returned to variety. Even the prestigious Grand Theatre turned cinema for seven weeks in 1917 to show D. W. Griffith's classic *Birth of a Nation*. The Theatre Royal continued as a theatre. When Francis Laidler took it over in 1909 he established a long-running tradition of pantomimes with his production of *Babes in the Wood*, a tradition which continued until the theatre closed in 1957.

For millions sport also helped to focus attention away from the difficulties so many people endured in everyday life and enabled them to associate with the successes of their heroes. Thousands packed Headingley to watch first-class cricket; dour Roses matches when Yorkshire and Lancashire met or when England and Australia were locked in a keenly fought test match. In winter such was the popularity of Rugby League in the city that three professional sides, Leeds, Hunslet and Bramley attracted great support. Professional Association Football appeared in 1904 when Leeds City was founded. Within a year it was playing second division football at Elland Road and continued to do so until it was expelled from the Football League in 1919 for making illegal payments to players. It was re-formed as Leeds United in 1920.

Entertainment and sport were both covered widely in the local press and Leeds was fortunate in the wide range of publications available. The old rivals the *Yorkshire Post* and *Leeds Mercury* were still available even though in 1923 the Yorkshire Conservative Newspaper Company and owner of the *Yorkshire Post* took over the *Mercury*, which was finally absorbed into its long-term competitor in 1939. The *Leeds Daily News* had become an evening paper renamed the *Yorkshire Evening News* in 1903 and supplementing these were several weekly papers, the most influential being the *Yorkshire Weekly Post*, the *Leeds Guardian* and, with specific readerships in mind, the *Leeds Catholic Herald*, the Labour publication the *Leeds and District Weekly Citizen* and for sports enthusiasts the *Sporting Pink* and the *Sports Echo*. Leeds never became the base for a national newspaper. The *Daily Chronicle* was an attempt to establish one in the city in 1925 but by 1930 it had failed.

But a new and speedier form of disseminating information had arrived on the scene and heralded a communication revolution. In October 1922 the British Broadcasting Company was founded as a private company and radio transmissions from London, station 2LO, began the next month. Listening to the wireless gradually became a national pastime. On 8 July 1924 the Leeds and Bradford Relay Station, 2LS, was opened in Basinghall Street. Three years later a charter of incorporation changed the company's nature and its name. It was replaced by a public corporation and became the British Broadcasting Corporation answerable to Parliament. On 18 January 1933 it opened Broadcasting House in Leeds on Woodhouse Lane.

The new service offered news and entertainment but equally important was its commitment to education. Nationally, education had become increasingly important since Forster's act of 1870 and Leeds City Council, of whatever political complexion, undertook a major role in improving the education services available to the people of the town. In 1902 Balfour's Education Act extended the opportunities for secondary education in the country and abolished the old school boards, placing responsibility for educational provision on local councils. Thus the new Education Committee in Leeds inherited 57,000 pupils in the 157 old elementary board schools and two established higher grade schools in Central and Thoresby. It also took over the new Cockburn High School which the board had just opened in 1902. A further 25,000 children were catered for in the voluntary sector in the city.

The council now embarked upon an ambitious programme of extending secondary education. West Leeds High School opened in 1907. Leeds Boys' and Girls' Modern Schools were taken over the same year and in 1932 moved to new premises at Lawnswood, the girls' school becoming Lawnswood High School and the boys' Leeds Modern. In 1914 Chapel Allerton Girls' High School was adopted and in 1920 another girls' school was absorbed to become Roundhay High. Provision for the boys was made in a second school on the same site in 1926.

The vast majority of Leeds children, however, attended local council schools leaving at twelve years of age until 1918 when the age was raised to fourteen. Thirty-nine Church of England schools and twelve Roman Catholic schools in addition to Leeds Grammar and Leeds Girls' High alongside a few private establishments made up the rest of the complement.

Secondary education in the new high schools was selective and available for those prepared to pay the fees. A limited number of places were available for children who passed scholarships. These paid the teaching fees and provided books but parents still had to provide clothing. To buy indoor, outdoor and gym shoes as well as blazer, cap or beret, uniform trousers or dresses and sports strip at a time of severe economic stress was impossible for some families. Thus many successful scholarship winners were unable to take advantage of the opportunity offered. The Greenhalgh family in Leeds faced such a dilemma. John, a local miner, saw his five daughters and one son pass their scholarships. Only being able to afford to send one on to higher education he opted for the son. His decision today would be seen by many as sexist but his argument was simple: the girls would probably get married whilst the son would have to provide for a family.

It was to help such needy families that the Leeds Poor Children's Holiday Camp Association was formed in 1904. It opened a holiday camp at Silverdale on Morecambe Bay where children whose parents could not afford a holiday were able to enjoy a break by the sea. By 1922 it had catered for 10,000 Leeds children. In March 1922, in order to provide funds for the camp, Leeds teachers suggested a novel way of raising money. A vast children's carnival was proposed which would include sports events, a fancy-dress parade and mass gymnastic displays. But its intention was not just to improve finances, it was hoped that the event would encourage more and more children to take part in sports and healthy exercise. The event became known as Children's Day. On that day the city came to a stop, the Lord Mayor supervised proceedings and one lucky girl, chosen to be Queen of Children's Day, rode in triumphal procession from the Town Hall to Roundhay Park to preside over the event. Children's Day ran until the 1960s, a resounding success for the teacher organisations that administered it and the local businesses and city council who supported it.

Adult educational provision was made by the university which itself grew in influence, particularly under its Vice-Chancellor Sir Michael Sadler. Two other vital adult education institutions in the city were the Workers' Educational Association and the Swarthmore Educational Centre which opened in 1909.

However, the bulk of adult education provision came from the council. Schools run by the Leeds Institute on Cookridge Street came under its auspices and were eventually formed into the College of Technology and the College of Art. Commercial evening classes were grouped into what eventually became the College of Commerce. The council provided a teacher training college at Beckett Park in 1907 and in 1934 Carnegie College of Physical Education for men, as at that time such colleges existed only for women. In 1907, the Yorkshire Ladies' Council offered the local authority their Yorkshire School of Cookery and Domestic Economy which trained teachers in those subjects and from 1921 became known officially as the Yorkshire College of Housecraft and unofficially as 'the Pud Club'.

The council's attempt to provide for a city worthy of the twentieth century was perhaps best symbolised by the building of the new Civic Hall and the widening of the Headrow. Not only did the new hall provide much-needed office accommodation for the departments of the Town Clerk, City Treasurer, City Engineer, Waterworks and Sewerage Engineer and the Baths Superintendent, its construction offered work to the unemployed building workers in the city. Supported by the Unemployed Grants Committee the Portland stone building was completed in three years at a cost of £360,000. It was officially opened by King George V and Queen Mary on 23 August 1933.

Since the 1840s people had discussed the need to build wider and healthier streets in Leeds. In May 1924 under Alderman Charles Lupton the council decided to embark upon an ambitious scheme to provide Leeds with an impressive and wide east-to-west route through the city centre. It meant sweeping away the old buildings on the north side of the road and replacing them with ones which conformed to a uniform style laid down by the architects. After toying with various new names for the thoroughfare the council opted for its original one and the Headrow it remained.

Two of the most popular new buildings on it were the Paramount Cinema, later to became the Odeon, and Lewis's Department Store. Lewis's, which opened in 1932, made its mark. Apart from the wide range of goods it carried, it claimed to have the first moving escalator in the North of England and the only one in Leeds.

Shopping in town at Lewis's or at the local Co-op,* visiting Golden Acre Park after its opening in 1932, dancing at Tom Bacon's Ballroom in Vicar Lane, taking coffee at the Kardomah Café in Briggate or attending socials and smoking concerts** at local churches and chapels were all part of the pattern of life in those inter-war years. By the 1930s drinking had become less of a social problem and some city-centre public houses remained closed on Sundays. The Chief Constable, Robert Matthews, expressed the view that the cinemas, theatres, dance halls, and the wireless had all contributed to this improvement. But it was also, no doubt, a success in part due to the inroads churches and chapels had been making in that area.

Although attendance at church or chapel was still high and for many still formed a focal point in their community, more and more people were slowly beginning to drift away from active involvement in religion. As early as 1909 the Vicar of Wortley was being attacked in the *Armley and Wortley News* for his fundamentalist opposition to Darwinism but by 1928 he changed his views and was forced to concede evolution as a fact.

Meanwhile the Church itself was slowly changing. It had had to help people make sense of the appalling losses of the Great War, organise what aid it could during the years of the Depression and offer guidance in a rapidly changing world. Attempts were made by certain churches and chapels in Leeds to co-operate more and more and break down the contentious elements which had so long divided Anglicans from Nonconformists. Nevertheless, among the Church establishment the free churches were still viewed with suspicion. When the Revd Richard Horton of Leeds spoke in a local Methodist chapel in February 1936 he was strongly reprimanded by his bishop.

In December that year another Yorkshire bishop in the person of Bishop Blunt of Bradford also took exception to the Nonconformists and the suggestion that they should play a part in the forthcoming coronation service of the new king, Edward VIII. When the Leeds-based *Yorkshire Post* reported his speech the world's press misconstrued his words. For some time Fleet Street had agreed not to mention the king's involvement with a married woman. Now it is believed the bishop had addressed the issue and thus was launched the political avalanche that became the Abdication Crisis. The nation was shocked when Edward gave up the throne to marry a divorcee, Mrs Wallis Simpson.

---

* In 1928 the LICS opened its hundredth branch in the city in Chapeltown Road.

** On arrival the men were given tobacco or cigarettes and the women chocolates.

Bishop Blunt was equally shocked. He had never even heard of Mrs Simpson!

The people of Leeds, along with the rest of the world, watched the drama of the Abdication Crisis unfold. It was not the only crisis they found reported in the Leeds press. They read with horror of Italian aerial attacks in Abyssinia. They saw for themselves the effects the Spanish Civil War was having on Leeds. Communist Party members collected funds outside Kirkgate Market to support the Republicans and some twenty volunteers left the city to fight against Franco and his Fascists. One of the saddest sights was that of Spanish refugee children arriving in Leeds to be housed at Hill Top, Bramley. They were not the only refugees reaching the city. Within a year of Adolf Hitler assuming power in 1933 the Leeds Jewish Refugee Committee had been formed. The brutal anti-Semitism that Nazism spawned led to an increasing number of German Jews being driven out of their homeland. By 1939 some 700 had been helped by the local committee to find refuge in Leeds. But groups sympathising with Fascism existed in Britain and anti-Semitism at times manifested itself in the city.

Although Jews had contributed considerably to the economic well-being and the cultural development of Leeds anti-Semitism surfaced in the town in various ways. Local golf clubs refused to admit Jewish members.* The 101 dance club advertised for 'English clientele only'. Some tea-rooms at times refused to serve Jewish customers. Certain firms, particularly in engineering and building, applied a selective policy on employment to the point that some Jews even changed their names in order to get jobs. Little of this appeared in the local press. The editor of the *Yorkshire Post* explained that certain prominent Jews felt the less said about the question the better.

But anti-Semitism was the ideological linchpin of the burgeoning Fascist movement. In Britain the British Union of Fascists had been founded by Sir Oswald Mosley in 1932 after his return from Mussolini's Italy. Mosley's anti-Communist and anti-Semitic views echoed the vicious attacks Adolf Hitler was heaping on Marxists and Jews whilst Mosley's uniformed black-shirted followers mirrored Hitlers' brown-shirted legions.

Leeds became an obvious target for anti-Jewish action and propaganda. Mosley's blackshirts and their supporters conducted a campaign of harassment and insult on any passing Jew. Cinema queues were tar-

---

* The first Jewish golf club in Leeds was formed in 1923. By the 1930s it played fixtures with non-Jewish clubs.

geted as Fascists flaunted their publications in front of them. Physical attacks were made on individuals though a small group of Jewish volunteers retaliated by returning violence with violence.

In September 1936 Mosley announced a mass meeting was to be held on Holbeck Moor. The windows of Jewish shops on North Street were covered with Fascist propaganda and swastikas. Objections came from both Jews and Gentiles when it was realised that Mosley and his followers intended to march in their black-shirt uniforms through the most densely populated Jewish area of the town. Churchmen and other prominent citizens also raised their deeply felt concern at such a provocative act. The Watch Committee listened to their fears, changed the route but allowed the marchers to wear their uniforms.

On Sunday 27 September Mosley led about 1,000 blackshirts, drawn from the West Riding, onto the moor. A massive crowd had gathered to witness the event. At the same time a counter-demonstration organised by the Communists and supported by some Leeds Jews arrived. As the Fascists marched hecklers yelled abuse, stones were thrown and fighting broke out. Police did their best to restrain the crowd. Three people were arrested and Mosley and several other Fascists were injured. Mosley and his blackshirts were for the moment silenced but the forces that had been unleashed on the world and which they represented were gathering momentum. The Second World War was about to begin.

CHAPTER NINE

EUROPEAN CITY

On Friday 30 September 1938 the *Daily Express* announced to a hopeful world, 'Britain will not be involved in a European war this year, or next year either.' There were many, however, who feared that it would be. On page eight of that same edition, the paper described what steps were being taken in the event hostilities should break out. In Leeds it reported how the corporation Engineers' Department had discovered a disused water main under the city centre in which it was estimated that 5,000 people could be accommodated in the event of an aerial attack. And it went on to suggest that some 3,000 householders in the town, both men and women, were busy digging trenches and preparing air-raid shelters.

From 1936 the deteriorating situation in Europe saw Leeds City Council taking preliminary steps to organise civil defence and air-raid precautions (ARP). The bombing of the Spanish town of Guernica in 1937 by German aircraft emphasised to the world just how devastating such attacks could be on a civilian population. That same year a recruiting drive for ARP wardens was launched in Leeds and 3,968 volunteers enrolled within twelve months. In July 1938 the government created the Auxiliary Fire Service (AFS) to augment local fire brigades and in Leeds volunteers were trained to supplement the Leeds City Police Fire Service.

There were many in Britain who rejoiced in 1938 when Prime Minister Neville Chamberlain returned from Germany with the Munich Agreement. They believed that it really guaranteed, as he claimed, 'peace in our time'. Others, like Alderman Bretherick of Leeds, had their doubts. In October that year he sent a circular letter to the City Engineer and others suggesting the construction of an underground monorail tramway system in Leeds which, because it could double up as air-raid shelters, would be eligible for government grants. In the event it was never built but steps were taken to protect the general public by placing air-raid shelters at strategic positions across the city. By 1939 over 14,000 domestic air-raid shelters had been erected in Leeds, capable of protecting some 300,000 people.

At the beginning of 1939 gas masks were issued in Leeds schools and plans drawn up to evacuate to safe locations those children whose parents agreed. Schools in Leeds were summoned back from the summer holidays early. On 1 September, two days before war was declared, special trains took 18,250 children, 1,450 teachers and a further 1,350 voluntary helpers to secret destinations. Some were taken to nearby Ilkley and Pateley Bridge, others were transported further afield to places such as Retford, Lincoln, Gainsborough and Worksop. The following day 8,167 mothers, expectant mothers, blind and disabled people were also moved. But many Leeds parents remained suspicious of the scheme and the secrecy that surrounded it. In October only fifty per cent of the children registered for evacuation were actually relocated. In all, the evacuation option was taken up by only thirty-three per cent of the school population of the city.

Schools in Leeds remained closed during the whole of that autumn term. They reopened in January 1940 and by that time almost half the evacuees had returned home. Evacuation had proved unpopular with many and was considered unnecessary by those who may well have been lulled into a false sense of security. After the fall of Poland in 1939 little military action was forthcoming and Britain endured what became known as the 'phoney war'. Nevertheless, Leeds was not inactive. Men registered for the armed forces and women enrolled for the women's services. But the mistakes of the last war were learned and no longer were 'pals' battalions, formed entirely of local men, created.

In May 1940 the Local Defence Volunteers (LDV) was established. In Leeds units of the LDV, later known as the Home Guard and more affectionately today as 'Dad's Army', were created in the city centre and at Kirkstall, Silver Royd, Bramley, Farnley, Low Mills and Wellington Bridge. They were used to protect industrial sites, water supplies, man anti-aircraft batteries at Knostrop and Adel and guard enemy prisoners.

In Leeds the political parties established a truce and at the by-election for the North East constituency held in March that year, Professor J. J. Craik-Henderson, the Conservative candidate, was returned with a resounding majority of 23,160; his single opponent, a Fascist, raised only 722 votes.

Then in April 1940 the invasion of Norway was launched and the 'phoney war' was over. The advancing Wehrmacht armies swept across Europe and what could be saved of the British Expeditionary Force was evacuated from Dunkirk. For the first time Leeds people saw the sombre reality of the present conflict. Some 20,000 Dunkirk evacuees were brought to the city and billeted with civilians. The wounded were accommodated in St James's Hospital.

It was obvious to anyone walking through Leeds that the country was in a state of war. Sandbag barricades were erected at the entrances to places like Kirkgate Market. Windows of schools, trams and some shops were draped with adhesive netting to prevent the glass shattering in the event of an explosion. Metal railings and gates were removed and pots, pans and all manner of scrap metal were collected to be used for the war effort. The roofs of the arcades were painted black and each evening the streets became chasms of darkness as the black-out took effect. Air-raid shelters and static water tanks were placed across the city. And in the event of any heavy raids taking place the Leeds Public Assistance Committee established eighty-five centres across the town which would provide food and shelter. All manner of buildings were utilised: the Lakeside Café at Roundhay Park, Alwoodley Church Hall, the Scouts Hut at Moortown, Leeds University Sports Pavilion at Weetwood, and St Cyprian's School at Coldcotes were all designated sites.

And yet life did continue in the city. Children still gazed at the windows of the Dolls' Hospital in County Arcade, football continued at Elland Road, albeit using guest players, people still went to the cinema, ladies met for tea and cakes at Betty's Café. And shoppers in Leeds still pointed out 'Woodbine Lizzie', the lady tramp with her three overcoats and walnut face shuffling through the city streets or gave a penny to the legless beggar crouching outside Trinity Church on his wooden bogie.

In June 1941 the government recognised that better co-ordination and uniformity of training were required between the different local fire brigades and it created the National Fire Service (NFS). The Leeds City Police Fire Service and the AFS, like 1,400 other local fire brigades, were incorporated into one of the newly formed forces of the NFS.* Throughout the war, the NFS in Leeds had to deal with twenty-four major fires as a result of enemy bombing. Aerial attacks on the city also destroyed 197 buildings and damaged a further 7,623. Leeds was fortunate, however, in that despite having several munitions factories just eighty-seven alerts were sounded and only nine actual raids occurred. One heavy raid took place on 1 September 1940 when between 3,000 and 4,000 incendiaries and fourteen high explosive bombs were dropped on the town, but the *Yorkshire Post* was able to report that 'little damage' had been inflicted.

However, the night of the 14/15 March 1941 saw the worst attack on Leeds. At 8.28 p.m. that Friday night the sirens gave the alarm. The raiders arrived shortly after 9 p.m. and commenced raining down first incendiary bombs and then high explosives. In the city centre the Town

---

* When Leeds City Fire Brigade resumed responsibility in 1948 it was no longer part of the police service.

Hall, the museum in Park Row, Kirkgate Market, the Metropole Hotel and Quarry Hill Flats were among buildings hit. Railway goods yards were targeted and the factories of Fairbairn and Lawson, and Greenwood and Batley's suffered damage. Among the suburbs hit were Holbeck, Gipton, Woodhouse, Headingley, Roundhay Road and Armley.

Next day, censorship allowed the *Yorkshire Evening News* merely to report 'Fire Blitz on NE Town Beaten'. Ironically, it was able to carry the German communiqué which stated that Leeds, along with other towns, had been bombed the previous night. Leeds people could certainly confirm that. About 4,600 houses were damaged during the raid; 100 were wrecked beyond repair. Over 200 people were injured and sixty-five or sixty-six, the figures are uncertain, were killed. None of the deaths was more tragic than that of June Margaret Oddy, nine years-old, who had been brought for safety from London to Leeds in order to escape the blitz. The street where she was lodging received a direct hit and she was killed that Friday night. The tragedy was compounded when the ARP wardens were called in to recover the bodies. The warden who found her was John Oddy, one of her relatives. By the end of the war, the number of people killed in the city by enemy action totalled seventy-seven.

But the spirit of the people of Leeds, like the rest of the country, was not daunted by the struggle. When Prime Minister Winston Churchill stood on the steps of Leeds Town Hall and addressed a crowd of 25,000 in May 1942 he made it clear that Britain was engaged in that struggle as a 'people not only with the resolve and cause, but who also have the weapons'. And the Leeds response was to raise what funds it could to help provide those weapons. 'Wings for Victory Week' raised £7.2 million and, to publicise it, a Lancaster bomber from 97 Squadron which had flown forty-seven sorties was put on display outside Quarry Hill Flats. 'War Weapons Week' raised £3.5 million, 'Salute the Soldier Week' £2 million, but undoubtedly the greatest achievement was '*Ark Royal* Week'. The *Ark Royal* aircraft carrier had been torpedoed and sunk in 1941. Leeds adopted the new *Ark Royal* and raised £9 million during '*Ark Royal* Week'. In all, Leeds contributed £72 million to the war effort. It also ensured its fire and rescue services were available to cities like Hull, Coventry and London which fared much worse from the bombing than Leeds ever did. Then in July 1944, as the flying bomb or 'doodle bug' campaign was taking its toll on the south of England, Leeds took in some 800 refugees from the capital.

It also took in prisoners of war. Wounded enemy prisoners were treated in Leeds Infirmary where they were watched over by the Home Guard. Healthy prisoners were held at two prisoner of war camps in the city. The Germans were held at Camp No. 244 at Butcher Hill in Horsforth, where they worked on road building schemes and published their own magazine *Die Brücke* (*The Bridge*). The second camp, No. 91, was at Post Hill, Farnley where a few German but mainly Italian prisoners were held. The Italians were employed on local farms and in nearby engine sheds but on an evening were allowed to play football by Farnley Beck or walk down to Armley to visit the local cinemas.

The war in Europe ended in May 1945. In Leeds, factories and schools were shut, thanksgiving services were held, street parties organised and a flag-waving crowd bore an effigy of Hitler down Briggate. But even before hostilities against Japan had been concluded party politics began to reassert themselves. In the general election of July 1945 Clement Atlee's Labour Party was swept to power in a landslide victory.

Voters in Leeds reflected the national trend. Labour took five of the existing six seats in the town with the Conservatives only holding on to Leeds North after a recount by a majority of 128. Among the new MPs were Alice Bacon, a Normanton teacher and the only woman member to represent the city until the twenty-first century, and Hugh Gaitskell. Gaitskell went on to become both leader of the Labour Party and Leader of Her Majesty's Opposition. All parties acknowledged that his tragic and untimely death in 1963 deprived the nation generally, and Leeds South specifically, of a true statesman. The rarity of the disease which killed him and the fact that Anatoli Golitsin, a KGB defector, claimed that the Russians had planned the assassination of a west European opposition leader led to concern that the death may not have been natural. The matter has never been satisfactorily resolved.

The general election of 1950 set a trend which continued until the reorganisation of Leeds into a metropolitan borough in 1974. The Conservatives held Leeds North and won the new Leeds North West constituency; Labour held the other five. When Leeds reverted to six constituencies in 1955 the Conservatives held Leeds North East and Leeds North West, Labour the remaining four. Some of those MPs were extremely long standing with Denis Healey, the Labour MP for Leeds East, serving for thirty-seven years and Donald Kaberry, the Conservative MP for Leeds North West, for thirty-three.

In the same *Yorkshire Evening Post* that announced Labour's historic electoral victory in 1945 the paper looked to the future and identified the issues which now faced the new government: 'demobilisation, resettlement, housing and social progress'. There were others, however, arriving in Leeds in the months ahead who faced a bleak and uncertain future and for whom resettlement was crucial. At the end of the war millions of homeless refugees and ex-prisoners of war crowded the roads of western Europe. Many did everything in their power to avoid being sent home to the newly dominated Soviet eastern bloc. These displaced persons, as they were known, were ferried to different destinations in the west. Some came to Leeds.

The old POW camp at Post Hill was billeted with Ukrainians, Poles, Lithuanians and Latvians, though many of the refugee women were able to lodge in the homes of families in the Bramley area. These displaced persons began to rebuild their shattered lives, working in the local mills, mines and quarries. One small farmer from Ukraine, Fred Waselenko, was typical. His wife had died after having been incarcerated for three and a half years in a Siberian gulag. He fled to the west and spent the rest of his life working in the quarries at Bramley Fall, living in perpetual fear of being repatriated to the Soviet Union. As a boy 'Ted' Piscaszo literally walked to Leeds with his mother and younger brother from central Europe. He applied himself well in his adopted country and eventually became a draughtsman in Rodley.

The end of the war was a watershed in history as the world divided between the eastern Communist block and that of the western democracies. An uneasy peace developed as the so-called Cold War posed the threat of atomic warfare wreaking catastrophic devastation on the rival societies. The memory of Hiroshima and Nagasaki was still in people's minds and the government drew up contingency plans to deal with any possible nuclear attack. In 1952 it was estimated that if a bomb such as had demolished Nagasaki, the equivalent of 20,000 tons of TNT, were detonated above Leeds Bridge, combustible materials up to a mile from the spot would ignite and the bridges as far away as Woodlesford and Kirkstall be destroyed.

Robert Crute, the Town Clerk, recommended to the government that people made homeless in an attack should be compulsorily billeted in both private and council houses. Some sixty-five per cent of the homeless north of the river were to be moved to Otley, Harrogate, Wetherby and York; a further 20,000 south of the river were to gather in Middleton Park before being directed to Wakefield. If their homes were not too badly damaged, it was hoped that many would remain and cook on open fires. Drinking water was to be ferried from Eccup reservoir, special food convoys were to be established at Wetherby and Sheffield. Staffed by a crew of fifty, each convoy would contain two water tankers, four vans for stores, eight canteens and the capability to serve 7,000 helpings of stew at a sitting.

If the international future looked bleak for the nations of the world it did not deter the British people from taking a major step towards eradicating poverty and deprivation as the Beveridge Report was introduced proposing welfare from the cradle to the grave. It included comprehensive social insurance, a free health service, family allowances and free secondary education. Much of its implementation in Leeds was the responsibility of the city council.

Up to the introduction of the Leeds Metropolitan District Council in 1974 control of the city alternated between two periods when the Conservative Party was in power from 1951 to 1953 and 1967 to 1972, and three occasions when the Labour Party were in the majority: 1945–51, 1953–67 and 1972–4. In those years between the end of the Second World War and metropolitanisation there were no major ideological differences between the parties. Politicians of both parties saw their role as being one which encouraged local authority officers to utilise their professional expertise. The continuation of slum clearance, housing development, concessionary fares for old people, the introduction of one-man buses, the provision of bus shelters, the preservation of the Grand Theatre were all Conservative initiatives with which Labour agreed. The only major areas of disagreement were over the sale of council houses and the cleaning of the Town Hall. The Civic Trust also opposed that proposal believing it should be retained in its begrimed condition as both a symbol of the city's industrial heritage and a constant reminder of what pollution can do to the environment.

From 1945 several services provided by the city council were taken over by national bodies. In 1948 provision of electricity was transferred to the regional Yorkshire Electricity Board and the 'safety-net' of public assistance to the National Assistance Board. The following year gas supplies became the responsibility of the North Eastern Gas Board. One of the most significant changes, however, occurred in health.

The National Health Service (NHS) Act of 1946 set up a free medical service for all. Existing hospitals, whether run as voluntary establishments, or under local authority control became part of the NHS. Leeds had made considerable efforts to improve the quality of health provision in the borough and no man was more responsible than Dr J. Johnston Jervis, the Medical Officer of Health. Thanks to his gifted leadership infectious diseases diminished and life expectancy improved in the town. In 1925 the old Poor Law Hospital at Beckett Street had been renamed St James's Hospital, not after either St James the Just or St James the Great, but after two men: Dr James Allen, a long-serving medical superintendent, and Mr, later Sir, James Ford, the influential Clerk to the Guardians. Under Dr Jervis's direction St James's

Hospital was becoming recognised as one of the major hospitals in the country.

The introduction of the NHS saw the administration of Leeds hospitals come under the aegis of three new bodies. Leeds (A) Group Hospital Management Committee took responsibility for five hospitals: St James's, St Mary's, Cookridge, and the two voluntary ones, the Dispensary and the Jewish Herzl Moser Hospital. Group (B) administered specialist hospitals like Seacroft, Killingbeck, Meanwood Park, Crooked Acres and the Hollies along with the Leeds Chest Clinic. They also had responsibility for several units outside the Leeds city boundary such as Gateforth Hospital near Selby and Arthington Hospital near Otley. Leeds Infirmary, Ida and Robert Arthington Convalescent Hospital, the Hospital for Women, the Maternity Hospital and the Dental Hospital were supervised by the Board of Governors of United Leeds Hospitals.

Jervis also turned his attention to the provision of nurseries and made an effort to combat the ever-increasing problem of pollution as Leeds suffered from one of the heaviest soot deposits in the country. He was fortunate in that the chief public health inspector, J. Goodfellow, was also committed to ridding the town of the nuisance. It was a problem the citizens of Leeds had faced for over a century as the letter from 'Septimus' to the *Leeds Times* in 1845 had shown. In the 1950s 'the dark and murky cloud' he had written about was still choking the lungs of Leeds people. The exhaust fumes from the increasing number of vehicles on the streets of Leeds compounded the problem.

Time and again the city was brought to a standstill by impenetrable smog, an offensive mixture of smoke and fog, which left a filthy deposit of grime on people, choked their lungs and seriously affected their health. The killer fog, which claimed almost 4,000 people's lives in London in 1952, led to the passing of the Clean Air Act four years later. This sought to control smoke emissions from factories and domestic fires in urban areas. Leeds took the first necessary steps in 1959 to introduce zones where only smokeless fuel could be used. Even so, from 3 to 6 December 1962 Leeds endured a blanket of smog which paralysed the city, saw the sulphur dioxide content in the air reach eight times above normal and led to thirty-seven people being treated in hospital for respiratory diseases. However, by 1973 there were 109 smokeless zones established in the city and by the end of the century Leeds, if not totally pollution free, could rightly claim a success in ridding itself of one of its greatest scourges.

It was obvious that to create a healthy environment a major step forward was needed to provide better housing conditions. Robert Baker's reports had graphically shown the squalor which had existed in nineteenth-century Leeds. The pre-war slum clearance programmes had already started to make inroads into the problem and now with the war over Leeds accelerated its efforts. In the immediate post-war years 1,106 houses were demolished and by about 1964 the original 1934 plan for slum clearance had been completed. But council house provision always lagged behind demand. The problem was eased somewhat by renovating some of the existing back-to-backs. The small bedroom was converted into a bathroom and toilet whilst dormer windows were fitted into the attic to create an additional bedroom.

Major new estates were built at Armley Heights, Spen Lane, Cow Close, Moor Grange and Tinshill with extensions being added to the existing Belle Isle and Seacroft ones. In an attempt to solve the housing shortage Leeds followed the national trend by erecting multi-storey and high-rise blocks of flats. Though these offered far better equipped homes than tenants had previously enjoyed, they proved to be an alien environment for many. Used to the close proximity of neighbours in their old communities large numbers of people moving into these new surroundings felt isolated. They were frustrated by structural faults and at times felt threatened by recurrent vandalism. It became clear that the new strategy was not the solution its enthusiasts had hoped for. The situation deteriorated to such an extent that tenants eventually refused to occupy them and, after only twenty years in existence, Hunslet Grange flats on Leek Street had to be demolished.

Resentment turned to downright opposition when the Conservative Housing Programme of 1971–5 was launched. When the proposals to sweep away 30,000 houses in Armley, Bramley, Burmantofts and Stanningley were leaked to the press, residents across the city formed protest groups. The Conservative leader, Alderman Sir Frank Marshall, explained that the policy was to be simply a rolling programme over the next twenty years. However, the proposal generated such opposition that it was ultimately modified. By the end of the twentieth century there were still some 23,000 back-to-backs in use in Leeds.

Private house provision continued the pre-war trend by concentrating particularly in the north of the city. Alwoodley, Shadwell, Oakwood, Lawnswood, Roundhay, Moortown and Cookridge saw considerable developments with the Holt Park estate at Cookridge combining both private and council housing on the same site.

Perhaps the most far-reaching effect of the post-war years occurred in education thanks to the Education Act of 1944. This opened up the opportunity of free secondary education for all children according to their age, aptitude and ability. In turn, it enabled those who were capable of benefiting from higher education to go on to university or college and thus for the first time the professions were opened up to working-class aspirants. In Leeds all children attended county primary schools and then sat a selection examination, the Eleven Plus. The result of this determined whether a child attended a secondary grammar school like Roundhay High, a secondary technical school like Central High, or a secondary modern school like Parkside.

Leeds was fortunate in that all political parties generally set party differences aside to allow the education service to develop under the guidance of professionals. Two of the most prominent chairmen, Alderman Joshua Walsh, Labour, and Alderman Patrick Crotty, Conservative, saw their role as facilitating local authority officers to implement the plans needed to improve the education services of the city. Foremost of these was George Taylor, the Chief Education Officer.

The mass migration of the population to the suburbs from the city-centre areas necessitated the building of new primary and secondary schools. In 1905 some 30,000 children lived within a mile radius of the city centre and only 6,700 dwelt on the city fringes. By 1966 the position was reversed with only 2,400 living within a mile of the centre and over 30,000 in the peripheral suburban areas.

One of the more imaginative education schemes introduced was undertaken in conjunction with the Nuffield Foundation in 1961, and sought to teach French in certain Leeds primary schools to children from the unusually early age of eight. Another, literally life-saving, strategy was launched some years earlier when a scheme was introduced to teach every child in the city to swim.

To cater for the increasing school population Leeds also opened a second teacher training college, the James Graham College at Farnley. It was specifically created to utilise the skills and experience of mature students. Higher education was further developed in Leeds when, in January 1970, Dr Patrick Nuttgens was asked to begin the amalgamation of the colleges of Technology, Commerce, Home Economics and eventually the two training colleges to form the Leeds Polytechnic. In 1992 it became Leeds Metropolitan University. Meanwhile the University of Leeds, with its site expanding across the Woodhouse Lane and Hyde Park area, became one of the largest and most prestigious universities in post-war Britain.

Change was in the air. The burgeoning housing estates of the city, the new modern schools which were being built and the expanding higher and further education institutions transformed the face of Leeds. But possibly the most noticeable change which affected every man, woman and child in the city was seen on the roads. Increasing traffic congestion led to the council having to take a serious look at the problem and review its transport policy. In just four years, car registrations in the city increased from 42,974 in 1960 to 61,690 in 1964. It was a national problem and the government commissioned Colin Buchanan to consider solutions. Leeds was one of his case studies and, in 1967, when the Buchanan Report was published it suggested a bold strategy should be pursued.

Even before the Buchanan Report appeared, the council had taken some action. As early as autumn 1945 a survey was carried out to determine what future problems the projected increase in traffic would pose for the city. Then, in 1951, it proposed an inner ring road to be built north of the city centre that would divert through traffic away from the central area and link up with major arterial roads. In 1965 it introduced a fixed penalty system for parking offences in the city centre. That same year the City Engineer's Department installed parking meters on the streets. But congestion brought about by traffic travelling through the city centre or parking there were the major problems. From 1965, working in partnership with Ministry of Transport and the Ministry of Housing and Local Government, the council undertook a major survey and launched what became known as the 'Leeds Approach'. This aimed at providing a series of long-term multi-storey car parks to accommodate commuters, an efficient bus service that used bus lanes and pedestrianising areas of the city centre. The last recommendation was no new idea. Proposals to divert traffic away from places in the town heavily congested with pedestrians had been suggested in the Leeds press as early as November 1805.

The northern section of the new Inner Ring Road became fully operational in 1975 and was a resounding success, though the completion of the full road did not begin until the early years of the twenty-first century. The 1975 section linked to the new motorways, the M1 and the M621 but their arrival in the city was to prove both a boon and a disaster. Certainly Leeds became a major focal point of the motorway system of Britain, linking north and south and east and west and justifiably it was given the name the 'Motorway City of the Seventies'. But it was achieved at a price as great areas south of the city were carved up by the new concrete highways and only the prompt action of the Middleton Railway Trust preserved the line of the 'oldest railway in the world'.

Another radical change in Leeds transport policy occurred in the

1950s when Alderman John Rafferty, Chairman of the Transport Committee, pointed at the junction of Park Row and the Headrow and turned to the young *Yorkshire Evening Post* reporter who was with him. 'Tha sees yon trams, lad?' he asked simply, 'We're getting shut of the buggers.' It gave a young Keith Waterhouse his first journalistic scoop and announced to the people of Leeds a bold new transport strategy. Like every other town in England it had cast its lot on a transport future solely dependent upon buses.*

Leeds had run one of the most efficient tramway systems in the country, reaching its peak in 1933 when 476 trams operated on 124 miles of track. But it had not always run smoothly. In 1943 women workers staged an unofficial strike refusing to work on Sundays because of their increased workload. Grievances over working conditions and new schedules continued to grow until, in September 1945, the work-force struck. The Conservative council led by Alderman Croysdale, and supported by Alderman Brett of the Labour Party, refused to negotiate until the workers returned to work. A call went out for volunteers to help maintain the service and servicemen on leave and university students were among those who came forward. However, it was an act which exacerbated the situation.

Protest marches were held, tram depots picketed, trolley ropes cut and over 2,000 strikers gathered in the Albert Hall to protest. Some tram and bus services were maintained, with the operators either praised as being civic-minded citizens or condemned as villainous blacklegs. One side-effect of the strike was a drop of fifty per cent in cinema audiences in the city centre, and huge queues formed at hotels, restaurants and cafés in the town at lunchtimes when people found they were unable to get home to the suburbs for dinner, which was the usual practice then.

The stoppage lasted nine days and resulted in a severe dislocation of the city. Following that strike of Leeds transport workers, never again in any British town were members of the public asked to drive trams. The council's intransigence in dealing with the strikers and allowing such disruption of the city to occur only weeks before the local elections may well have been significant. Coupled with the anti-Conservative mood in the country in 1945 it no doubt contributed to produce the biggest majority Labour had ever enjoyed on the city council.

With hindsight, fifty years later many people regretted the decision to abandon the system and places like Manchester and Sheffield rein-

---

* Not strictly true. Blackpool became the only authority in England which retained trams.

21. Traffic in the 1950s

Trams in Boar Lane in the 1950s. By then it was felt that increasing traffic congestion and cheap fuel rendered them obsolete. The last one ran in November 1959. With hindsight many now see it as a serious miscalculation.

troduced trams on restricted routes towards the end of the century. Eventually, as the new century dawned Leeds itself revealed plans for a super tram service to be introduced. But in the 1950s, when the decision was taken, trams were regarded by most people as being out of date and the cause of increasing road problems as people had to hold up traffic simply to board them. Added to that was the fact that fuel was cheap. A phased withdrawal of services began and was completed on Saturday 7 November 1959. The evening was cold, damp and foggy in Leeds but it did not deter crowds of enthusiasts from gathering to watch the last convoy of trams leave Selby Road junction. At about 7.15 p.m. the last of them, No. 178, clanged its way into the Swinegate depot.

In some ways that last tram journey could be seen as symbolic. It was the end of an era, just as the 1950s represented the end of an age. Some see the 1960s as probably the most radical decade in the history of the world as conventional values were questioned, the establishment lampooned and traditional social mores rejected. Those changes, allied to advancing technologies in industry, medicine and science, the introduction of the contraceptive pill and a revolution in communications liberated individuals in the same way the changing world order was to liberate colonial peoples.

In Leeds new glass and concrete office blocks began to dominate the skyline. In the enthusiasm to a build a vibrant modern city, old buildings were mindlessly swept away in what many believe to have been no more than acts of senseless architectural vandalism. To combat these trends, the Leeds Civic Trust was established in 1965 and from then on waged a successful battle against those planners and developers who showed scant regard for the architectural heritage of the city.

Fortunately John Barran's Park Square warehouse and the 1862 Bank of England on South Parade were two buildings saved for the city. What infuriated the people of Leeds was that many of the so-called functionally designed buildings proved to be anything but functional and the glass and concrete office blocks, known colloquially as 'glass and concrete upended shoe boxes', were considered to be eyesores. The government, appreciating the problem, passed the Civic Amenities Act of 1967 allowing local authorities to designate certain parts of the city as 'Conservation Areas'. Leeds used the legislation effectively and, by the 1990s, sixty-three areas were so protected.

Change too was noticeable in the industrial pattern of Leeds but throughout the 1960s and 1970s the industrial diversity which had always been a boon to Leeds saw the city grow in prosperity. However, many of the town's traditional industries like textiles and leather fell into decline. In 1955 there were fewer than thirty-five cloth manufacturers in Leeds and not one in Hunslet, once the centre of the industry. The decline continued and by the 1980s only six firms remained. Even clothing and footwear saw an eighteen per cent drop in employment from the end of the war to the mid-1960s. Nevertheless, the clothing trade was still the largest employer in the city although, by the mid-twentieth century, it was concentrated principally into four major firms as a result of amalgamations carried out in the 1950s. Burton's, with 6,000 employees was the largest with Hepworth's, John Collier's and Alexander's making up the quartet. Several smaller firms concentrated on bespoke quality provision.

Fashions themselves altered. In the years that followed, suit wearing became less popular and more casual clothes became fashionable, but many Leeds firms were slow to adapt to those changing demands. Heaton's collapsed, Barran's was taken over, Hepworth's was absorbed into the Next chain and Burton's ceased to manufacture clothes and concentrated solely on retailing.

But engineering, electrical and metal goods firms were important contributors to the local economy with Yorkshire Imperial Metals employing a workforce of 8,000. Printing, publishing, timber and furniture manufacture all provided large numbers of jobs but the largest employers in the city were the service industries. Of these, the most dominant were professional and banking services and the distributive trades.

In Leeds, as elsewhere in the country, the pattern of retailing changed dramatically with the advent of supermarkets. Asda, now one of the nation's most successful chains, began its operations in Leeds at Cross Gates in 1965. It started as Hindells' Dairy Farmers Ltd in Leighton Lane, Leeds in 1920, went on to found other companies like Craven Dairies and, in 1949, changed its name to Associated Dairies – hence its current name. In 1984 Asda opened its one hundredth store nationwide, but its headquarters remained in the city. It became part of the American company Wal-Mart in July 1999 and, by the end of the century, was able to boast 240 stores and nineteen depots across the United Kingdom.

When Harold Macmillan remarked in 1957 that 'most of our people have never had it so good' he was stating what became a truism for the later years of the twentieth century. As in the rest of the country, the 1960s and 1970s saw many people of Leeds enjoying a material wealth they could never at one time have envisaged. By the 1970s most families in the city owned television sets, fridges, freezers and washing machines, whilst a growing number bought cars, enjoyed the benefits of central heating and had telephones installed. But Macmillan had referred to 'most of our people', and there were still significant numbers of Leeds inhabitants who were part of an economic underclass.

Unfortunately, as the nation generally began to enjoy an increase in the standard of living, crime also began to increase. In Leeds the city police carried out research and planning to combat the trend but criminals became more mobile and their techniques more sophisticated. In January 1963, the Leeds Sub-Regional Crime Squad was established and staffed by officers of the Leeds, Bradford and West Riding forces who were able to ignore local boundaries and supplement whichever of the three forces required assistance in a particular investigation.

Crimes of violence increased and, in 1966, the highest number of murders ever recorded in the city to that date was reported. Of the six, five were solved but the culprit who shot the assistant in the Bridge End

Post Office in June of that year was never arrested. Drugs too were beginning to present a major problem both nationally and locally. To that end, a drug squad was formed in Leeds in May 1967 and, in 1970, as car thefts became more prevalent a specialist CID squad was formed. But of all crimes committed during the 1960s and 1970s the most mindless was that of football hooliganism which manifested itself at various grounds across the country.

Sociologists have tried to analyse the reason why football violence erupted as it did during those years. However, no satisfactory explanation has ever been forthcoming as to why this brutal tribalism appeared at so many football grounds. Leeds was certainly not immune. The success of Leeds United under Don Revie in the late 1960s and early 1970s saw the team become one of the major clubs in Europe as Leeds United won the FA Cup, the First Division Championship and the European Fairs Cup. However, from time to time, its triumphs were marred by the violent acts of a small minority of Leeds supporters clashing with the like-minded supporters of opposing teams. On some occasions, 300 police officers were needed to control games at Elland Road and unfortunately, despite every effort by the directors and genuine supporters, the club gained an unsavoury reputation.

What puzzled many people was that during these years, at the three rugby league stadia and the various rugby union grounds in the city, there was little if any trouble. Nor was any reported from the vast crowds which gathered at Headingley to watch test cricket. The only criminal act of any severity at that ground occurred in 1975 when vandals gouged the test wicket and poured crude oil over it to draw attention to the alleged wrongful imprisonment for armed robbery of a convicted criminal, George Davis. The match had to be abandoned.

Many observers felt that the increasing obsession with materialism and the alarming increase in crime were related to a general decline in religious belief. Leeds reflected that national trend. Many churches and chapels became defunct, their buildings utilised as carpet warehouses or community centres. A few were taken over by other faiths and used as temples. Chapels that had so jealously guarded their own preserves, and viewed their neighbours with some suspicion at the beginning of the century, now found that declining congregations forced them to amalgamate. Probably less than 50,000 active participants in Christian worship remained in both church and chapel in the city but those who did provided a vibrant and valuable asset to the community at large. That contribution was clearly demonstrated in 1978, when churches working with local charities opened Wheatfields, a hospice at Headingley, and the Roman Catholic Church opened another, St Gemma's, at Moortown.

But for most people the 1960s and 1970s were times for law-abiding pleasure. The Holme Moss transmitter began beaming in BBC TV programmes to Leeds in October 1951 and by 1953 the number of sets in the city had trebled in anticipation of the coronation of Queen Elizabeth II. With the advent of television, the popularity of the cinema dramatically waned. From a total of sixty-eight cinemas in 1939, the number plummeted to fifteen by 1980. The introduction of independent television added to the cinemas' woes. Originally the Leeds public took Granada's ITV transmissions until 1968, at which time Yorkshire Television began operating from its new studios on Kirkstall Road. The same year BBC TV established its Yorkshire base at Woodhouse Lane, appropriately located on the site of film pioneer Louis le Prince's studio, and also opened its local broadcasting station, Radio Leeds. In 1981 a commercial radio station, Radio Aire, began operations on Kirkstall Road.

Throughout the 1950s and 1960s dancing was still well patronised both at ballrooms in the city such as the Majestic and Mecca, or in the suburbs at the Capitol and Astoria. Ice skating, ten pin bowling, and the ubiquitous bingo, often played in one-time cinemas like the Harehills and Western or at the Top Rank Bingo in Cookridge Street, were all popular. By the 1980s restaurants in Leeds had proliferated and offered a range of Chinese, Thai, Indian, Greek, Italian and other foreign fare, making eating out one of the more regularly pursued pastimes in the city. Traditional fish and chip shops, too, changed their habits. Whereas fish and chips had always been a cheap and popular meal for lunchtime or supper, a tendency grew in the town to open fish shops at teatime rather than later in the evening. They also faced growing competition, particularly from Chinese takeaways, and, by the end of the last decade of the century, from international brands such as Kentucky Fried Chicken, McDonalds and Pizza Hut.

The growth in popularity of foreign cuisine in the city reflected to some extent the change in the nature of British society. From the 1950s a substantial number of people from the Indian subcontinent, Hindus, Moslems and Sikhs, and Afro-Caribbeans from the West Indies began arriving in Britain. The first Indian immigrants to Leeds, Nur Mohammed Kotia and B. Singh, had arrived in the city as early as the 1930s. But the new Commonwealth immigrants of the 1950s and 1960s arrived in considerable numbers. Leeds had long experience of absorbing immigrant communities. Irish and Jewish immigration in the nineteenth century had shown that over a period of time newcomers to the city could be absorbed into and become valued members of Leeds society. Following the pattern of previous migratory groups the new Commonwealth immigrants settled initially in the less affluent areas of Leeds: West Indians in the Chapeltown area and Asians in the Harehills and Holbeck areas, whilst in the Burley area the social mix was multi-racial. Many found employment in heavy industries, the manufacture of surgical boots and shoes and in running garages and operating corner shops, mini-supermarkets and restaurants. A further surge of Asian refugees arrived from Uganda when President Idi Amin expelled 50,000 in August 1972.

By the end of the century second-generation immigrants were found in most occupations in the city and, as owners of corner shops, became a by-word for efficiency. Numbers of young people from these communities went on to higher education at college or university. Consequently many Asians sought professional careers. Several became magistrates and, in 1993, Ujjal Singh Rayat became the first Sikh councillor in the city. Though absorption into the general community was acknowledged to be important by all ethnic groups it was also recognised that it was important to preserve individual cultures and beliefs. To this end several mosques and temples opened. One particular difficulty which caused some concern in schools was the conflict young people from ethnic minority groups faced. They found themselves caught between the tra-ditional and strict moral values of their own faiths and the greater free-doms and at times moral laxity that they saw pervading much of life in late twentieth-century Britain.

Though at times small factions of the indigenous white and ethnic minority groups clashed in the city in racist incidents and claims of racial discrimination were made against some individuals, the new immigrants settled into Leeds and were accepted by the community at large. Considerable efforts were made to achieve this. From the 1970s inter-faith strategies were devised to bring people of different religious groups together. In 1985 the Concord Multi-Cultural Resources Centre was opened to provide facilities for teachers and students and to help disseminate ideas about other faiths. In 1990 and 1991 'One City, One World' festivals were organised in Leeds to bring large numbers of peo-ple into Asian places of worship. The council encouraged every effort for different groups to become better acquainted and involved with each other. Indeed, one of the great events in the city became the annual Chapeltown Caribbean Carnival held each August Bank Holiday Monday.

But the areas the newcomers settled in were often run-down and suf-fered from years of neglect. Those areas and Burmantofts, Gipton,

Seacroft and the swathe of districts south of the river predominantly constituting the area from Armley in the west to Middleton and Belle Isle in the south and inhabited by the indigenous white population, were designated Urban Priority Areas. It was here in these regions that poverty and social deprivation were most rampant and where crime flourished at its worst. In 1986 there were still 2,600 houses in these areas without a bath, inside lavatory or hot and cold water.

But by this time responsibility for the city no longer lay with the old Leeds council. In 1974 Sir Charles Wilson's imperialistic dream of half a century before became a reality. The Local Government Reorganization Act of 1972 changed the face of local government in Britain by establishing six metropolitan county councils across the country which incorporated the major conurbations. West Yorkshire was one and contained five metropolitan districts: Bradford, Calderdale, Kirklees, Wakefield and Leeds, the second largest metropolitan district in the United Kingdom.

Leeds itself now stretched from Otley in the north-west to Rothwell in the south-east; from Wetherby in the north-east to Morley and Pudsey in the south-west. The battle Pudsey had fought in 1922 to remain independent was finally lost and understandably its inhabitants were furious. They were not alone and protests were raised across the nation. In the West Riding the old authorities fought valiantly to retain their independence and avoid becoming absorbed into this new amorphous local government leviathan called Leeds. Nor was the situation helped when Alderman Frank Marshall commented somewhat arrogantly to the dissenting councils that they should 'broaden their minds'.

The Leeds City Police Force was also scheduled for reorganisation. A deputation from the Watch Committee led by Councillor Bernard Atha presented its case to the Home Office, stressing that it represented the views not only of itself but also of the majority of serving officers. It was to no avail. In the old county borough of Leeds many people resented the loss of the local force and overall believed that to provide an efficient local government service, an authority needed an optimum population of no more than 500,000. Large numbers of people across the whole county of Yorkshire also bitterly objected to the replacement of the ancient place names of the North, East and West Ridings with the more prosaic North, South and West Yorkshire and Humberside. However, the new metropolitan district of Leeds with a population of 738,931 was formed on 1 April 1974. It was a date not lost on the local wits!

The three-day week introduced by Edward Heath's Conservative government between December 1973 and March 1974 as a result of the miners' overtime ban and a major rise in oil prices saw the streets of Leeds plunged into darkness and factories and offices put on short-time working. Disruption again affected Leeds during 1978–9. The city suffered during the so-called 'winter of discontent' when industrial unrest, particularly by council workers, dislocated services in the city. James Callaghan's Labour government fell at the general election in 1979 and, although no Leeds seat changed hands, the country returned Margaret Thatcher and the Conservatives to power.

The late 1970s and 1980s was a watershed in British politics as the two main political parties began to polarise. Under Margaret Thatcher the Conservatives moved to take up a more right-wing position whilst Labour under their new leader, Michael Foot, took a more deeply entrenched position on the left. The policies of the new government, known collectively as Thatcherism, were a radical attempt to reinvigorate an economic system which had been severely disrupted by the world recession of the 1970s. Its supporters saw it as laying the foundation of a new and more efficient and vibrant economy in which entrepreneurs were encouraged and individuals urged to be more responsible for their own lives. Its enemies condemned it for creating massive unemployment, a greater disparity between rich and poor and overemphasising materialism.

Rising unemployment during the 1980s was a major problem but in Leeds it was more muted than in many cities. Nevertheless the lack of jobs was still a serious problem for large sections of the city and, in some streets, it was reported that not one adult male was employed. The increase in unemployment, dissatisfaction with the government and a surge of mindless racism led to civil protests. Riots broke out in inner-city areas in Brixton, Toxteth, Southall and Leeds.

For two nights during July 1981 crowds of teenagers, mainly black youths but supported by a large number of young whites, rampaged through the streets of Chapeltown, the predominantly West Indian area of the city. Police were attacked with petrol bombs and stones and eventually some 300 officers with riot shields were required to maintain order. It was estimated that £2 million of damage was caused as properties were burned and shops looted. Allegations were later made that outside *provocateurs* had been involved and that looters came from a wide area with the sole intention of theft. Whatever the cause, the whole city was shocked and George Mudie, the council leader, sought to develop a municipal strategy with ethnic minority representatives to remove some of the conditions which lay at the root of the trouble.

As the nature of national politics changed so too did local politics in Leeds. Both leading parties controlled the council at various times, Labour from 1972 to 1976 and from 1980 to the end of the century. The Conservatives held power from 1976 to 1980. Under the various leaders – Sir Frank Marshall and Irwin Bellow (later Lord Bellwin) for the Conservatives, and George Mudie and Jon Trickett for Labour – councillors began to be more actively involved in running the corporation rather than leaving it to officers.

One policy both parties agreed upon was the need to introduce comprehensive education. This would discard the selection process at eleven and concentrate children of all abilities into the same school. In 1972 the Labour Party introduced the Conservative plan for a three-tier system in which children attended primary schools from age five to nine, middle schools from nine to thirteen and high schools from thirteen to eighteen. It was introduced in the old county borough area but the city's school population declined and it was felt necessary to reorganise once again. In 1991–2 the three-tier system was abandoned, and a two-tier system of five to eleven and eleven to eighteen introduced.

In Leeds disillusion among many council employees surfaced over certain government policies and was further intensified by the council's own strategies. Education in particular was in a state of turmoil, both nationally and locally. Industrial disputes with central government over a number of years, compounded by the government's attempt radically to reform education, led to strikes and large numbers leaving the profession. In Leeds this was further exacerbated by the failure of the council to recognise some of the difficulties which schools were facing.

Nevertheless, concern about the quality of education had been growing nationally for several years and in 1992 the government set up the Office of Standards in Education (OfSTED). Though claims were made that the new inspection system had produced an improvement in general academic standards across the country, an inspection of the Leeds Education Authority by OfSTED in November 1999 reported that the local authority had provided a less than satisfactory service. In consequence a new company, Education Leeds, was established. This was owned solely by Leeds City Council but drew on the expertise of a private company, CAPITA, which had government approval.

The council had other major issues to deal with. In the mid-1980s three-quarters of the houses in inner-city Leeds were in need of major repairs. Fifty per cent of unmarried mothers lived here as well as sixty per cent of the local unemployed. Unemployment in the city overall stood at about ten per cent, but in the Urban Priority Areas it went as high as twenty-five per cent. Adding to these problems was a rising crime rate. East Leeds, particularly the Halton Moor, Gipton and Seacroft districts registered some of the highest crime rates in the country. Prostitution was particularly noticeable in the Chapeltown area although this had reduced somewhat by the end of the 1990s. The drug culture which became endemic in England during the latter two decades of the twentieth century was first predominant in Chapeltown but by the end of the century posed a major problem across the city as a whole. Child crime, particularly burglary, car theft and solvent abuse began to grow during the late 1970s and 1980s. To this end, police juvenile liaison officers worked with schools and welfare officers to combat the problem, just as the West Yorkshire police generally worked hard at establishing good community relations in an effort to reduce crime.

The increase in violent crime in Britain was evident in many ways and Leeds was not immune from its effects. Despite the sterling efforts of Leeds United Football Club to eradicate anti-social behaviour amongst its supporters, football hooliganism again reappeared in the early 1980s in the form of a small group of Leeds United supporters known as the Service Crew. They engaged in running battles with both the police and the supporters of other teams, though serious trouble usually occurred away from Elland Road. By the end of the century the hooligan element had been mostly contained thanks to the efforts of the police and the club. But an element of racism did manifest itself in Leeds, as it did at Headingley, where racist taunts at times marred the usually calmer atmosphere of the cricket ground.

Another feature of the changing nature of society which emanated from the 1960s was the women's liberation movement. Its agenda was to correct the unequal position which existed between men and women in legal, economic, professional, domestic and sexual matters. One issue which was highlighted in the 1970s was the plight of so many women who were subjected to domestic violence. Once again events in Leeds mirrored the national pattern. By 1978 volunteers had set up a refuge for such women and children in the Burley area of the city and to draw attention to the situation nationally, Women Against Violence Against Women drew 500 delegates from across the north to a weekend conference held in that district in November 1980.

Earlier that same week the so-called Yorkshire Ripper had committed his thirteenth murder in the Leeds and West Yorkshire area, this time at Headingley. Angry at the failure of the police to arrest anyone over the four-year period during which the murders had been carried out, a mass demonstration by the delegates took place.* The protesters attacked men and cars on the street, attempted to break in to the BBC TV studios, fought with police and assaulted reporters whether they were from right-wing newspapers like the *Yorkshire Post* or left-wing newspapers like the *Morning Star*. The violence culminated with an attack on the Odeon 2 cinema where demonstrators hurled red paint at the screen. Their spokeswomen claimed, 'We have made our point.' The *Yorkshire Post* loftily commented they had proved themselves 'at best second rate men'.

Though such demonstrations of violence were rarely seen on this scale, nevertheless the street violence, crime, and outbursts of racism Leeds had to face through the latter years of the century did no more than replicate the problems faced by every major city in the country. Poverty was another case in point and a considerable number of unemployed men and women during the 1980s and 1990s suffered accordingly. But if that was a downside of society there were other more positive signs of the growing prosperity in Leeds. Those in employment enjoyed a higher standard of living than ever before and the city itself reflected that success.

Leeds had always enjoyed the reputation for being a major shopping centre and had the added bonus that it was concentrated into a relatively small area. Over thirty years shopping centres like the Bond Street, Merrion, St John's and Headrow Centres were developed, while encouragement was later given to establishing large out-of-town shopping complexes like the White Rose Centre at Beeston. By the end of the 1990s Leeds could boast a thousand retail outlets. The pedestrianised areas of the town, in particular of Briggate, its principal street, were a further encouragement to shoppers, and induced companies such as the London-based Harvey Nichols to open its first provincial shop in the city.

The physical appearance of Leeds was also changing. For a time the city centre had developed a decidedly shabby appearance. But the regeneration process had begun and a new style of architecture, the 'Leeds Look', appeared in the 1980s. On the site of the old Quarry Hill Flats the national headquarters of the Department of Health and Social Security was opened. It was a huge, impressive structure, impishly referred to by local wits as 'The Kremlin'. But the architectural vandalism that marred Leeds in the 1960s was replaced by a sensitive reclamation

---

* In January 1981 Peter Sutcliffe, a thirty-five years-old Bradford lorry driver, was arrested and admitted the murders.

of old and disused buildings, which were turned into hotels and luxury apartments. The vast increase in the number of hotels in the city over the last ten years of the century indicated its dynamic growth and reflected the success of establishing a corporate city where private enterprise and city council worked closely together.

22. Leeds Waterfront
Once a derelict eyesore, Leeds Waterfront was dramatically reclaimed during the 1980s. Today it symbolises a rejuvenated Leeds offering desirable riverside residences and itself has become a popular and impressive tourist attraction. The Parish Church can just be seen on the left.

To this end, in 1990, the Leeds Initiative was set up by the council, the Leeds Chamber of Commerce, numerous organisations, institutions, businesses, government departments and the Leeds Development Corporation. In 1988 the Conservative government set up the Leeds Development Corporation to bring about a regeneration of neglected areas of the city. Initially the move was bitterly opposed by both the Labour council and the Chamber of Commerce who condemned it as interference by an unelected quango. The planning powers granted to it over much of south and central Leeds created outrage. However, after an uneasy beginning the city council and the Development Corporation came together to work more amicably for the benefit of the citizens of Leeds. Money made available from central government was used imaginatively. The neglected riverside and its dilapidated warehouses, an echo of the old port of Leeds, were reclaimed during the 1980s and Leeds Waterfront became a desirable place to live and a popular tourist attraction. By 2001 over 4,600 people were living in the city centre with this number projected to increase to 10,000 in a few years.

It was not the only place by the River Aire to attract tourists. The river which had played such a vital part in the development of Leeds had degenerated over the years into a polluted watercourse flanked by broken-down and derelict eyesores. It was now given a new lease of life. In addition to the Leeds Waterfront development, Granary Wharf and its craft market, and the Royal Armouries built on the thirteen-acre site of the derelict Clarence Dock and opened in 1996 by the queen, all had for their backdrop the regenerated river.

The banks of daffodils in spring, its hanging baskets in summer and the introduction of sponsorship of its roundabouts over the last twenty-five years turned the once drab and gloomy looking streets of the 1950s and 1960s into a bright and colourful environment. The £6 million refurbishment of Queen Victoria Street, and Cross and County Arcades into the Victoria Quarter by Prudential, the conservation of Brodrick's Corn Exchange, the £165 million investment in the reconstruction of City Station by Railtrack, its largest single station investment, and an ongoing policy of architectural reclamation demonstrated the energy shown in the city. By the beginning of the twenty-first century some £647 million had been spent on major office developments and Leeds had been transformed from a grimy, industrial, provincial town into a major European conurbation.

It had become a conurbation which, by the end of the twentieth century, was the third-largest manufacturing centre in the United Kingdom. Engineering and printing had long occupied an important position in the Leeds economy but by the 1990s packaging, food, medical and information technology products were also prominent. It had also become one of the major centres for financial and legal services outside London with the principal employment centred in solicitors' offices, insurance companies and financial houses. A further 15,000 people were employed in call centres as telephone banking and related services multiplied. By 2001 the city had become Britain's e-commerce capital, handling thirty-five per cent of the country's e-mail traffic whilst Leeds employed the largest information technology workforce outside London.

The city's popularity was reflected by the growing number of hotels needed to cater for its visitors and by the fact that its two universities now had around 59,000 students. In cultural terms Leeds was also able to boast a diverse range of activities as the century moved to its close. The West Yorkshire Playhouse and the Henry Moore Sculpture Gallery, opened by the queen in 1982, had both achieved international recognition. Since Victorian times Leeds had enjoyed a reputation for music. Its acclaimed Leeds Triennial Music Festival, the Leeds International Pianoforte Competition held in the city every three years since 1961 and, from April 2001, the Leeds New Music Festival have all made a major contribution to its reputation.

To facilitate entertainment and cultural pursuits the council took over the City Varieties and the Grand Theatre, which in 1978 became the base for Opera North. They also bought the Hyde Park cinema which played an important role in the annual Leeds Film Festival. The introduction of the annual Valentine's Fair brought a vitality to the city-centre streets and the construction of the Millennium Square in front of the Civic Hall enabled concerts and other large-scale activities to be held, though many were critical of the disruption such activities brought to the city centre and the cost entailed. What was universally approved, however, was the fact that two-thirds of the Leeds metropolitan area was made up of parkland, green belt, golf courses and gardens.

Leeds had regularly been on the itineraries of touring stars: Laurel and Hardy, Judy Garland and the Beatles have all played to packed houses in the city. From the 1980s the Leisure Services Department inaugurated a series of highly successful popular concerts in Roundhay Park to cater for the youth of the city. Among those who performed there were the Rolling Stones, Michael Jackson and Madonna. But it also continued its long-established tradition of providing regular concerts and recitals of classical music.

As the twenty-first century dawned, Leeds boasted that it was a lively twenty-four-hour city. In the city centre alone there were 105 bars, sixty-two restaurants and twenty-five clubs, all of which attracted people from across the country each weekend. On the streets continental style cafés became a common sight. The advent of satellite television and the transmission of live football matches on a regular basis saw crowds gathering in local public houses to watch games on large screens. The increasing use of the world wide web and e-mail stimulated the opening of internet cafés where people who did not own a personal computer could access what was often referred to as the 'information superhighway'.

The last thirty years of the century saw sport gain in popularity in the city. The 'glory days' of the Don Revie era of the late 1960s and early 1970s were recreated when, under manager David O'Leary, a young Leeds United side reached the semi-final of the European Champions' League in season 2000/01. As a sign of its growing strength the club, with the overwhelming support of fans, decided to leave its old ground at Elland Road and move to a purpose built 50,000 seater stadium south-east of the city adjacent to the M1, for the 2004/05 season. For people wishing to participate in sport a number of high quality private golf courses, supplemented by several municipal courses, were available as were football and cricket pitches and bowling greens. Various sports centres were established across the city and the Leeds International Pool, which opened in 1967, hosted national and international fixtures.

Many people argued that such dynamic success was a direct result of the Conservative government's policies of the 1980s and 1990s which had encouraged enterprise and local initiatives. Others responded that it was the result of a visionary council succeeding despite government interference and cutbacks. The right to buy council houses was taken up enthusiastically by many tenants but its success placed both the local authority and the recently created housing associations under great pressure to provide more homes for rent. It was estimated that of the 1,900 houses that were needed each year only some 500 could be provided.

As in every major city in Europe the increase in volume of traffic in Leeds during the 1980s and 1990s was a particular difficulty that the city had to face. It was essential that a strategy be developed which would answer those growing problems. When Leeds lost control of local transport in 1974 to the West Yorkshire Metropolitan Council it no could longer devise and control a unified transport policy. Then in 1986 the system was privatised and deregulated. For a while repeated changes to bus routes and the failure to maintain adequate regular services caused considerable criticism of the move and hopes to encourage people to use public transport were not as successful as had been hoped for.

Several bold attempts were launched to overcome the increasing difficulties road users were experiencing and the council was conscious that in the first decade of the twenty-first century it was estimated that a further 40,000 jobs would be created in the greater Leeds area and with them would come associated problems of traffic congestion. To improve traffic flow through the city a one-way system known as the Loop was introduced. Backed by European Union funding an experiment, commencing in 1998, was carried out on Stanningley Road to increase car occupancy. Cars with two or more people in them were allowed to travel in a designated high occupancy lane. It was based on successful schemes used in the United States.

Another transport initiative was the introduction in 1998 of a super-bus lane on Scott Hall Road in which buses used guideways to enable them to bypass traffic queues. In 2000 work began on a similar bus lane on York Road. A year later an ambitious £500 million scheme was also announced which would provide Leeds with a super-tram system servicing Headingley, Middleton and Seacroft and which, it was hoped, would carry twenty-two million passengers a year, most of whom it was thought would have been car commuters. But residents in West Leeds complained that their needs were being overlooked.

Though these were regarded as much-needed strategies, considerable criticism was voiced by ratepayers that the maintenance of suburban roads in the city had been badly neglected and that the state of Leeds roads was worse than that in many other local authorities. By the end of the twentieth century the government admitted that the local roads in the country generally were 'in their worst condition for thirty years'. It was a situation worsened by the fact that councils only received one-third of the funds needed for road maintenance from central government.

Leeds never suffered the political extremism which characterised the left-wing Labour councils in Liverpool and certain London boroughs during the 1980s, and its policies to galvanise industry and commerce and support minority groups were welcomed. However, by the end of the century, numbers of businesses based in the city centre felt penalised by excessive rate charges, many council workers claimed morale had been seriously undermined and large sections of the community felt that basic services were being neglected in the suburbs by what was perceived at times as a less than efficient administration.

Public debate over local issues in Leeds had for over two hundred years always been stimulated by a competitive press. The closure of the *Leeds Mercury* in 1939 was a sad community loss but for the next twenty-four years the *Yorkshire Evening Post* and the *Yorkshire Evening News* offered the opportunity for Leeds readers to see two sides of various arguments. In November 1963, however, the *Evening News* was taken over by the *Post* and Leeds found itself with only one newspaper.

The *Post* newspapers themselves were taken over by the United Provincial Newspaper Group in 1969. The following year the Prince of Wales opened their new state-of-the-art printing plant on the site of Benjamin Gott's mill at Bean Ing.

During the 1970s a revolution in the world of newspapers took place when publishers began to issue free sheets. As would be expected these papers carried a considerable amount of advertising but they also featured numerous articles and reports. In September 1980 the UPN Group launched the *Leeds Weekly News*, a newspaper which carved a niche for itself in the fabric of the city's society in that it was able to feature issues of a more prosaic and local nature than could find expression in other newspapers. But the fact that the same company produced the *Yorkshire Post* and *Evening Post* led a small group of individuals to attempt to redress the balance by publishing a weekly leftwing newspaper. The *Leeds Other Paper* appeared from 1974 to 1991.

It had been launched to countermand, in however small a way, the Conservative views expressed by the *Yorkshire Post* and it reflected the extent of the political divisions in the country as a whole. Dissatisfied with the polarised position of the two main parties, a centrist party emerged in January 1981. The hope of the Social Democratic Party (SDP) was to occupy the middle ground between the Conservatives and Labour. Several MPs defected to it and in Leeds some Labour councillors did likewise. However, the SDP made little headway in Leeds and in 1982 had only one councillor. The following year, in the general election of 1983, dissatisfaction with both leading parties was noticeable in Leeds West where the Liberal candidate, Michael Meadowcroft, registered the first Liberal victory in the city since J. Murray won the same seat for the Liberals in 1922.

Through the 1980s and 1990s the Labour Party held power in Leeds as the Conservative Party did at Westminster. Slowly, however, the national Labour Party reorganised itself by discarding many of its left-wing policies and ideologies and even referred to itself as New Labour. By the mid-1990s the British public generally felt that the Conservative Party had become jaded after eighteen years in power. It was racked by several major crises and corruption scandals and a groundswell of public opinion built up against it. That was reflected in Leeds during the council elections of 1996 when Labour held on to power by registering the largest number of seats it had ever achieved in the city. For the first time since 1913 the Liberals, now the Liberal Democrats, became the official opposition party albeit by only one seat.

There were other political records made in Leeds in the years which followed. In the general election of 1997 the city of Leeds, now made up of eight constituencies, failed to return a single Conservative member. It was the first time since December 1910 that such an event had occurred. This trend continued; no Conservatives were returned in the general election of 2001. In 1998 David Blackburn was elected for Wortley Ward to became the first Green Party councillor in the city's history. The following year the untimely death of Derek Fatchett, the MP for Leeds Central, led to a by-election in which Hilary Benn, the Labour candidate, was elected. It was an election which entered the record books, as the 19.6 per cent turnout was the lowest in any parliamentary election since the Second World War.

Perhaps such results indicated a change in political attitudes, just as over the centuries Leeds had seen its political position change from the heyday of the Tory and Anglican dominated town council of the eighteenth century, through the Whig–Liberal supremacy of Victoria's reign to the Labour Party's domination during the latter half of the twentieth century. Each party in turn was eulogised by its supporters for its achievements and bitterly condemned by its opponents for its failings. Each in its turn sought to stimulate the town's growth during their terms of office. It was a growth which owed much to the flair and enterprise of Leeds businessmen and women and also to the diversified and talented workforce upon which they could draw.

At the dawn of a new millennium seers will try to anticipate what changes the future will bring to the city. In March 1941 Stuart Hirst of the *Yorkshire Evening News* did just that. He considered 'Leeds in 2000 AD' and wrote: 'We shall make slums and smoke a painful memory . . . This dream of Leeds as a regional centre . . . is worth planning for now as the rightful heritage of an elevated and industrious people.' The people of the town, of every political persuasion, have followed that dream. It began a millennium and a half ago and, despite the weaknesses and failings of the past, the citizens of Leeds facing the twenty-first century could look back on the efforts of those industrious people with gratitude and with hope. From a small medieval village clinging to the banks of the River Aire their town had become not simply a regional centre but a major European city with a robust economy and an encouraging future. The debt owed to the past generations of men and women who made that possible is incalculable. The way to repay it is by the people of present-day Leeds cherishing the legacy they have inherited and preserving for generations yet unborn the precious heritage they enjoy.

BIBLIOGRAPHY

Leeds is fortunate in that its Local and Family History Library offers a magnificent collection of books, documents, census records, directories, maps and photographs. Its copies of local newspapers on microfilm stretch back to the eighteenth century.

The following books are all available in libraries and though many are now out of print the local history student will find them invaluable sources of reference. Among the foremost is Steven Burt and Kevin Grady's very comprehensive study *The Illustrated History of Leeds* (Derby) 1994. There are two collections of academic essays that are most useful. In date order of publication they are *Leeds and Its Region* (Leeds) 1967 edited by Maurice Beresford and G. R. J. Jones and *A History of Modern Leeds* (Manchester) 1980 edited by Derek Fraser. An invaluable collection of extensive quotations on Leeds is to be found in Ann Heap and Peter Brears's *Leeds Describ'd; Eyewitness Accounts of Leeds 1534-1905* (Derby) 1993. In more specialist areas Maurice Beresford's 'East End, West End: the Face of Leeds During Urbanisation, 1684-1842': *Thoresby Society Publications* monograph vols LX and LXI 1988 on housing, and Jim Soper's two volume *Leeds Transport* (Leeds) 1985 and 1996 on Leeds trams are invaluable reference sources. Tom Bradley's *Old Coaching Days in Yorkshire* (Leeds)1889 gives a graphic account of coaching in Leeds. R. J. Morris in *Class, Sect and Party; the Making of the British Middle Class, 1820-1850* (Manchester) 1990 bases his study on Leeds and E. P. Thompson in *The Making of the English Working Class* (London) 1991 draws heavily on the town's history for examples.

Visual records of the city have been produced in abundance, the two most impressive being Peter Brears's *Images of Leeds 1850-1960* (Derby) 1992 and Brett Harrison's *A Century of Leeds; Events, People and Places over the Last 100 Years* (Stroud) 1999. No student of Leeds history can afford to ignore such classic references as M. L. Faull and M. Stinson's edition of Domesday Book; Yorkshire (Chichester) ed 1986 in two parts or Ralph Thoresby's *Ducatus Leodiensis* (London) 1715. Equally invaluable are the annual *Thoresby Society Publications* that have been produced for over a century on a multitude of local history topics. For children's reference, David Thornton's *The Picture Story of the City of Leeds* (Leeds) 1983 offers a simple yet comprehensive guide.

As this publication is a general history it was felt that detailed footnotes were not essential. The following have all been consulted in the production of this work:

Newspapers, Magazines and Journals
Absolute Leeds
Armley and Wortley News
Cistercian Studies Quarterly
Daily Express
Leeds Guardian
Leeds Independent
Leeds Intelligencer
Leeds Mercury
Leeds Other Paper
Leeds Patriot
Leeds Times
Leeds and District Weekly Citizen
Leeds Wednesday Journal
Leeds Weekly News
Morley Advertiser
News Chronicle
Northern History
Northern Star
Railway Magazine
Reynolds News
The Times
University of Leeds Review
Yorkshire Archaeological Journal
Yorkshire Evening News
Yorkshire Evening Post
Yorkshire History Magazine
Yorkshire Library News
Yorkshire Post

Reports
Baker R. *Report of the Leeds Board of Health* (Leeds) 1833
Baker R. *Report on the Condition of the Residences of the Labouring Classes in the Town of Leeds in the West Riding of the County of York* (Leeds) 1842
Employment of Children in Factories; Royal Commission Report 1834 vol XIX

Leeds Extension Railway Act (1865)
Leeds Poll Book 1834
'Reports from the Select Committee – Woollen Trade': *Parliamentary Papers* 1806 III
Report of the Special Committee on the Strike of Municipal Workmen 11 December 1913 to 13 January 1914 (Leeds) 1914
Town Council Borough of Leeds Annual Report - Public Library Annual Report 1870-1872
Town Council Borough of Leeds Annual Report - Public Library Annual Report 1877-1878
Town Council Borough of Leeds Annual Report - Baths and Cemeteries Committee 1889-1890
Town Council Borough of Leeds Annual Report - Public Library Annual Report 1893-1894
Town Council Borough of Leeds Annual Report - Public Library Annual Report 1900-1901
Town Council Borough of Leeds Annual Report - Property Committee 1900-1901
Town Council Borough of Leeds Annual Report - Parks Committee 1904-1905
Town Council Borough of Leeds Annual Report - Parks Committee 1906-1907
Town Council Borough of Leeds Annual Report - Parks Committee 1909-1910
'West Yorkshire Poll Tax Returns 1379': *Yorkshire Archaeological Journal* vol VII 1882

Directories and Guides
Baines E. *The Leeds Directory for 1809* (Leeds) 1809
Baines E. *Directory General of the Town and Borough of Leeds for 1817* (Leeds) 1817
Baines E. *History, Directory and Gazetteer of the County of York - West Riding* vol I (Leeds) 1822
Baines and Newsome *General and Commercial Directory of the Borough of Leeds* (Leeds) 1834
Charlton R.J. *Directory of the Borough of Leeds 1847* (Leeds) 1847
Goodall C. *Leeds Official Year Book for 1879* (Leeds) 1879
Hamilton J.B. *Official Guide to the Tramway Routes of the City of Leeds* (Leeds) 1911
Jackson R. *Guide to Leeds* (Leeds) 1889
Leach J.H. *A Walk Through Leeds or Stranger's Guide* (Leeds) 1806

Lee J. *Leeds; a Guide and History* (Leeds) nd

Parsons W. *General and Commercial Directory of the Borough of Leeds* (Leeds) 1826

Parsons W. and White W. *Annals, History and Guide to Leeds and York* vol I (Leeds) 1830

Ryley J. *The Leeds Guide including a Sketch of the Environs and Kirkstall Abbey* (Leeds) 1806

Ryley J. *The Leeds Guide; Giving a Concise History of the Rich and Populous Town, and the Circumjacent Villages and Kirkstall Abbey* (Leeds) 1808

White W. *History, Gazetteer and Directory of the West Riding of Yorkshire* vol I (Leeds 1837)

Books and Articles

Aiken J.A. *Description of the Country from Thirty to Forty Miles Around Manchester* (London) 1795

Allott W. 'Leeds Quaker Meeting': *Thoresby Society Publications* vol L 1968

Anning S.T. *The General Infirmary at Leeds; the First Hundred Years 1767-1869* (Edinburgh/London) 1963

Anning S.T. *The General Infirmary at Leeds; the Second Hundred Years 1869-1965* (Edinburgh/London) 1966

Anning S.T. *The History of Medicine in Leeds* (Leeds) 1980

Anon *An Address to the Members of the Stranger's Benevolent Society and to the Inhabitants of Leeds* (Leeds) 1797

Anon *Leeds and Its History* (Leeds) 1926

Anon *Education in Leeds* (Leeds) 1926

Anon *Leeds the Industrial Capital of the North* (Leeds)1954

Anon *Early Photography in Leeds 1839-1870* (Leeds) 1981

Anon *Ancient Monuments in Leeds; Leeds City Council Dept of Planning* (Leeds) 1986

Anon *Temple Newsam* (Leeds) 1989

Anon *Tetley's Brewery, Leeds* (Leeds) nd

Ashley M. *The Life and Times of William I* (London) 1973

Ashley M. *The Life and Times of King John* (London) 1984

Atkinson D.H. *Old Leeds; Its Bygones and Celebrities* (Leeds) 1868

Atkinson D.H. *Ralph Thoresby the Topographer; His Town and Times* vol I (Leeds) 1885

Atkinson D.H. *Ralph Thoresby the Topographer; His Town and Times* vol II (Leeds) 1885

Baines E. (Jun) *The Life of Edward Baines: Late MP for the Borough of Leeds* (London/Leeds) 1851

Barber B.J. 'Aspects of Municipal Government': *A History of Modern Leeds* (Manchester) 1980

Barnes G.D. 'Kirkstall Abbey 1147-1539; an Historical Study': *Thoresby Society Publications* vol LVIII 1984

Bates D. '55BC-AD1068': *The History Today Companion to British History* (London) 1995

Beckwith F. 'The Population of Leeds During the Industrial Revolution': *Thoresby Society Publications* vol XLI 1954

Beckwith F. *The Leeds Library 1768-1968* (Leeds) 1994

Bede *History of the English Church and People* trans Sherley-Price L. (Harmondsworth) 1968

Bedford P. and Howard D.N. *St James's University Hospital, Leeds; a Pictorial History* (Leeds) 1989

Belchem J. *Orator Hunt - Henry Hunt an English Working Class Radical* (Oxford) 1985

Beresford M.W. *The Leeds Chamber of Commerce* (Leeds) 1951

Beresford M.W. 'Prosperity Street and Others; an Essay in Visible Urban History': *Leeds and Its Region* (Leeds) 1967

Beresford M.W. 'The Face of Leeds 1780-1914': *A History of Modern Leeds* (Manchester) 1980

Beresford M.W. 'East End, West End: the Face of Leeds During Urbanisation, 1684-1842': *Thoresby Society Publications* monograph vols LX and XLI 1988

Beresford M.W. and Jones G. R. J. ed *Leeds and Its Region* (Leeds) 1967

Bergen A. 'Leeds Jewry, 1930-1939: the Challenge of Anti-Semitism': *Thoresby Society Publications* (Second Series) vol 10 2000

Black J.B. *The Reign of Elizabeth 1558-1603* (Oxford) 1985

Bonser K.J. 'Spas, Wells and Springs of Leeds': *Thoresby Society Publications* vol LIV 1974

Boud R.C. 'The Great Exodus; the Evacuation of Leeds Schoolchildren 1939-1945': *Thoresby Society Publications* (Second Series) vol 10 2000

Bradley T. *Old Coaching Days in Yorkshire* ed (Otley) ed 1988

Brears P. *Kirkstall Abbey; Leeds' Cistercian Monastery* (Leeds) 1982

Brears P. *Images of Leeds 1850-1960* (Derby) 1992

Brears P. *Leeds Waterfront Heritage Trail; A Guide to Historic Sites and Buildings along Eight Miles of the Aire Valley Through Leeds* (Leeds)1993

Brears P. *A Taste of Leeds* (Derby) 1998

Briggs A. ed *Chartist Studies* (London) 1958

Briggs A. *Victorian Cities* (Harmondsworth) 1977

Briggs A. *The Age of Improvement 1783-1867* (London) 1987

Broadhead W.H. 'Houses in Leeds Bearing Knights Hospitallers Crosses': *Thoresby Society Publications* vol IX Part 2 1898

Bryant A. *King Charles II* (London) 1931

Bryant A. *Years of Endurance 1793-1802* (London) 1942

Bryant A. *English Saga 1840-1940* (Glasgow) 1961

Buckman J. 'Later Phases of Industrialisation to 1918' : *Leeds and Its Region* (Leeds) 1967

Bushell J. *The World's Oldest Railway* (Sheffield) 1975

Burt S. ed *Old Leeds Inside Out* (Leeds) nd

Burt S. 'Leeds Manor House: the Development and Changing Function of a Central Site': *Thoresby Society Publications* (Second Series) vol 5 1994

Burt S. and Grady K. *War, Plague and Trade; Leeds in the Seventeenth Century* (Leeds) 1986

Burt S. and Grady K. *The Illustrated History of Leeds* (Derby) 1994

Butler B. *The Football League 1888-1988; the Official Illustrated History* (London) 1987

Butler L. and Given-Wilson C. *Medieval Monasteries of Great Britain* (London) 1983

Bye S. *A History of Middleton Railway* (Leeds) 1994

Caunce S. and Honeyman K. 'Introduction; the City of Leeds and its Business': *Leeds City Business* (Leeds) 1993

Chadwick S.J. 'The Farnley Wood Plot': *Thoresby Society Publications* vol XV 1909

Chambers J.D. *The Workshop of the World* (London) 1964

Charing D. *Glimpses of Jewish Leeds* (Leeds) 1988

Charing D. 'The Jewish Presence in Leeds': *Religion in Leeds* (Stroud) 1994

Chartres J. and Honeyman K. ed *Leeds City Business* (Leeds) 1993

Chaucer G. *The Canterbury Tales* trans Wright D. ed (Oxford) 1998

Chippendale B. and Thornton D. *The Story of St. John the Evangelist Church, Wortley-de-Leeds* (Leeds) 1998

Clark E.K. trans 'The Foundation of Kirkstall Abbey': *Thoresby Society Publications* vol IV 1895

Clay E.W. ed *The Leeds Police 1836-1974* (Leeds) 1974

Claye A.M. *A Short History of the Hospital for Women at Leeds 1853-1953* (Leeds) 1953

Cole D. *Cookridge; the Story of a Yorkshire Township* vol 1 (Leeds) 1980

Collingwood W.G. 'The Early Crosses of Leeds': *Thoresby Society Publications* vol XII 1914

Collyer C. 'Yorkshire and the Forty-Five': *Yorkshire Archaeological Journal* vol XXXVIII 1955

Connell E.J. and Ward M. 'Industrial Development 1780-1914': *A History of Modern Leeds* (Manchester) 1980

Cooke A. *Six Men* (London) 1977

Court W.H.B. *A Concise Economic History of Britain from 1750 to Recent Times* (Cambridge) 1954

Crawford E. *The Women's Suffrage Movement; a Reference Guide 1866-1928* (London) 1999

Crompton T. *A True and Plenary Relation of the Great Defeat Given by my Lord Fairfax Forces unto my Lord of Newcastle's Forces in Yorkshire January 23* (London) 1642/1643

Crossley F.H. *The English Abbey* (London) 1935

Crump W.B. ed 'The Woollen Industry of Leeds 1780-1820': *Thoresby Society Publications* monograph 1931

Crump W.B. 'A Jubilee Review':*Thoresby Society Publications* vol XXXVII 1945

Dalton H.W. 'Walter Farquhar Hook, Vicar of Leeds: his Work for the Church and the Town, 1837-1848': *Thoresby Society Publications* vol 19 (Second Series) 1990

Davies G. *The Early Stuarts 1603-1660* (Oxford) 1985

Defoe D. *A Tour Through the Whole Island of Great Britain* vol II (London) ed 1966

Dickinson G.C. 'Passenger Transport Developments': *Leeds and Its Region* (Leeds) 1967

Dillon T. 'The Irish in Leeds, 1851-1861': *Thoresby Society Publications* vol LIV 1974

Douglas J. and Powell K.I. *Leeds; Three Architectural Walks* (Leeds) 1983

Douglas J. and Powell K. *St John's Church Leeds* (Leeds) 1993

Driver C. *Tory Radical; the Life of Richard Oastler* (Oxford) 1946

Elton A. 'Leeds Cyclists and Cycle Makers' 1880-1901': *Thoresby Society Publications* vol 5 (Second Series) 1994

Elton A. *The House that Jack Built; the Story of Marshall & Co of Leeds Flax Spinners and School Managers 1788-1886* (Leeds) 1994

Englander D. '1801-1914': *The History Today Companion to British History* (London) 1995

Engels F. *The Condition of the Working Class in England* (Moscow) ed 1977

Fairfax F. *The Good and Prosperous Successe of the Parliaments Forces in Yorkshire* (London) 1642

Faull M.L. and Moorhouse S.A. ed *West Yorkshire: an Archaeological Survey to AD 1500* vol 1 (Wakefield) 1981

Faull M.L. and Moorhouse S.A. ed *West Yorkshire: an Archaeological Survey to AD 1500* vol 2 (Wakefield) 1981

Faull M.L. and Moorhouse S.A. ed *West Yorkshire: an Archaeological Survey to AD 1500* vol 3 (Wakefield) 1981

Faull M.L. 'The Roman Period'; 'The Post-Roman Period': *West Yorkshire: an Archaeological Survey to AD 1500* vol 1 (Wakefield) 1981

Faull M.L. and Stinson M. ed *Domesday Book; Yorkshire* (Chichester) ed 1986 Part One

Faull M.L. and Stinson M. ed *Domesday Book; Yorkshire* (Chichester) ed 1986 Part Two

Feiling K. *A History of England; from the Coming of the English to 1918* (London) 1969

Fisher H.A.L. *A History of Europe* (London) 1936

Fletcher J.S. *Picturesque History of Yorkshire* vol II (London) nd

Ford J. *This Sporting Land* (London) 1977

Forsaith P. *A Kindled Fire: John and Charles Wesley, and the Methodist Revival in the Leeds Area* (Leeds) 1988

Forster G. 'From not so Splendid Isolation to Association: The Leeds Library 1768- 1996': *Yorkshire Library News* 1996

Forster G.C.F. 'Parson and People; Troubles at Leeds Parish Church': *University of Leeds Review* vol VII 1960-1961

Forster G.C.F. 'From the Foundations of the Borough to the Eve of the Industrial Revolution': *Leeds and Its Region* (Leeds) 1967

Forster G.C.F. 'The Foundations': *A History of Modern Leeds* (Manchester) 1980

Forster G.C.F. 'The Early Years of Leeds Corporation': *Thoresby Society Publications* vol LIV 1976

Foster R.F. *Modern Ireland 1600-1972* (Harmondsworth) 1989

Fowler J.T. 'Introduction to Cistercian Statutes': *Yorkshire Archaeological and Topographical Journal* vol 10 1886

Fraser A. *King James* (London) 1974

Fraser A. *Cromwell; Our Chief of Men* (London) 1973

Fraser D. 'The Leeds Churchwardens 1828-1850': *Thoresby Society Publications* vol LIII 1971

Fraser D. 'Improvement in Early Victorian Leeds': *Thoresby Society Publications* vol LIII 1971

Fraser D. 'Poor Law Politics in Leeds 1833-1855': *Thoresby Society Publications* vol LIII 1971

Fraser D. 'The Fruits of Reform; Leeds Politics in the 1830s': *Northern History* vol VII 1972

Fraser D. ed *A History of Modern Leeds* (Manchester) 1980

Fraser D. 'Politics and society in the nineteenth century': *A History of Modern Leeds* (Manchester) 1980

Fraser D. 'The Life of Edward Baines: a Filial Biography of the "Great Liar of the North"': *Northern History* vol XXXI 1995

Freedman M. 'The Leeds Jewish Community; a Sketch of its History and Development': *Aspects of Leeds* (Barnsley) 1998

Frere S. *Britannia; a History of Roman Britain* (London) 1974

Gamble G.C. 'A History of Hunslet in the Late Middle Ages': *Thoresby Society Publications* vol XLI 1954

Garbett M. and Goulding B. *Lancaster at War; Fifty Years On* (London) 1995

Gardham W. ed *Handbook of the Old Leeds Exhibition* (Leeds) 1926

Gardiner C. *From Acorn to Oak* (Leeds) 1985

Gardiner J. and Wenborn N. ed *The History Today Companion to British History* (London) 1995

Garmondsway G.N. trans *The Anglo-Saxon Chronicle* (London) ed 1978

Gibb M.A. and Beckwith F. *The Yorkshire Post; Two Centuries* (Leeds) 1954

Gildas F.M. 'Cistercians'; *The Catholic Encyclopaedia* trans Trippett L. (New York) 1908

Gillingham J. '1068-1485': *The History Today Companion to British History* (London) 1995

Gilyard-Beer R. *Fountains Abbey, Yorkshire* (London) 1970

Gimpel J. *The Cathedral Builders* (London) 1981

Gliddon P. *But Who Was Don Robins?* (London) 1949

Grady K. 'The Georgian Public Buildings of Leeds and West Riding':*Thoresby Society Publications* monograph vol LXII 1989

Grady K. 'Commercial Marketing and Retailing Amenities, 1700-1914': *A History of Modern Leeds* (Manchester) 1980

Green J.R. *Short History of the English People* (London) 1891

Greenia C. 'Cistercian Lay Brothers in the Twelfth and Twentieth Centuries': *Cistercian Studies Quarterly* vol 27.4 1992

Hadfield C. *British Canals: an Illustrated History* (Newton Abbot) 1969

Hagerty J.M. *Leeds at War 1914-18: 1939-45* (Leeds) 1981

Hall R. and Richardson S. *The Anglican Clergy and Yorkshire Politics in the Eighteenth Century* (York) 1998

Hammerton H.J. *This Turbulent Priest; the Story of Charles Jenkinson* (London) 1952

Hammerton J. *The Second Great War; a Standard History* vol 5 (London) nd

Hammerton J. *The Second Great War; a Standard History* vol 9 (London) nd

Hand T.W. *Leeds Public Free Libraries* (Leeds) 1903

Hand T.W. 'Early Leeds Printing and Printers': *Handbook of the Old Leeds Exhibition* ed Gardham W. (Leeds) 1926

Hargrave E. 'The Leeds Volunteers 1794-1802': *Thoresby Society Publications* vol XXVIII 1928

Harrison B. *Drink and the Victorians; the Temperance Question in England 1815-1872* (London) 1971

Harrison B. *A Century of Leeds; Events, People and Places over the Last 100 Years* (Stroud) 1999

Harrison J.F.C. 'Chartism in Leeds': *Chartist Studies* (London) 1958

Harrison J.F.C. 'Social Reform in Victorian Leeds': *Thoresby Society Publications* Monograph III 1954

Hartley O. 'The Second World War and After, 1939-1974': *A History of Modern Leeds* (Manchester) 1980

Harvey B. *Living and Dying in England 1100-1540: the Monastic Experience* (Oxford) 1993

Heap A. *Briggate; a History in Pictures* (Leeds) 1988

Heap A. *The Headrow; a Pictorial Record* (Leeds) 1990

Heap A. and Brears P. ed *Leeds Describ'd; Eyewitness Accounts of Leeds 1534-1905* (Derby) 1993

Hendrick H. 'The Leeds Gas Strike 1890': *Thoresby Society Publications* vol LIV 1975

Hey D. *Yorkshire from AD 1100* (London) 1986

Hill C.P. *British Economic and Social History 1700-1882* (London) 1986

Hodson M.O. *Leeds Parish Church: its History and Memorials* (Leeds) 1905

Hoggart R. *The Uses of Literacy* (Harmondsworth) 1957

Hole J. *Light More Light* (London) 1860

Holyoake G.J. *The Jubilee History of the Leeds Industrial Co-operative Society from 1847 to 1897* (Leeds) 1897

Hope W.H. St John and Bilson J. 'Architectural Description of Kirkstall Abbey': *Thoresby Society Publications* vol XVI 1907

Howard D.N. *St James's University Hospital, Leeds. A Pictorial History* (Leeds) 1989

Hullah K. et al *A Portrait of Farnley* (Leeds) nd

Hutton R. *The Restoration; a Political History of England and Wales 1658-1667* (Oxford) 1985

Illing E.J. *A History of the Parish of Middleton and of its Parish Church 1846-1971* (Leeds) 1971

Innes J. '1660-1801': *The History Today Companion to British History* (London) 1995

Jackson E. *A Pastor's Recollections* (Leeds) No 5 1890

Jenkins E.W. '*A Magnificent Pile*'; *a Centenary History of Leeds Central High School* (Leeds) 1985

Jewell H.M. *A School of Unusual Excellence; Leeds Girls' High School 1876-1976* (Leeds) 1976

Keighley J.J. 'The Prehistoric Period': *West Yorkshire: an Archaeological Survey to AD 1500* vol 1 (Wakefield) 1981

Kilburn-Scott E. *Leeds Church Middle Class School; Records from 1870-1927* (Leeds) 1927

Kilburn-Scott E. *Matthew Murray, Pioneer Engineer; Records from 1765-1826* (Leeds) 1928

Kee R. *Ireland; a History* (London) 1981

Kelsey P.H. *Four Hundred Years 1552-1952; the Story of Leeds Grammar School* (Leeds) 1952

Kirby J.W. 'The Manor and Borough of Leeds; 1425-1662: an Edition of Documents': *Thoresby Society Publications* vol LVII 1983

Kirby J.W. 'The Rulers of Leeds: Gentry, Clothiers, Merchants c1425-1626': *Thoresby Society Publications* vol LIX 1986

Kirk P. ed *Bramley; the Village that Disappeared* (Leeds) nd

Kitson S.D. and Pawson E.D. 'Early History of Temple Newsam': *Temple Newsam House* (Leeds) 1951

Knott K. and Kalsi S.S. 'The Advent of Asian Religions': *Religion in Leeds* (Stroud) 1994

Krausz E. *Leeds Jewry; its History and Social Structure* (Cambridge) 1964

Lancaster W.T. 'The Possessions of Kirkstall Abbey': *Thoresby Society Publications* vol IV 1895

Lancaster W.T. 'Bramhope': *Thoresby Society Publications* vol IX 1899

Lancaster W.T. and Baildon W.P. ed 'The Coucher Book of the Cistercian Abbey of Kirkstall': *Thoresby Society Publications* vol VIII 1904

Lancaster W.T. 'A Fifteenth Century Rental of Leeds': *Thoresby Society Publications* vol XXIV 1915

Lawrence C.H. *Medieval Monasticism: Forms of Religious Life in Western Europe in the Middle Ages* (London) 1989

Lee C.E. 'The Steam Locomotive in 1812': *Railway Magazine* June1962

Lefroy W.C. *The Ruined Abbeys of Yorkshire* (London) 1882

Lekai C.J. *The Cistercians; Ideals and Reality* (Ohio)1977

Liddington J. and Norris J. *One Hand Tied Behind Us: the Rise of the Women's Suffrage Movement* (London) 1978

Linstrum D. *Historic Architecture of Leeds* (Newcastle-upon-Tyne) 1969

Linstrum D. *West Yorkshire Architects and Architecture* (London) 1978

Lockhart J.G. *Cosmo Gordon Lang* (London) 1949

Lockyer R. *Tudor and Stuart Britain 1471-1714* (Harlow) 1985

Logan F.D. *Runaway Religious in Medieval England c 1240-1540* (Cambridge) 1996

Lonsdale A. 'The Last Monks of Kirkstall Abbey': *Thoresby Society Publications* vol LIII Part 3 1973

Lovell V.M.E. 'Benjamin Gott of Armley House, Leeds 1762-1840; Patron of the Arts': *Thoresby Society Publications* vol LIX 1986

Lumb G.D. ed 'Justice's Notebook of Colonel John Pickering': *Thoresby Society Publications* vol XI 1904

Lumb G.D. ed 'Extracts from the Minute Book of the Committee of Charitable Uses, Leeds': *Thoresby Society Publications* vol XXII 1914

Lumb G.D. 'Leeds Manor House and Park': *Thoresby Society Publications* vol XXIV 1915

Lumb G.D. 'Extracts from the *Leeds Intelligencer* and the *Leeds Mercury* 1769-1776': *Thoresby Society Publications* vol XXXVIII 1938

Lumb G.D. and Crump W.M. ed 'The Leeds Steam Carriage Company':*Thoresby Society Publications* vol XXXVII 1945

Lumb G.D. and Place M.F. 'Extracts from the *Leeds Intelligencer* and the *Leeds Mercury* 1777-1782': *Thoresby Society Publications* vol XL 1955

Lumb G.D. and Beckwith F 'Extracts from the *Leeds Intelligencer* and the *Leeds Mercury* 1791-1796': *Thoresby Society Publications* vol XLIV 1956

MacCulloch D. '1465-1660': *The History Today Companion to British History* (London) 1995

MacLean F. *A Concise History of Scotland* (London) 1973

Mackie J.D. *The Earlier Tudors: 1485-1558* (Oxford) 1985

McKisack M. *The Fourteenth Century; 1307-1399* (Oxford) 1959

Marshall T. 'Chartae Leodienses': *Thoresby Society Publications* vol IV 1895

Marson D. *Children's Strikes in 1911* (Oxford) 1973

Martin E.J. 'The Templars in Yorkshire': *Yorkshire Archaeological Journal* vol XXIX 1929

Martin E.J. 'The Templars in Yorkshire': *Yorkshire Archaeological Journal* vol XXX 1930

Mason A. ed *Religion in Leeds* (Stroud) 1994

Matthew H.G. *Gladstone 1875-1898* (Oxford) 1995

Matthews R.D. *The History of Freemasonry in Leeds* (Leeds) 1954

May T. *An Economic and Social History of Britain 1760-1970* (Harlow) 1992

Mayhall J. *The Annals and History of Leeds* (Leeds) 1860

Meadowcroft M. 'The Years of Political Transition 1914-1939': *A History of Modern Leeds* (Manchester) 1980

Mee F.W. *The Poor Law; its Principles and Work* (Leeds) 1910

Meiklejohn A. *The Life, Work and Times of Charles Turner Thackrah, Surgeon and Apothecary of Leeds (1795-1833)* (Edinburgh/London) 1957

Meiklejohn J.M.D. *A New History of England and Great Britain* (London) 1896

Merton T. *The Waters of Siloe* (New York) 1949

Michelmore D.J.H. 'The Rural Medieval Landscape': *West Yorkshire: an Archaeological Survey to AD 1500* vol 1 (Wakefield) 1981

Michelmore D.J.H. 'The Rural Medieval Landscape': *West Yorkshire: an Archaeological Survey to AD 1500* vol 3 (Wakefield) 1981

Michelmore D.J.H. 'Township and Tenure; Township Gazetteer': *West Yorkshire: an Archaeological Survey to AD 1500* vol 2 (Wakefield) 1981

Micklethwaite J.T. 'The Cistercian Order'; *Yorkshire Archaeological Journal* vol 15 1900

Miller J. *The Life and Times of William and Mary* (London) 1984

Milner L. *Leeds Pals* (Barnsley) 1991

Mitchell P. *Momento Mori; the Flats at Quarry Hill, Leeds* (Otley) 1990

Mitchell W.R. *A History of Leeds* (Chichester) 2000

Moorhouse S. 'Boundaries': *West Yorkshire: an Archaeological Survey to AD 1500* vol 2 (Wakefield) 1981

Moorhouse S. and Wrathmell S. *Kirkstall Abbey; the 1950-64 Excavations, a Reassessment* (Wakefield) 1987

Moorman J.R.H. *A History of the Church in England* (London) 1973

Morgan J. 'Demographic Change': *A History of Modern Leeds* (Manchester) 1980

Morris R.J. 'The Rise of James Kitson: Trade Union and Mechanics' Institution': *Thoresby Society Publications* vol LIII 1973

Morris R.J. *Class, Sect and Party; the Making of the British Middle Class, 1820-1850* (Manchester) 1990

Morris R.W. *Yorkshire through Place Names* (London)1982

Mortimer J. 'Thoresby's Poor Deluded Quakers: the Sufferings of the Leeds Friends in the Seventeenth Century': *Thoresby Society Publications* vol 1 (Second Series) 1991

Mortimer J. 'Joseph Tathum's School, Leeds': *Thoresby Society Publications* vol 1 (Second Series) 1991

Morton M. 'The Cliff Family; Fact or Fiction': *Yorkshire History Magazine* nd

Mott R.A. 'Kirkstall Forge and Monkish Iron-Making': *Thoresby Society Publications* vol LIII 1972

Muir R. *Old Yorkshire; the Story of a Yorkshire Landscape and People* (London) 1987

Mulready W. *History of Kirkstall Abbey, Yorkshire* (London) 1847

Nelson B. *The Woollen Industry of Leeds* (Leeds) 1980

Nichols B.M. ed *Whingate School Centenary Celebrations; 1886-1986* (Leeds) 1986

Nuttgens P. *Leeds; the Back to Front, Inside Out, Upside Down City* (Otley) 1979

Owen D.E. *Kirkstall Abbey* (Leeds) nd

Palmer A. ed *The Penguin Dictionary of Modern History* (Harmondsworth) 1982

Pankhurst C. *Unshackled; the Story of How We Won the Vote* ed Pethick-Lawrence F. W. (London) 1987

Parsons E. *The Civil, Ecclesiastical, Literary , Commercial and Miscellaneous History of Leeds* vol I (Leeds) 1834

Parsons E. *The Civil, Ecclesiastical, Literary , Commercial and Miscellaneous History of Leeds* vol II (Leeds) 1834

Patourel J. le 'The Manor and Borough of Leeds 1066-1400': *Thoresby Society Publications* vol XLV 1957

Patourel J. le 'Medieval Leeds': *Thoresby Society Publications* vol XLVI 1963

Paz D.G. 'William Aldam, Backbench MP for Leeds, 1841-1847:

National Issues Versus Local Interests': *Publications of the Thoresby Society* (Second Series) vol 8 1998

Pemberton 'Two Hundred Years of Banking in Leeds': *Thoresby Society Publications* vol XLVI 1963

Pennock P.M. 'The Evoluion of St James's, 1845-1894: Leeds Moral and Industrial Training School, Leeds Union Workhouse and Leeds Union Infirmary': *Thoresby Society Publications* vol LIX 1986

Petrie C. *The Jacobite Movement; the Last Phase 1716-1807* (London) 1950

Pickering H.S. 'Part 1 1907-1933': *A Short History of the City of Leeds Training College* (Leeds) 1957

Pincher C. *Their Trade is Treachery* (London) 1981

Pogson J.N. 'Ralph Thoresby's House in Kirkgate': *Old Leeds Inside Out* (Leeds) nd

Poole A.L. *From Domesday to Magna Carta 1087-1216* (Oxford) 1955

Preedy R.E. *Leeds Cinemas Remembered* (Leeds) 1980

Preedy R.E. *Leeds Theatres Remembered* (Leeds) 1981

Preedy R.E. 'At the Flicks': *Aspects of Leeds* (Barnsley) 1998

Price A.C. *Leeds and its Neighbourhood* (Oxford) 1909

Price A.C. *A History of Leeds Grammar School from its Foundation to the End of 1918* (Leeds) 1919

Proudfoot N. *Leeds; a History of its Tramways* (Leeds) 1991

Raistrick A. *Prehistoric Yorkshire* (Clapham) 1976

Raistrick A. *Roman Yorkshire* (Clapham) 1974

Read D. *Peterloo: The 'Massacre' and Its Background* (Manchester) 1958

Read D. *Press and People 1790-1850; Opinion in Three English Cities* (London) 1961

Reid R. *Land of Lost Content - the Luddite Revolt of 1812* (London) 1986

Riley P. *The Amazing Varieties* (Leeds) 1997

Rolt L.T.C. *A Hunslet Hundred* (London) 1964

Rimmer W.G. *Marshalls of Leeds, Flax-Spinners 1788-1886* (Cambridge) 1960

Rimmer W.G. 'The Evolution of Leeds to 1700': *Thoresby Society Publications* vol L 1967

Rimmer W.G. 'Occupations in Leeds 1841-1951': *Thoresby Society Publications* vol L 1967

Robertson A. *Atkinson Grimshaw* (Oxford) 1988

Robertson P. ed *The Shell Book of Firsts* (London) 1986

Robinson P. *Leeds Old and New* (Leeds) 1926

Rosen A. *Rise Up Women! The Militant Campaign of the Women's Social and Political Union 1903-1914* (London) 1974

Rusby B. *St Peter's at Leeds; Being an Account Historical and Descriptive of the Parish Church* (Leeds) 1896

Ryott D. *John Barran's of Leeds 1851-1951* (Leeds) 1951

Samuel M. ed *School Centenary; Queens Road / Royal Park* (Leeds) 1992

Schroeder W.L. *Mill Hill Chapel 1674-1924* (Leeds)1925

Scott P. *The History of Selby and District* Part Two (Leeds) 1987

Scott W.H. *Leeds in The Great War 1914-1918* (Leeds) 1923

Shannon R. *Gladstone: Heroic Minister 1865-1898* (London) 1999

Shaw M. *Frank Meadow Sutcliffe, Photographer; a Third Selection* (Whitby) 1990

Shimmin A.N. 'The Ninety-Seven Industries of Leeds': *Leeds and Its History* (Leeds) 1926

Shimmin A. *The University of Leeds; the First Half Century* (Cambridge) 1954

Singleton F.B. and Rawnsley S. *A History of Yorkshire* (Chichester) 1986

Smith A.H. *Place Names of Yorkshire* vol XXXII (Cambridge) 1961

Smith A.H. *Place Names of Yorkshire* vol XXXIII (Cambridge) 1961

Smith B. 'Was there a Castle at Armley': *Armley Through the Ages* (Leeds) 1983

Smith F.H. *Proud Heritage; a History of Thomas Smith & Sons (Rodley) Ltd* (Leeds) nd

Soper J. *Leeds Transport; 1830-1902* vol 1 (Leeds) 1985

Soper J. *Leeds Transport; 1902-1931* vol 2 (Leeds) 1996

Spark F.R. and Bennett J. *History of Leeds Music Festivals 1858-1889* (Leeds) 1892

Sprittles J. 'Links with Bygone Leeds': *Thoresby Society Publications* vol LII 1969

Sprittles J. *Leeds Parish Church; a History and Guide* (Gloucester) nd

Stansfeld J. 'Rent Roll of Kirkstall Abbey'; *Thoresby Society Publications* vol I 1891

Stead G. 'The Moravian Settlement at Fulneck 1742-1790': *Thoresby Society Publications* monograph (Second Series) vol 9 1999

Stenton F.M. *Anglo-Saxon England* (Oxford) 1950

Stephens W.B. 'Elementary Education and Literacy, 1770-1870': *A History of Modern Leeds* (Manchester) 1980

Stevenson J. '1914-1979': *The History Today Companion to British History* (London) 1995

Stevenson-Tate L. ed *Aspects of Leeds* (Barnsley) 1998

Stones J. *Wortley; Past and Present* (Leeds) 1887

Stratton J.M. *Agricultural Records AD 220 - 1977* (London) 1978

Taylor A.J.P. *English History 1914-1945* (Oxford) 1965

Taylor G. 'Education in Leeds': *Leeds and Its Region* (Leeds) 1967

Taylor J. ed 'The Kirkstall Abbey Chronicles': *Thoresby Society Publications* vol XLII 1952

Taylor R.V. *Biographia Leodiensis* (Leeds) 1865

Thackrah C.T. *The Effects of Arts, Trades and Professions ... on Health and Longevity* 2nd ed (London) 1832

Thompson A.H. *English Monasteries* (Cambridge) 1923

Thompson A.H. 'The Story of Leeds': *Leeds and Its History* (Leeds) 1926

Thompson B. *Portrait of Leeds* (London) 1971

Thompson E.P. *The Making of the English Working Class* (London) 1991

Thoresby R. *Ducatus Leodiensis or the Topography of the Ancient and Populous Town and Parish of Leedes* (London) 1715

Thoresby R. *The Diary of Ralph Thoresby FRS: Author of the Topography of Leeds* ed Hunter J. vol I (London) 1830

Thoresby R. *The Diary of Ralph Thoresby FRS: Author of the Topography of Leeds* ed Hunter J. vol II (London) 1830

Thornton D. *The Picture Story of Kirkstall Abbey* (Leeds) 1978

Thornton D. *The Picture Story of Middleton Railway* (Leeds) 1978

Thornton D. *The Picture Story of the City of Leeds* (Leeds) 1983

Thornton D. *A Century at Headingley; the Story of the Leeds Cricket, Football and Athletic Co Ltd* (Leeds) 1989

Thornton D. *The National Tramway Museum* (York) 1989

Thornton D. 'A Letter to the Editor; Readers' Letters to the Leeds Press 1795-1850': *Aspects of Leeds*(Barnsley) 1998

Trevelyan G.M. *England under Queen Anne; Peace and the Protestant Succession* (London) 1946

Trevelyan G.M. *England under Queen Anne; Blenheim* (London) 1948

Trevelyan G.M. *English Social History* (London) 1973

Turberville A.S. completed by Beckwith F. 'Leeds and Parliamentary Reform, 1820- 1832': *Publications of the Thoresby Society* vol XLI 1954

Wade J.B. *One Hundred Years of Odd Fellowship* (Leeds) 1989

Wardell J. *The Municipal History of the Borough of Leeds in the County of York* (Leeds)1846

Waterhouse K. *City Lights* (London) 1994

Watson J.S. *The Reign of George III; 1760-1815* (Oxford) 1964

Wedgwood C.V. *The King's War 1641-1647* (London) 1958

Weldrake D. *The Templars and Temple Newsam* (Wakefield) 1995

Wenborn N. ed *The Twentieth Century; the Pictorial History* (London) 1989

Wesley J. *The Journal of the Rev John Wesley AM* ed Curnock N. vol III (London) 1938

Wheaton W. *Temple Newsam; its History and Antiquities* (Leeds) nd

Whitelock D. *The Beginnings of English Society* (Harmondsworth) 1956

Whone H. ed *Fountains Abbey* (Otley) 1987

Wilkinson A.M. *The Fountains Story* (Ripon) 1957

Williams F. *Fifty Years' March; the Rise of the Labour Party* (London) 1949

Williams N. *The Life and Times of Elizabeth I* (London) 1972

Wilson C.A. *Food and Drink in Britain from Stone Age to Recent Times* (Harmondsworth) 1984

Wilson E. 'Leeds Law Suits in the Sixteenth Century': *Thoresby Society Publications* vol IX Part 3 1899

Wilson R.G. 'The Corporation of Leeds in the Eighteenth Century': *Thoresby Society Publications* vol LIV 1976

Wilson R.G. 'Georgian Leeds': *A History of Modern Leeds* (Manchester) 1980

Woledge G. 'The Medieval Borough of Leeds': *Thoresby Society Publications* vol XXXVII 1945

Wood R.J. 'Leeds Church Patronage in the Eighteenth Century': *Thoresby Society Publications* vol XLI 1954

Wood R.J. 'Further Notes upon Leeds Church Patronage in the Eighteenth Century': *Thoresby Society Publications* vol L 1968

Wood S. *English Monasteries and their Patrons in the Thirteenth Century* (Oxford) 1955

Wood S. *More Back-to-Back Memories* (Leeds) 1993

Woodhouse T. 'The Working Class': *A History of Modern Leeds* (Manchester) 1980

Wrathmell S. *Kirkstall Abbey; the Guest House* (Wakefield) 1987

Wright P. *Spycatcher: the Candid Autobiography of a Senior Intelligence Officer* (Victoria, Australia) 1987

Wroot H.E. 'Yorkshire Abbeys and the Wool Trade': *Thoresby Society Publications* vol XXXIII 1935

Yarwood R.E. 'The Distribution of Wealth': *West Yorkshire: an Archaeological Survey to AD 1500* vol 2 (Wakefield) 1981

Yates G. *A Daughter of Leeds* (Castleford) 1997

Yates N. 'Leeds and the Oxford Movement': *Thoresby Society Publications* vol LV 1975

Yates N. 'The Religious Life of Victorian Leeds': *A History of Modern Leeds* (Manchester) 1980

Young A.D. *Leeds Trams 1932-1959* (London) nd

Ziegler P. *The Black Death* (Harmondswoth) 1975

Unpublished Works

Fahey E. *Common Lodging Houses* (Leeds) 1996 (unpublished study in Leeds Local History and Family History Library)

Fraser D. *Politics in Leeds 1830-1852* (unpublished PhD thesis University of Leeds) 1969

Thornton D. *Mr Mercury – A Biographical Study of Edward Baines with Special Reference to his role as Editor, Author and Politician* (unpublished PhD thesis University of Leeds) 1999

Web Sites

http://www.asda.co.uk
http://www.bbc.co.uk
http://www.fortunecity.co.uk
http://www.leeds.chamber.uk
http://www.leeds.gov.uk
http://www.leeds.piano.com
http://www2.marksandspencer.com

INDEX